BOSTON
PUBLIC
LIBRARY

HUMAN RIGHTS AND GOVERNANCE IN AFRICA

CARTER LECTURE SERIES
CENTER FOR AFRICAN STUDIES
UNIVERSITY OF FLORIDA

CARTER LECTURE SERIES

Satisfying Africa's Food Needs
edited by Ronald Cohen (1988)

Structural Adjustment and African Woman Farmers
edited by Christina H. Gladwin (1991)

Apartheid Unravels
edited by R. Hunt Davis, Jr. (1991)

HUMAN RIGHTS AND GOVERNANCE IN AFRICA

EDITED BY
Ronald Cohen, Goran Hyden,
and Winston P. Nagan

UNIVERSITY PRESS OF FLORIDA
Gainesville / Tallahassee / Tampa / Boca Raton
Pensacola / Orlando / Miami / Jacksonville

Copyright 1993 by the Board of Regents of the State of Florida
Printed in the United States of America on acid-free paper ∞
All rights reserved

Library of Congress Cataloging-in-Publication Data
Human rights and governance in Africa / edited by Ronald Cohen, Goran
Hyden, and Winston P. Nagan.
p. cm.—(Carter lecture series)
Includes bibliographical references and index.
ISBN 0-8130-1220-1 (acid-free paper)
1. Human rights—Africa. 2. Africa—Social conditions.
3. Africa—Politics and government. I. Cohen, Ronald. II. Hydén,
Göran, 1938-. III. Nagan, Winston P. IV. Series.
JC599.A36H84 1993
323'.0968—dc20 93-14893

The University Press of Florida is the scholarly publishing agency for the
State University System of Florida, comprised of Florida A & M University,
Florida Atlantic University, Florida International University, Florida State University,
University of Central Florida, University of Florida, University of North Florida,
University of South Florida, and University of West Florida.

University Press of Florida
15 Northwest 15th Street
Gainesville, FL 32611

To
GWENDOLYN CARTER
(1906–1991)

CONTENTS

Contributors	ix
Foreword *Peter R. Schmidt*	xi
Preface *Ronald Cohen, Goran Hyden, and Winston P. Nagan*	xiii

PART I: THEORETICAL PERSPECTIVES

1. Endless Teardrops: Prolegomena to the Study of Human Rights in Africa *Ronald Cohen*	3
2. Human Rights and Precolonial Africa *Timothy Fernyhough*	39
3. Human and Peoples' Rights: What Point Is Africa Trying to Make? *H. W. O. Okoth-Ogendo*	74
4. The African Human Rights Process: A Contextual Policy-Oriented Approach *Winston P. Nagan*	87

PART II: SUBSTANTIVE ISSUES

5. Women's Rights and the Right to Development *Rhoda E. Howard*	111
6. African Refugees: Defining and Defending Their Human Rights *Art Hansen*	139

7. "Life Is War": Human Rights, Political Violence, and
   Struggles for Power in Lesotho   168
   Robert Shanafelt

8. The National Language Question and Minority Language
   Rights in Africa: A Nigerian Case Study   191
   F. Niyi Akinnaso

9. Education and Rights in Nigeria   215
   Ajuji Ahmed and Ronald Cohen

10. Academic Freedom in Africa: A Right Long Overlooked   235
    Goran Hyden

11. The Challenges of Domesticating Rights in Africa   256
    Goran Hyden

Index   281

CONTRIBUTORS

AJUJI AHMED is senior lecturer of education at the University of Maiduguri, Borno.

F. NIYI AKINNASO is associate professor of anthropology at Temple University.

RONALD COHEN is professor of anthropology and African studies at the University of Florida.

TIMOTHY FERNYHOUGH is senior lecturer of history at the West London Institute of Higher Education, College of Brunel University, London.

ART HANSEN is associate professor of anthropology at the University of Florida.

RHODA E. HOWARD is professor of sociology at the McMaster University, Hamilton, Ontario.

GORAN HYDEN is professor of political science at the University of Florida.

WINSTON P. NAGAN is professor of law at the College of Law, University of Florida.

H. W. O. OKOTH-OGENDO is director of African Family Studies and professor of public life at the University of Nairobi.

ROBERT SHANAFELT is a folklife specialist at the Florida Department of State, Bureau of Florida Folklife.

FOREWORD: HUMAN RIGHTS AND GOVERNANCE

PETER R. SCHMIDT

Human Rights and Governance in Africa presents what most readers will find to be one of the most critical and comprehensive examinations of human rights issues on the continent. This book arises from a Carter Lecture Series held during 1988–89 in the Center for African Studies. The Carter Lectures at the University of Florida have come to be known as ground-breaking excursions into intellectual territory that most individual scholars eschew. Because the lectures seek to challenge convention and to develop new ways of seeing important problems that face Africa today, the final products, such as this book, are usually marked by an absence of theoretical doctrine and a refreshing willingness to question popular ideas.

We find both attributes abundantly present in *Human Rights and Governance in Africa*. For example, one of the most stimulating contributions is Timothy Fernyhough's argument that human rights in precolonial societies were widely expressed as individual rights, a view that challenges the commonly held notion that human rights in African societies are "communal." He also shows that this is an idea that issues more from political ideology than from a clear reading of African history. The relativistic argument that special circumstances and cultural differences require special definitions and applications of human rights standards in Africa is clearly confronted and weighed by Goran Hyden and found to be inappropriate. The reader will also find clear statements about second-generation human rights, such as the right to a decent education explored by Ajuji Ahmed and Ronald Cohen.

It is no accident that five of the contributors were members of the African studies faculty when the Carter Lectures were held. This is a commentary on the degree of involvement that Florida faculty have in human rights and governance issues. The three editors represent part of a core group of faculty known as the Governance Working Group, who regularly meet and participate in a number of research projects that have developed out of the intellectual ferment created by this lecture series. The legacy of this particular Carter Lecture Series can already be seen in the East Africa Governance Project, the Enhancement of Human Rights project in Uganda—a collaboration with the new Centre for Human Rights and Peace at Makerere—and the Governance and Democracy project with Obafemi Awolowo University in Nigeria.

The Center for African Studies is grateful for the leadership provided by Ronald Cohen as chair of the Carter Lectures Committee since 1985. He spearheaded initial fund-raising for an endowment and has been involved in oversight and planning of all subsequent lecture series. Thanks also go to University of Florida Provost Andrew Sorensen, who has provided administrative support for this volume, and to George Bedell and Walda Metcalf of the University Press of Florida for their constant encouragement of the Carter Lecture Series publications.

PREFACE

Recent events in the independent states of Africa attest to widespread problems associated with human rights abuses. Whether they concern the excesses of an Idi Amin or a Boukassa, the expulsion of nationals of one country living in another, the plight of people suffering at the hands of their own governments, or interethnic strife, reports of human rights abuses are increasing. The complaints form a rising chorus from journalists, from Amnesty International reports, and from more in-depth analyses of conditions in particular countries. On the other hand, until the late 1980s the topic has been off-limits. Authorities in power generally interpret such research as illegitimately critical, defamatory, and potentially unsettling to public order. If it is applied for at all, permission to carry out such research is usually turned down on grounds of being "too sensitive." Many expatriate scholars have simply shied away, focusing instead on safer topics, important in their own right but calculated not to close off access to countries whose goodwill is needed if long-term relations are to be maintained. In the case of nationals, refusals are also common and can lead to career problems, even to threats to personal safety.

During the 1980s conditions changed. For a variety of reasons researchers began to focus their attention on internal factors as primary causes of Africa's development problems. And from that shift emerged the problem of a peculiarly African perspective on human rights. A primary reason for it was the promulgation in 1981 of the Banjul Charter, or the African Charter on Human and Peoples' Rights, which, while overlapping with previous universal declarations by the United Nations, also argues for a human rights viewpoint or perspective consistent with African traditions and values. Theoretically, this peculiarly African quality creates important distinctions between human rights in Africa and elsewhere. And herein lies a fundamental issue. Are *human* rights to be defined as claims provided to all persons because they are alive, or should we recognize a number of major variants among these claims based on differences among cultural traditions? This disjuncture—the claims for uniquely African conceptions of human rights, along with specific human rights issues and abuses—has formed the starting point for this book.

These problems, especially the issues raised by the claims to African uniqueness, have attracted the attention of legal scholars for some time. However, much of this attention has been concerned with the legalistic exegesis of specific rights peculiar to one list or another. Our quest lies elsewhere: we are primarily interested in the processes by which rights items find their way onto lists. This process presupposes some civil and governmental means by which these claims (or rights) come to be accepted as legitimated rules. Both the scope and the protection of human rights depend on the state and how its institutions interpret such rules or even accept them. Hence the linked notions of human rights and governance in our title.

One other point about our approach is important. The book is purposely eclectic. We have a stubborn commitment to real-world issues and to the search for as complete a set of solutions as possible. No particular theory or paradigm has guided the choice of issues or authors. Given the complexity of the problems involved, along with what we see as a lack of agreement about theoretical and substantive issues, we believe the best way to move forward is to establish a forum representing as many views as possible. In other words, we assume human rights and governance problems are open to a number of interpretations and explanations. At this early stage of knowledge claiming, it is impossible to assume a priori that any one paradigm—i.e., a particular set of causal relationships or variables—is more valid or explanatory than any other. Not yet, anyway. And so as editors we have eschewed paradigmatics and taken on an eclectic perspective.

In more general terms, this rationale stems from our view that African studies involves a commitment to both emergent and chronic issues on the continent and the attempt to search for and create understandings applicable to their solution. Under these circumstances, commitment to a particular theory or paradigm tends to limit observations and to slant research conclusions. Almost monotonously over the past decades since African independence, unforeseen events have consistently squashed what once seemed to be incisive and sensible explanations.

For human rights this means trying to see the problem both by appreciating older approaches and searching for newer ones. It has taken a long time for research and theory to free normative concerns of the prepackaged outrage inherent in older, often zenophobic theories in favor of a calmer, more open search for the causes and processes by which

Africans are denied their human rights. So now we are able to look in all directions, to the international community and within African states themselves, for human rights issues and the means to explain them.

The importance of the human rights concern, and our approach to the subject, have led us to plan this volume of essays. It includes coverage of general theoretical issues—different ways of viewing and explaining the problem—plus a number of chapters on specific human rights issues. At the theoretical level we want to present, interpret, and challenge the traditional approach that argues for a specifically African quality to human rights in contrast to a universalist view. In addition we hope to demonstrate the utility of a processual approach to rights issues—looking at how and why rights emerge and become accepted—rather than arguing about the rectitude, or lack of it, of specific rights or rights lists.

The structure of the book follows from this plan. Cohen puts the problem into perspective in chapter 1. After discussing general conditions that affect rights issues such as collective versus individual rights, basic needs, and personal insecurity under statist regimes, Cohen argues that rights evolve continuously from "rights talk," that is, through a process of grievance aggregation in which social criticism in a civil society produces the capacity to recognize and make legitimate the need for rights protection. In the next few chapters that follow we examine the widely discussed claim that African societies are primarily "communal" rather than individualistic as they are in Western capitalist states. Looking into African history, Fernyhough shows that in fact much of the collectivist-oriented scholarship and political ideology has created a myth of "Merrie Africa" by overlooking the indigenous and ubiquitous development of individual rights in precolonial societies. This widely used conception assumes a simplistic evolutionary progression in which three different syndromes of rights—individual, social welfare, and communal—have evolved over time.

Up to now the process has been a Western one, but the needs of the Third World have created a new, more collective view of human rights. Much of what developed earlier is deemed valuable, but a collectivist set of societal rights is now added to and in some cases abrogates what went before.

Okoth-Ogendo deepens this argument by explaining why and how African scholars and jurists have come to see the human rights problem from the so-called third-generation or collectivist point of view in which the rights of the group, and ultimately the state, can have priority over those of the individual. Nagan fits this African perspective into an international setting. He also tries to find ways and means by which these different conceptions can be merged through watchdog work (Amnesty International) on individual rights around the world. On the other side of the argument he suggests worldwide efforts to create greater equality in standards of living between the have and have-not collectivities of North and South, a gap he sees as the root cause of conditions producing human rights abuses.

In part two, these theoretical differences are raised for a number of specific human rights concerns. Howard looks at women's rights in light of the African Charter and asks whether and to what extent gender issues can be put aside if all peoples' rights to development are to be met. Although she recognizes how cultural differences sustain male dominance in much of Africa, she argues ultimately for a more universalistic and emancipatory position that recognizes women as individuals whose rights as humans transcend culturally inherited gender roles. Hansen describes the plight of refugees and contends their rights should not be taken from them based solely on their forced relocation. More contentiously, he claims that given the youth of African states, refugees' rights transcend or "trump" the rights of state sovereignty, especially when refugees are moving across state boundaries but remaining within their own ethnic territory. Shanafelt's chapter describes the difficulties that accompany life for ordinary people under conditions of insecurity when the state cannot or will not ensure the rights of individuals against arbitrary attack by both public and private molesters. Under such conditions, more widespread than is presently admitted, personhood and its very survival are at stake.

The next three chapters discuss questions of culture and education. Akinnaso looks at the question of language rights—does a group of people, no matter how few it includes, have a right to speak and foster their own tongue and have the right protected by the state? And Ahmed and Cohen ask what rights people (both individuals and groups) in contemporary Africa have to a decent education, especially since Western education is the gateway to vast increases in income for the person lucky enough and persistent enough to qualify. Finally, Hyden discusses the constraints that have been laid on academic freedom and freedom of expression in Africa as a whole. The conference he reports on has moved toward a Western, not an African, conception of the right of people to work freely on problems of their own choosing and to express their thoughts freely even when they are critical of the regime in power.

In the final chapter, looking back over the theoretical and the substantive contributions, Hyden reassesses the African claim that there are peculiar circumstances, cultural differences, and developmental restraints in Africa that make the curtailment of human rights legitimate. His conclusion, as well as the thrust of the book as a whole, is that once it is examined closely, the plea for a special African position on human rights is indefensible. Most of the papers that discuss specific substantive issues, and many of the theoretical arguments, support his conclusion. On the other hand, the few that do not represent an important position must still be considered seriously. Only time and events will settle the issue.

A work like this book is the result of many hands. A grant from the Ford Foundation added to a large number of small donations to the Carter Lectures at the University of Florida made it possible for those contributors not resident on campus to come and deliver early versions of their papers as part of the Carter Lecture series. Joint discussions on human rights issues among a group of us at the University of Florida (Fletcher Baldwin, Ronald Cohen, Goran Hyden, Winston Nagan, and Peter Schmidt, joined on a number of occasions by Okoth-Ogendo) led eventually to a workshop in Nairobi in 1988 that clarified many areas of agreement and disagreement. This meeting helped us see how to orient the book and provided the basis for our joint efforts at a more extensive set of empirical studies on both rights issues and the capacity of African governments to govern and implement policy successfully within the rule of law.

We are indebted to the Center for African Studies at the University of Florida and its director, Peter Schmidt, for unflagging support of the work leading up to this volume and to our authors who tolerantly suffered and cooperated with our editorial demands. As with the other volumes in the Carter Studies on Africa, Cody Watson has carried out her copyediting with grace and dispatch, and we are in her debt. The death of Gwendolyn Carter during the final days of preparing this manuscript for publication led to our decision to dedicate this volume especially to her memory—and to Africa, which she served so well throughout her life.

Ronald Cohen
Goran Hyden
Winston P. Nagan
Center for African Studies, University of Florida

PART I

Theoretical Perspectives

1

Endless Teardrops: Prolegomena to the Study of Human Rights in Africa

RONALD COHEN

Rights and Wrongs at Issue

Human rights in Africa have surfaced as a respectable subject of inquiry. A decade ago few authors wrote of such things. And when they did the tone was generally more censorious than probing.[1] As the ramifications of the democracy movement unfold, it is becoming apparent that many development goals are tied in to rights issues. People are less likely to contribute to the common good in an atmosphere of personal and familial insecurity that includes danger to safety and property as well as unpredictable and prejudicial outcomes to their hopes and plans. The promise of a better life by self-selected military and civilian elites exerting arbitrary power, often for exploitative reasons, is bound to breed cynicism and mistrust no matter how plausible development strategies sound when promulgated from above. Besides the widely reported aberrations of an Idi Amin or a Boukassa, artists like Chinua Achebe (see especially *Anthills of the Savanna*), scholars like Schatzberg (1988) in his disturbing account of oppression in Zaire, and organizations such as Africa Watch and Amnesty International in their periodic reporting of human rights conditions in African states have heightened the internal and external awareness of the problem. As Hyden points out in the chapter on academic freedom (chapter 10), older shibboleths about the need to work first on more immediate priorities obscure questions about the relations of human rights issues to outcomes like economic stagnation, poverty, underdevelopment, and the routinization of "kleptocracy." In other words, rights issues are an essential part of today's, not tomorrow's, African predicament.

There are awesomely serious events and forces in Africa included under the broad rubric of human rights. Newspaper accounts and the evaluations of Amnesty International make it clear that the problem has measurable and tragic results.[2] But the work of accounting, recording, and publicizing leaves aside a more probing task. Even when the importance of human rights concerns is acknowledged, there is little agreement about the scope of the problem or even which issue or domain to focus on. To help clear the way for what follows, I first examine definitional issues in order to derive a set of dependent variables that place human rights in the context of everyday life. I then relate these variables to factors that facilitate and restrain their emergence. In order of their appearance here they cover the effects of tradition, communalism versus individualism, ethnicity, basic needs, development, and statism. I show how each of these is in turn the result of complex forces, which I summarize. Finally, I move to a more abstract level and discuss what qualities of culture as a whole tend to create an environment that fosters rather than restrains all of the determinants. The chapters that follow then take up specific elements and delve more deeply into each one. We hope this is a good way to advance our understanding. However, it is also important to remember that in the area of human rights, as with so many topics in African studies, the questions abound, the answers are elusive, but the encounter is necessary.

Human Rights Defined

At its most basic level, a human right is a safeguarded prerogative granted because a person is alive. This means that any human being granted personhood has rights by virtue of species membership.[3] And a right is a claim to something (by the right-holder) that can be exercised and enforced under a set of grounds or justifications without interference from others. The subject of the right can be an individual or a group and the object is that which is being laid claim to as a right (cf. Vincent 1986: 8–9).

Although this seems simple enough, there are thorny issues just below the surface. Given that rights exist for everyone who is judged human, what are they, and how or why are they on this list? Even more important, it is necessary to ask how and why consensus and disagreements emerge when groups put forward lists and provide grounds for the legitimacy of the justifications. Other issues abound. To what extent do some human rights override all others—the so-called trump feature (Vincent 1986: 10)? Or again, can people have or be entitled to something that they have never known or enjoyed or that has been denied to them for generations and they are relatively well adapted to not having (Donnelly 1985: 16–17)? Moreover, even the most obvious human rights assertions contain fuzzy features leading to contestable propositions about their meaning or application, whether they are fundamental or derivative, and whether they ought to be included within a definition or list of universal rights.

Rights Lists

One of the most distinctive features of twentieth-century history has been the sudden proliferation of documents concerned with worldwide, regional, or specialized forms of human rights. After the failure by Japan in 1919 to have a human rights statement written into the League of Nations Covenant barring racial discrimination against alien nationals (Cassese 1990: 17), there was a virtual outpouring of rights agreements. Seighart (1986: 238–40) lists some thirty-six separate instruments produced from 1926 (the Slavery Convention) to 1981 (the African Charter on Human and Peoples' Rights). Not surprisingly, there is much overlap. In general, no matter what the context the lists include sets of civil and political liberties. These are historically rooted in the evolution of Western democratic traditions and ideal practices. That they are always "ideal" rather than "real" can be seen at a glance. For example, as early as 1930, 128 nations including the major European colonial powers signed the international convention banning any form of forced labor, which they agreed was to go into force in 1932. The widespread use of such labor in colonial Africa by major powers that signed the convention seems to have been either regarded as irrelevant or easily translated into language that simulated compliance with the terms of the agreement.[4]

Vincent (1986: 11) summarizes civil and political rights in terms of the right to life, liberty, security of person, privacy, property, marriage by choice, fair trial; freedom from slavery, torture, and arbitrary arrest; freedom to seek asylum and freedom of movement; rights to a nationality; freedom of thought, religion, conscience, opinion, expression, assembly, and association; free elections, universal suffrage, and participation in public affairs. Most rights lists enshrine these features or something very close to them.

Economic, social, and cultural rights are less clear, less easily agreed to. Most authors comment on these differences, especially those reflected in the African Charter, although many of the same issues first surfaced in the International Covenant on Economic, Social and Cultural Rights (1966, adopted 1976). For some commentators these rights appear to be secondary (Cranston 1977). Others take just the opposite view. How, they argue, can we even think of civil and political liberties if "there is no reliable expectation about the maintenance of life itself" (Vincent 1986: 13; see also Shue 1980)? In the African Charter the right to minimal sustaining economic well-being provides the justification for Article 22: 2, which declares that states have a right to ensure the development of their constituent peoples. And Chapter 2 of the Charter describes not just the rights of an individual but also his or her duties to collectivities including, most importantly, the state. The duty is described as every person's obligation "to serve his national community by placing his physical and intellectual abilities at its service" (Chapter 2, Article 29: 2). Thus, to be an individual African means not only safeguarded privileges but also obligations to collectivities including the state, whose corporate human rights include duties and expectations of service to and from members. Can human rights be corporate and collective? And is the language so loose as to form a justification for unchecked state power in the cause of everyone's obligatory concern for the public interest?

These disagreements among the lists and about their meanings are so great that it is wiser to treat particular rights as outcomes of a process of influences affecting rights claims rather than as rival claims to a definition. In that case it is necessary to rethink the notion of human rights, abstracting sufficiently from differences to isolate comparable qualities.

Rights Decentered

The inclusive notion of a human right as a safeguarded prerogative and Vincent's (1986: 8–9) idea of a justifiable claim to something expected by dint of being alive are good starting points. However, given the disagreements that follow it is important for theory and praxis that we *decenter* the concept. That is to say, we must try to create a category that places human rights outside a single cultural tradition, but one that, ideally at least, is applicable across specific historical experiences.

Given the experiences of everyday life in many African countries over the past few decades, it is necessary to begin our redefinition with the prerogative of personal security and safety from legitimated use of state power to intimidate and terrorize those being serviced by government agents (cf. Shue [1980], who defines rights as [a] subsistence, [b] security). Reasons for this are in the realm of causal variables and are discussed below. Suffice it to say here that the reports of Amnesty International, Africa Watch, and many others indicate that abuse of power by officials is widespread over the entire continent. It waxes and wanes, goes unpunished for periods of time, then a mild crackdown may occur, but the potential for abuse is always there. Anyone not aware of such a potential is quixotic, reckless, heroic, or all three. In Chinua Achebe's novels, the heroic message is clear: anyone who pronounces in favor of public virtue or acts virtuously in the face of official misuse of power runs serious personal risks under contemporary conditions in Africa. Everyday experience supports the belief in a pervasive but unpredictable and harmful intrusion of state power (local and central) and civil strife into the lives of ordinary people. As Shanafelt's chapter on Lesotho makes clear (chapter 7), this sense of personal insecurity is based on real events. In rights terms people anywhere have a right, by virtue of being alive, to be safe from arbitrary misuse of power by the state and from arbitrary violence in civil life. The frequency varies, but this statement assumes a widespread belief in Africa that interacting with officials whose duty it is to serve the public interest involves fear for personal safety, exploitation, and unpredictable but oppressive actions by officials unless unauthorized demands are met. Power not only corrupts, but in Africa it engenders the sentiment that personal and peoples' rights are customarily abrogated by those representing state power. This can be mediated through individual relations to someone influential whose personal intervention on one's behalf makes government work, but "big men" or those who can reach them are not always available, nor can they be asked to help cover the vast numbers of relations that ordinary people have with government.

Thus, the first and most fundamental human right in a world society of states is the right of individuals and collectivities to feel secure in the face of state power. And, as Hyden argues in the concluding chapter, it is becoming clearer as time goes on that Western ideals of individual rights and their protection through governance and autonomous civil actions are not simply ethnocentric. Both their expression as rights claims and their continuous reproduction under the rule of law (discussed by Okoth-Ogendo and Nagan in chapters 3 and 4, respectively) are a necessary foundation to a secure life in the modern state.[5] Indeed, the African experience since independence has made it clear that personal safety and security must be the starting point for any operational definition of human rights.

The concept of human rights refers to relations, laws, and constitutional principles, but more appositely for research purposes, it encompasses how rights develop and are put into practice. As already noted, the emphasis I wish to highlight is that of *process* rather than the presence or absence of specific items on the various lists of rights. Wrangling over the inclusion or exclusion of a particular right or set of them into lists or covenants is the way the subject bogs down.[6] The various lists attempt to reify rights, to create rights principles through legislative and judicial actions. As Hansen shows for the case of refugees (chapter 6), research and judicial review can be used to propose new items for international covenants. Although these formal processes help, we are also interested in the more informal actions and reactions by which human rights are brought into focus and take on importance in the public life of a country. By contrast, lists of rights, which attempt to codify particular rights and argue for their acceptance, are a later stage in the emergence and recognition-cum-legitimization of human rights. This being so, arguing over what is and what is not to be included on a listing of rights is not the place to begin. Rights change over time, they emerge where none existed before, and they can atrophy with time.[7] It is this processual quality that must be conceptualized first. This means trying to isolate those factors in social life whose activity produces the germination of rights out of the everyday life of people caught up in situations that make rights issues emerge as important goals.

Where Do Rights Come From?

More than any other species humans tend to assess. That is, they have a highly developed capacity to process information and experience by comparing what is expected (from past learning) with what is being perceived and experienced. This highly evolved ability to abstract—see similarities amidst differences—is the basis for evaluation and critical analysis. It is built into human intelligence through our capacity to process, recall, and compare information sets as an adaptive feature (Cohen 1981, 1991). It lies behind innovation in all realms of action by providing us with the capacity to see contrasts between what is and what ought to or could be if changes were to be made. Without going into the evolutionary and biological basis (Cohen 1981, 1991), suffice it to say that one of the most adaptive features of the ability to abstract is the capacity to make judgments about the fairness of actions and outcomes. People differ over what they may see as fairness and in how intensely they react to such assessments. There are vivisectionists and antivivisectionists, right-to-lifers and pro-choicers, those who would mobilize for development by manipulating public resources for the collective good and those who prefer to privatize by allowing market forces to provide incentives to individuals and groups. And each side of these opposing viewpoints believes in the justice or fairness of its assessment of means and ends. Although an enormously complex topic, fairness can be operationally and heuristically defined.[8]

The contradictory quality of such debate means that issues are being examined. Ultimately through natural (sociocultural) selection, some viewpoints or polarities are dropped, or more widely accepted, or even made lawful. Contrarily, some would say that until a law on the statute books or a court judgment mandates a particular human right, then recognition and discussion of this particular right remain inconsequential (Seighart 1986). My point is exactly the reverse. These discussions, conflicts, and disagreements about fairness assessments are the seedbed out of which rights are generated. It is a process that evolves from an infinite variety of judgments about human actions in which some logic or fairness criteria are applied consistently to individuals and groups, between these and governments, and even among governments in an international community. Once the assessments are made and actions proceed from fairness judgments, then interested groups work to obtain societal and legally binding acceptance and protection for particular rights. In more abstract terms, a human rights claim is born and the debate over its status in society becomes part of the social life. Given an Idi Amin, or the loss of life and property by Igbo people in 1960s Nigeria, or by both Tutsi and Hutu in central Africa, or by nonwhite Africans under apartheid, or the privatization of land and its alienation from primordial ways of gaining access to land, then fairness judgments are made by sufferers and critics. The criteria used in any particular situation are those that lead to unfairness assessments. How well the unfairness assessment thrives is the process by which rights become legitimated. In metaphorical terms, social process—the ongoing life within and between states—produces endless teardrops, reactions, and grievances about the fairness of our lives and those of others we know and hear of. If enough of these are similar to one another among one or more publics at a particular point in time and can be aggregated to include many others who either suffer the same fate or sympathize in some way, then we have the beginnings of a sense of a right. And if claimants argue that such a right is inherent in being alive, then it can be claimed as a human right. This being the case, it also follows that it must be campaigned for, as Nagan argues in chapter 4. And as the campaign goes on, whether it be for freedom of expression, rule of law, personal security against oppression, or whatever, ultimately a rights claim becomes established as a universal criterion for judging how individuals, collectivities, and governments ought to behave as members of the human community—suffering sanctions from that community when they fail to comply.

These, then, are human rights: the security of individuals and groups in the face of power, especially state power, and the justice claimed to be due to people, innately, when the results of social life are judged and their fairness outcomes legitimized. In theoretical terms this description lays out a general conception of the dependent variables for a researchable model of the human rights predicament in Africa and, it is hoped, elsewhere as well. The first quality—security of individuals and groups—varies with state power. With too little state power security of person is low; we can call this the "Lebanon effect." Personal security peaks with some as yet unknown optimum of state power, and it slowly declines in asymptotic fashion as state power continues to rise toward levels common in most contemporary African states. Fairness judgments are much more complex and vary with contexts and with issues. Within any particular context, the pattern is that of a normal S-shaped growth curve. That is to say, as a process rights claiming has historically started up rather slowly in the face of state power. Sometimes, as with language rights (see Akinnaso's discussion in chapter 8), matters are complex and it is difficult to find spokespersons who can articulate the issues to a wider public. Hyden's concluding chapter deals with why the process occurs either more or less easily across societies. For now, suffice it to say that fairness judgments leading to rights claims remain at a low level of legitimacy and interest aggregation when the issues are first discussed. However, as a particular issue becomes more significant, more salient to a wider population who agree with and participate in similar fairness judgments, it increases in acceptance, with more and more spokespersons and groups campaigning for its stable institutionalization in law and custom.

Understanding Human Rights in the African Context

Theoretically speaking, human rights are conceived here as patterns of personal security and the emergence and legitimization of fairness judgments on particular issues. I have pictured them in this way—as both normative and behavioral—in order to shift the debate about human rights in Africa. As already noted, the debate has been fueled by the differences that have surfaced, especially since the proclamation of the African Charter with its emphasis on "peoples'" rights. If research is restricted to this level, that of debate over similarities and differences among charters or lists, then rights are to some (arguable) extent universal, and to some (again unknown) extent culturally relative, i.e., dependent on genuinely evolved beliefs and values of the local and regional contexts. This moderate or compromise cultural relativism (see Howard 1983) places research into a murky arena in which the "reasonable" legitimacy of cultural differences, their universalist value, and the often invidious comparison of differing traditions of values and rights become the grounds for deciding what is and what is not a legitimate justification for human rights claims. Defining human rights as part of evolving social processes allows us to ask more comparative questions. First, what factors help explain differences among peoples concerned with human rights, including African as opposed to Western contexts? And second, how do these factors facilitate and restrain the emergence and achievement of enhanced human rights capabilities?

The Role of Tradition

The role played by tradition as a source of understanding and variance among human rights is controversial. All phenomena evolve, including traditions, societies, and states. This perspective assumes that all things change and that changes over time result from selective factors operating on variations. Rates vary. Some changes are quite sudden or revolutionary, others occur more incrementally; both are evolutionary (Cohen 1981). And early elements can hang on long after their functions have been taken over or replaced by later ones. Thus, in the evolution of the state customs and practices of earlier times remain in remote areas long after the major populations centers have dropped them or changed to newer ways of doing things. So too cultural traits buried deep in the early experience of peoples tend to be reproduced and sustained for very long periods of time with varying degrees of scale and scope.[9] From this perspective, many of the legitimate differences among peoples derive from much older historically extended adaptations—from symbols, common reactions, and ideals that form the assumptions and logic that determine agreements and "arguments about the meaning of the destiny its members share" (Bellah et al. 1985: 27). This is the heart of the relativist position. In effect it demands that we carefully consider rights claims that emerge from the roots of specific cultural traditions. Not to do so, it is argued, means using our own traditions as the only valid criteria for measuring performance in the rights field. Kantian judgments have real-world limitations.

On the other hand, our common humanity demands that certain fundamental features of existence be assured to all. Thus most writers agree that there are arenas or domains—civil-political, social-economic, and collective or group rights—that cut across almost all of the various lists available for study. Cultural traditions that deny rights in these arenas can be judged contrary to the overlapping of all traditions and their contemporary statements on human rights. Exactly what the details of these fundamental features are and, more specifically, their priority ordering are still controversial. However, it is also widely acknowledged that using cultural traditions to defend actions deemed prejudicial to the interests of individuals or groups is unacceptable within the purview of human rights logic. Condemning apartheid on the one hand and defending female mutilation on the other is an uncritical and illegitimate use of cultural relativism as rhetoric, rather than its legitimate application as a method to understand and overcome cultural differences and ethnocentricism.

Traditions are not written in stone. They respond to factors and conditions that promote a people's welfare within the orbit of their own understandings and practices. However, there are inexorable forces of change operating in the world—decolonization, urbanization, technological change and the accompanying intensification of production stemming from the industrial revolution and now encircling the planet, population expansion and control, the growing numbers of nuclear families, health, education, democratization, and the emergence of the state and the interstate environment as the universal political and economic domain within which older ones still operate. These are only a few of the massive changes wearing down the traditions that African societies bring to a shrinking world. And as it compacts, problems of all sorts converge. Most importantly for the relativist-Kantian dialectic, rights issues are beginning to fall within narrowing confines of solutions. In other words, the cultural relativism issue is also one that is not written in stone. In a world increasingly responsive to common problems, controversies over human rights stemming from (presently justifiable) differences in traditions will soon appear inappropriate and reactionary. We are not all the same, nor shall we ever be. But the differences among us are contracting. And human rights concerns are dependent on this process of evolving convergence.

Individualism and Communalism

Even with the declining justifiability of cultural relativism, it is still necessary to look at major cultural variables said to account for differences among human rights concerns when we seek to understand and contribute to the African viewpoint. For a number of decades it has been suggested that African cultures share a much greater concern for group interests than for those of the individual, the focus in Western societies. Individuals in Africa are said to be socialized into groups such that the "we of me," or group welfare, is part of the selfhood of the person (Cohen 1970). As one legal scholar puts it: "Social harmony . . . the preservation of the fabric of social life, comes first in African thought, and the threads in this fabric are either the connections among extended families, or other connections modelled upon them. Individuals are not visible in the fabric, only the duties they discharge, the functions they fulfill. To be a person, in a traditional African society, is to be incorporated in this way into a group. Personhood, in contrast to individualism in the West, is intelligible only in the group and not against it" (Vincent 1986: 39).

The author of this passage is not an African specialist. But this is now a widely accepted explanation for behavioral and attitudinal differences between Africa and the West. In the human rights field it is used to explain why there are explicit collectivist rights in the African Charter in contrast to their absence in rights documents emanating from the West. As Fernyhough points out in chapter 2, others suggest that African traditions with their central concern for group interests are preadapted to achieve more equality among groups and classes in matters of social justice. In contrast, Western cultures are weighed down by traditions of capitalist individualism that reward inequality and thrive on competition, personal success, and social differentiation. For many African leaders and intellectuals, these Western traditions must be resisted, even excised if possible, to achieve social justice, while African social policies need only reach back into their own traditions and expand what is already there (Legesse 1980: 125-26).

There are serious doubts whether this myth of "Merrie Africa" (see chapter 2) is as valid as theorists and ideologues suggest. It is true that group-centered life is heavily accented in African traditions. Many African cultures value the group—one should never die alone, live alone, remain outside social networks unless one is a pariah, insane, or the carrier of a feared contagious disease. Corporate kinship in which individuals are responsible for the behavior of their group members is a widespread tradition. But in addition, the individual person and his or her dignity and autonomy are carefully protected in African traditions, as are individual rights to land, individual competition for public office, and personal success. Even where first marriages are completely out of the hands of the young people concerned, there are rules that provide for child brides to abrogate the arrangement should they wish to do so. The value of individual effort, integrity, wealth, and achievement is as indigenous to Africa as it is to the West.

Similarly, the image of the capitalist West as the bastion of unrestricted individualism with no concern for group rights and social justice is a distorted caricature. Although traditions of untrammeled competition for individual gain and personal rewards, even moral strength, are strong in the West, there are equally strong antidotal values pulling in the opposite direction.[10] This contrary theme, from traditions of religion, democratic theory, and what I call below the civil society, promulgates the view that unchecked individualism is pernicious, that it can lead to despotism and chaos unless counterbalanced by a similarly strong tradition of participation in public affairs and a concern for community welfare as a condition for the durability and protection of individual rights and privileges (Bellah et al. 1985: 38).[11] And so along with the myth of "Merrie Africa" goes a corresponding and oversimplified fallacy depicting the West as a bastion of egoistic alienation fostering a traditional lack of social or collective concern—and hence a reluctance to foster social justice.

What about the relation of these variables to our dependent variables defining human rights? First, it is clear that the much-touted distinction or contrast of collectivist Africa versus an individualist West has been overdrawn. And from this less starkly different background even more convergence is evolving. As African economies develop, individual property rights in land, housing, and other forms of capital, never fully absent in Africa's past, are expanding. Add to this an accelerating rate of urbanization at twice the rate of population growth in which extended kin are being broken into smaller family units because of housing shortages, along with an urban-fed growth of individual responsibility in both criminal and civil law, to name only a few of the inexorable trends, and the outcomes are difficult to estimate. Without careful research that sets ideology aside, it is not a simple matter to say what the balance of individualism and collectivism will be as both of these ideologies are reproduced and changed in the years to come.

The invidious contrast of African and Western values has a more ominous side. As Nagan and Hansen point out (chapters 4 and 6, respectively), the emphasis on duties to the group in the African Charter stresses obligation to the community's rights, which may be interpreted as "trumping" individual rights when the two conflict. And if the state has a collective right and obligation to develop the society, economy, and polity (Article 29), then as an instrument it can be used to defend coercive state actions against both individuals and constituent groups to achieve state policies rationalized as social and economic improvement. Given the alleged primacy of collective or group life and welfare in African tradition, this claim gains legitimacy through its supposed rootedness in African historical experience. As already noted, this is an overgeneralization when compared with the actual facts of indigenous individualism. More importantly, the dangers of supporting state power as a fundamental "right" are obvious. Indeed, the African record to date on that score provides serious grounds for concern.

The argument so far leads to a number of hypotheses. African societies and nation-states emphasize both communal and individual rights, although there is a traditional tilt to communalism. Social conditions are selecting for and increasing the importance of individual merit and accountability while correlatively weakening the protection of the extended kin group and increasing personal insecurity and alienation. The stresses and insecurity of these changes are alleviated by creating and/or maintaining older-style linkages, new memberships, "old boy" associations, and ethnic associations. But most importantly for our purposes, these stresses have produced a new awareness of the need for rights protection across a wide range of social and cultural domains such as gender (chapter 5), language (chapter 8), and educational and academic rights (chapters 9 and 10). In effect (as Hansen notes in chapter 6), the need for rights protection within or between states increases once a person is outside the traditional sources of security in kin, village, and ethnic associations. For many fortunate enough to find viable linkages to power, utilizing well-established patterns such as patron-client relations can bridge the gap. But there are simply too many situations that require protection of one's capacity to succeed or even survive. Patron-client relations were never designed to take care of the vast numbers of transactions between ordinary people, or between persons and groups on the one hand and empowered officials on the other. Even a market for favors (corruption) or special "fixers" who can help expedite licenses, permits, school entrances, and the like cannot expand to meet the demand. As the following chapters demonstrate, such safeguards ultimately fail to keep pace with emergent problems among the wider population and the recognition of rights issues becomes an inevitable part of the development process.

At the level of the state, the use of tradition to justify the priority of collective over individual rights as obligation to the state is an intervening variable supporting increased state power. And to the degree that this quality overrides other forms of protection, it is relevant to the prediction of human rights conditions. In this sense, collectivist human rights claims used as a rationale for government policies are hypothesized to increase personal insecurity to the degree they are actually implemented, when *insufficiently checked* (or "trumped") by laws and practices defending the rights of individuals and constituent groups within the state.

Ethnicity

On its own, ethnicity has little or no relation to human rights. Some ethnic groups, usually the traditionally less stratified ones, have greater protection for individual rights, showing less inequitable treatment of individuals and women. But this is only a matter of degree. Thus, as an institution slavery was practiced as frequently among the unstratified as among the stratified African societies (Cohen and Schlegel

1968). In all indigenous African societies, or parts of them, individual or group grievances could be articulated by supporting more sympathetic leaders, or by voting with one's feet, or both. Although the topic is a complex one, ethnic differences per se are not necessarily related to rights issues.

However, once the scene shifts to interethnic relations, rights matters change significantly. Pluralism, the presence of distinctive groups (cultural, occupational, political, regional, etc.) within a single polity, involves the widespread issue of ethnic stratification. As widely noted (Schermerhorn 1970; Young 1976), this quality includes differential dominance, often with the denial of even the most fundamental human rights. Indigenous and even contemporary African societies have been no better or worse than most in their treatment of conquered or neighboring ethnic groups and their relations to foreign and/or pariah groups in their midst. However, the weakness of the state and the lack of a strong civil society mean that interethnic rivalries may easily flair into serious conflicts. On a number of occasions from the 1950s to the end of the civil war, colonial and postcolonial Nigerian governments were unable to prevent or even easily contain interethnic or interclan (Tiv) violence in the northern part of the country. (Similarly, the state did not prevent Hutu-Tutsi conflict in Rwanda and Burundi.) Whether or not some key state officials were in sympathy with the outbreaks, the upshot was the same: the state failed to prevent the violence. And it is noteworthy that since the civil war the Nigerian government has forcefully prevented any recurrence of such outbreaks.

Wherever ethnic stratification is a serious impediment to social justice, individuals are confronted by the reality of a shared fate with coethnics and must either defend or attack others for this reason. Africa is not unique in this respect. But from a human rights perspective this is important because both personal security and aggregated grievance reactions (our conception of the process of human rights emergence) are strongly related to ethnic stratification. As noted in chapters 8 and 9, it is difficult to travel anywhere in Africa and not encounter discussions, debates, and strong feelings about various forms of distributional rewards such as development investments, languages of instruction, quota hirings, and scholarships that are said to be influenced by ethnic criteria. The more favored groups demand greater importance for merit and achievement criteria; the less favored argue for some form of affirmative action policies to support a more equitable distribution of societal rewards. This trend is especially strong where ethnic stratification is an active component of the contemporary society, such as in Ethiopia, Sudan, Nigeria, and Kenya. Countries such as Tanzania and Botswana are less predisposed to these forces, having histories of less intense ethnic stratification.

However, the most relevant component of ethnicity for the understanding of human rights is not that of ethnic stratification, albeit this quality is the most noticed and commented on. The most important feature is that of the moral universe. This refers to the boundaries to which an individual is entreated ideally and trained in real-world terms to extend moral rules governing human interactions. Some cultural traditions preach moral rules of universal relevance; many others preach loyalty first to coethnics, and enmity, mistrust, and giving no quarter to those outside the ethnic boundaries stipulated as the end of the "we" and the usually penumbral beginnings of the "they." Once over that border all's fair. Moral rules do not apply; indeed people in the "they" category may hardly be seen as human or deserving of membership in a common field of action to which moral rules apply. Warfare, slave taking, and predatory raiding of settlements, trading caravans, and cattle herds, described in detail by nineteenth-century travelers, document this point repeatedly. In Hausaland it was possible for political leaders to settle foreign debts by declaring their own citizens to be apostate in Islamic faith in order to sanction punitive raids for booty and slaves (Richardson 1853).

More generally, universalistic beliefs are often curtailed by real-world ethnic boundedness. Most of the world religions—Islam, Christianity, Buddhism, and many others—stress the point that their moral teachings refer to all humanity or even to all living things. In practice, however, both in Africa and elsewhere these moral-religious beliefs often cannot overcome a more restricted application either to coreligionists or to coethnics based on older grounds of inclusion and exclusion. The problem of a conflict between belief and praxis of religious-moral principles that Marx (1977) saw for Christendom in Europe is even more severe for Africa, where older traditions of ethnic membership have only recently been overlaid by more universalistic religious beliefs and where experience teaches that the distribution of scarce rewards may be strongly influenced by ethnicity.

The moral universe is also influenced by economic and political relations. Economic relations require a level of mutual trust sufficient to support transactions even when these are interethnic. In Africa, blood brotherhood relationships, fictive kinship, joking relations, and negotiated mutual trust (*amana*) to structure and protect trading and other relations across ethnic boundaries have been recorded. Today many companies working in the private sector try to employ sales and service personnel who can represent the company to their own ethnic groups. Customers feel more comfortable with company representatives who are coethnics. But the company itself must learn to cope with its own multiethnicity. Ultimately, when push comes to shove its survival depends on people whose loyalty to and trust in this new economic unit are just as strong or stronger than their ethnic ties. Similarly, the state, starting with the colonial structure, initiated a set of laws, taxes, and administration at least at a minimal level and across ethnic lines. In both these instances ethnicity can affect appointments, promotions, and dismissals, but the organization is more efficient and more productive and has greater potential for survival when ethnicity is ignored. Here, then, are the organizational developments necessary for selecting and retaining expanded moral boundaries. Even so, their specificity is still acute—they started out as impositions from above and have always been applied to restricted arenas of behavior, ameliorated by the belief and experience that under present conditions in most of Africa the individual still shares his or her fate with his or her socially defined ethnic grouping.

In terms of human rights, this argument leads logically to the hypothesis that human rights practices and beliefs are dependent on the scale of the moral universe. And the moral universe is in turn dependent to some extent on the scale and scope of ethnicity. There is no end to ethnicity. It is propagated by politicians looking for constituencies among those wanting guaranteed protection of their shared fate in a plural society (Cohen 1978). But as already noted, memberships in new organizations such as private-sector firms and in the colonial and then as citizens in the independent state have increased memberships and made them cross-cut older ethnic units. As this happens, the importance and relevance of citizenship as a new ethnic marker has historically increased to include not just coethnics or coreligionists but fellow nationals as well. There come to be Kenyans, and Nigerians, and Senegalese, and so on, who must associate as fellow citizens and organization members within a common moral universe. Given religious, political, and economic factors that foster this process, there is a potential always to expand the moral universe beyond that of the "primordial" groupings and hence to make human rights praxis meaningful among a widening scale of social memberships. And, as Hyden concludes in the last chapter, the process occurs predictably in response to a number of factors.

Basic Needs

The criterion of personal security as the baseline human right is strongly determined by whether the conditions of life are sufficient to sustain existence itself. This means that being alive provides each individual with a claim on resources for his or her maintenance and survival; for many it means that the satisfaction of basic needs is a human right. However, the quantity and quality of that survival and of needs satisfactions are not matters of basic needs, as much of the literature suggests (Vincent 1986), but of development, which I discuss below. Nevertheless, to some degree "basic needs" are real. Using the statement above, a minimal level of food, drink, and other factors necessary to survival is a debt owed to humans for personhood.

Who holds the debt? We all do, but the responsibility for such security is inversely proportional to social distance. Family, extended kin, community, region, the state, and the international community are all involved, but the relative helplessness of newborn, disabled, and very old humans demands first and foremost that those closest to them protect their basic needs. Those at increasingly greater remove can aid in the process by supplying enabling resources such as clean water and health services and by providing emergency help when needed. This sets the stage and provides resources for magnifying the needs to be satisfied. Obviously, then, help capacities expand with development. But the actual delivery of basic needs requires information available only to those in intensive interaction with one another. In order to function at all, institutional and other wider-scaled agencies cannot operate unless they condense information flow from persons in need to needs supply. Enlarging the scale of responsibility for direct delivery of basic needs restricts its quality and quantity. Basic needs are most efficiently supplied by family, kin, and community organization. They are potentially more equitably and widely distributed by institutions dealing with publics. However, once the scale goes beyond primary group levels, standardization, bureaucratization, lack of identification with the public good, and information loss concerning the specific needs of individuals and local groups decrease the quality, often in the name of social justice.[12] In Africa, however, all scarce goods and services distributed by authorities are potentially and actually marketable by those with the discretionary capacity to administer programs. Decisions about bureaucratically regulated distributions can be bought and sold. From bedpans in hospitals to licenses, to fertilizers or places in law school, distribution policies oriented toward fairness are distorted by market forces governing who gets what and why. The goal of social justice has proven too often to be the open door to corruption and inequity of distribution—the African predicament.

In sum, basic human needs condition the possibility of a population achieving its human rights. Their satisfaction is dependent on the degree to which such needs can be met at the local level. Their delivery is weakened by any long-term removal from local control. Larger-scaled efforts can aid in delivery and cases of emergency but should not replace this requirement. In the long run, outside agencies can help by insisting that national and international standards (nutrition, health, etc.) are met. But if they assume long-term responsibility for supplying basic needs, they decrease the capacity for basic needs satisfaction by taking over local functions.

Development

Development refers to changes in a society that are directed to achieving self-sustaining improvements and prosperity for the greatest possible numbers. These changes are *directed* insofar as they result from actions and policies of the leading institutions in the public and private sectors. They are also *undirected* in that sustainable change requires adaptation—the possibility of wide ranges of choices and degrees of freedom for individuals and collectivities who are maximally free to select further developments stimulated by an environment of directed change and the demands of local contexts.

Development is also related to the increased importance of rights issues. This is not the place to discuss a full-blown theory of development, even if that were possible. It is useful, however, to examine how and why rights concerns have become more noticeable under conditions of development.

The relevant aspect of development for this analysis is that of differentiation, a mainstay of earlier theoretical approaches. Logically and empirically, differentiation involves the notion of whole societies in the form of new states that evolve more parts. These latter include new groupings, institutions, and so on, while simultaneously retaining and atrophying older ones, all the while trying to create and carry on workable and productive relations among them. This obvious quality has been set aside in the flurry of theorizing of the 1970s and 1980s in which equity and social welfare have moved onto center stage as more prominent criteria for defining development. From this point of view, differentiation has been a problem to be counteracted rather than a result and a stimulus to further the cause of development itself. To paraphrase one Nigerian agricultural expert, "You intellectuals from the West have confused us by lumping equitable rural social welfare with increased production—when in fact they are quite different and both pose important but quite separate problems for us in Africa." What he meant was that aid to rural smallholders provoked their differentiation into larger and smaller farmers, more and less commercialized, and that aid to very large farmers already commercialized was also important for increasing the nation's food supply. For him development means increasing the food supply to meet national shortfalls. And that goal means in turn that the rural population must inevitably become much more differentiated, resolving some problems while creating new ones (Cohen 1988: 22–23).

In macro terms, development has brought with it a bewildering amount of new groupings and new interests. Each grouping clambers, competes, and cooperates for access to resources and rewards; each has interests that both resonate and conflict in a confusing, often chaotic, and exciting world of change. These groupings and interests include rural versus urban demands for resources; labor unions and their demands; regional, ethnic, and linguistic demands; farmer organizations; women's associations; business organizations; students, especially university student organizations; the modern press; churches; teachers and university faculties; occupational organizations, both public and private; regional and town associations composed of people from a particular area or group—all juxtaposed and crosscut by patron-client relations that connect followers to ambitious "big men" with power in the government of the new state. In effect, then, the ubiquitous search for successful development produces increased demands that accelerate at a much faster rate than the capacity of the society to satisfy them. This is a benefit in that it provides a driving force for change that is internal and sustained. It is a cost in that these new nation-states verge constantly on the edge of destructive internal conflicts, the obvious remedy for which is the ready application of coercive control by the state, especially in the form of military regimes. But the shortfall of this solution is long-term legitimacy and orderly regime change. As Talleyrand noted long ago, the one thing one cannot do with a sword is to sit on it. Ultimately, as I discuss more thoroughly below, a "civil society" that evolves a cultural consensus about competition and social justice is the only durable means to counteract the conflicts engendered by Africa's ubiquitous dedication to development.

For present purposes, it is clear even from the brief remarks above that our two qualities said to define human rights, personal security and the capacity to aggregate and express fairness grievances, are deeply dependent on the development process. The greater the competition and conflict over scarce resources (constantly fed and expanded by new demands and the fear of losing what were thought of as safeguarded older privileges) among the rapidly expanding numbers of new groupings added to older ones, then the greater the concern for personal and group safeguards to security, and the greater the likelihood that rights issues will become paramount matters of public policy and private concern. Given the forces of change set in motion by the development commitment, it is inevitable that outbreaks and demands over unfair allocations from the past, the present, or planned for in future will become an ever more pressing set of issues. In this sense, development is a stimulus and a constant arena for the emergence and dramatization of human rights issues.

This same argument applies to the international community and the competition for resources within it. New states create more voices in the world system. The inequities in this system among states characterized by interdependent and semi-independent voices and interests, rather than subdued colonies and subordinated hegemonies, predict to many international issues being seen and expressed in fairness terms. In other words, part of the world system interaction is the emergence of arguments about grievances and interests by those who are less favored, all justified in terms of "human rights." This is exactly what has happened with the so-called third-generation rights discussions that translate world systems theory into international rights talk (Nagan takes a somewhat different view on this topic in chapter 4).

African States and Statism

Most African states are sovereign political systems derived as successor regimes to colonial governments. In the few exceptions (such as

Liberia and Ethiopia), the state was more or less set up by an outside power with results strikingly similar to those imposed by colonial conquest. This structural feature is the key to the contemporary crises and predicaments of African nations. More precisely, the colonial origins for statehood provided a heritage whose most significant characteristic is a relatively low level of vertical and horizontal integration under a distant and undemocratic regime at the center with authoritarian connections to local politics. The only way to change such a regime is by peaceful or armed rebellion that "liberates" the territory and supplants the government. No matter how it obtained power, the new postcolonial regime proclaimed total dedication to rapid development, national welfare, and the will of its constituent groupings and peoples.

However, liberation did little to change the colonial structure, even if it was packaged in the "Westminster," the Paris, or even the Peoples' Democracies models. Whatever the specific details, the colonial heritage lived on as a major element of the modern African state. It is important to note that this form of political underdevelopment is similar to the structure of the early (preindustrial) state. In both the new postcolonial and the early states, the core-periphery relations are not clearly delineated with neat hierarchies joining them to one another. The early state is a core, usually centered on a capital-citadel city with outlying areas more or less integrated. Over long periods of time state organization becomes a major ethnic marker, although constituent cultural differences remain both as vestiges and as potential fault lines for conflict. Political and economic networks adjust to state structures, and the process of vertical and horizontal integration serves to support a more developed state whose reproductive success is based on its own systemic quality, i.e., its adapting structure, its boundedness, and its capacity as a unit to cope with its own internal problems and external environments. In Africa, by contrast, the state structures hang partially suspended above the polity (Hyden 1983). Interpenetration of the state and the peoples it governs is weak, underdeveloped, and allows local groups an easy exit option while making national goals difficult to implement. In this regard the early state, the colonial state, and its successors all share a common trait. Social control and political allegiances are not well developed unless they are personal, based on older, more trustworthy associations or on newer class formations and other groupings not fully incorporated into society and polity.

Paradoxically, in Africa this weakness of the "soft" state has been correlated throughout much of the post–World War II period with an ideological commitment by political leaders and intellectuals to theories of statism—centralized planning and a managed economy. This *dirigisme* (Lal 1985) follows from a laudable desire to mobilize resources for rapid development while fostering social justice rather than inequality and social differentiation along with the multiple effects of individual and corporate profit orientations. The belief in *dirigisme* was widely promulgated as an antidote to the immorality of Western capitalist development, whose history of economic success also involved colonialism, racism, and the emmiserating exploitation of Africa's wealth for the welfare of the capitalist core. Socialism, centralized planning, and social justice geared to an assumed African tradition of collectivism were arguably more rational and more humane. And this approach was supported by the widespread belief especially among elites that private-sector development meant allowing foreign intervention using local lackeys rather than the pursuit of social justice through state-run distribution of the benefits of increased prosperity. The colonial successor state soon came under the control of an elite dedicated to statist ideology. Members of the elite saw clearly the African condition of political underdevelopment with its lack of integration. Many even realized its origins in the colonial form of state structure. And they also saw themselves as the solution—fathers of the new Africa, instruments of state formation and economic well-being whose empowerment could be used to achieve prosperity and avoid recapitulating the evils of Western development. In so doing they hoped to marry Western socialist theories with Africa's idealized communal past under one-party rule. The latter was justified as more traditionally African and as more stable in these underdeveloped and potentially conflict-laden polities. The goal under collectivist ideology was an accelerated and humane development arranged for by a progressive integration of state and society necessary for the mobilization and governance of a modern state. Using this ideology, governments would, it was hoped, build on what they believed to be the characteristically African concern for social welfare amidst a paternalistically led growth of economy and polity.

This was the vision. Given what the elites had to work with in terms of the colonial separation of government and society, underdeveloped theories, and little or no real-world experience of the internal and external constraints they faced, we can sympathize and understand their vain but human hope that the state in the hands of the well-intentioned could produce the societies they longed for. It didn't; instead African nations rocked and reeled from one venal regime to another within a rising frequency of military coups, takeovers, and, in several notable cases, notoriously suppressive periods. As Nagan points out in chapter 4, even within the framework of nobly phrased constitutions and legal processes that created an apparently independent judiciary, it is easy to pay lip service to these distant, foreign, and easily controlled and corrupted institutions. Indeed, the very notion of a truly independent judicial system is inimical to the structure and ideology of statist theory and praxis. And in practice the only thoroughly independent legal processes are those at the local levels whose primordial roots in the community act as they always have to administer a living law familiar and legitimate to those who live under it but for the most part unrelated to the new state. In any event, there is today widespread and growing awareness that statism is not the elixir it seemed when independence began and the future was new.

This awareness harks back to early antistatist theories. Building on his earlier work in the 1940s, Hayek (1971) based his ideas of statehood on the neoclassical notion of an infinite number of marketlike interactions that he called "spontaneous negotiations." These are partially free, partially guided, but never fully determined by decrees, legislation, rules and regulations of the state, plus the cultural traditions of constituent societies. Assuming this to be true, then overcentralized planning has two built-in tragic flaws. First, such planning must be based on enormous losses of the very kind of information required to make the planning a success. This, he argued, is normal for all bureaucratically led and centrally organized attempts to direct development. The hierarchy required by statist organization is therefore structured to shrink and squander its most necessary ingredient, the information necessary to make policy choices and implementation a success. Second, centralized directives are generally distorted as they move down a state-run command system past decision nodes in which each agency and every official involved have some discretionary capacity to interpret and renegotiate the implementation of policy. As Pressman and Wildavsky (1971) have demonstrated, the greater the interests of the local officials in the policy and its effects, the greater the distortions from top down, followed by increased distortion of the information flow back to the central government. In Africa the same problem supports and fosters the constant frustration of central planning, exit options at local levels, private or parallel markets, and corruption. It means that local plans and continuity of tradition along with resistance to change are made easy. It means that central planning and implementation always have limits. And in Africa this is doubly true since the successor regimes to colonialism had an early premodern state structure of underdeveloped coordination between command centers and their peripheries sustained by cultural, linguistic, communication, and transportation differences, to name only a few.

No matter how free or coercive the regime, all states contain an irreducible quantity of freely negotiable interactions along with a constant pressure to expand such freedom to ever-wider spheres as these affect people's interests and concerns. And this logic leads to a startling and apposite deduction. Given any validity at all to Hayek's theory and my reformulation of it for the African context, we can make an important knowledge claim about the hidden or intrinsic impulses in social life that nurture human rights. Because all human interactions contain minimal degrees of freedom with a constant tendency to expand it, there is also an unquenchable and inherent tendency to democratize built into human society. There is always some exit option, some degree of "uncapturedness" within *dirigisme* that people can informally use to create parallel or underground economies, even judicial procedures, leadership, communications, indeed almost any form of social and cultural life. The freedom to negotiate outcomes within the rules provides a constant dialectic or tension at the grass roots to expand freedom available in localized contexts. On the one hand, regulated and centralized directives of statist ideology and praxis operate to constrict interactions. But, and this is the point, those living in such systems and carrying out the interactions tend to increase their own degrees of freedom by bending, breaking, or avoiding the rules. Statist controls seek to decrease personal and group degrees of freedom in domains of activity often considered vital. Normal social interactions contain a constant tendency to work in the opposite direction. In this sense democratization is not simply an ideological goal. It is instead an inherent and fundamental attribute of human interactions. Its locus is universal. It resides in negotiations carried out by gratification-seeking and sympathizing actors who must deal with each other as persons and groups if they are to obtain from one another those resources and reactions necessary to survive and flourish. Given the sorry record of statist development policy, and its reality in newly independent Africa, then these factors—information loss and its resultant regime failures along with the democratization effect built into complex human interactions—predict to what is already happening: the failure of statist development policy and a pendulum swing toward privatization and increased democratization (Wunsch and Olowu 1990). I am aware, of course, that outside pressures from the lender and aid sources among capitalist nations and banks and the failure of statism in eastern Europe are also serving to stimulate these reactions. All that is obvious. However, the African response is not simply reactive and imitative. African policy moves away from statist ideology are also homegrown, stemming out of each state's own painful experience.

Furthermore, the trend is in no way complete, which is why and how this set of variables enters to influence our dependent phenomena of human rights. In effect, statist policies lead to regime insecurity (Schatzberg 1988). As already noted, statist regimes in Africa suffer from significant impediments to information flows between center and peripheries and are therefore underdeveloped in their capacity to choose adaptive policies and successful implementation. Programmed for high probabilities of failure, statist regimes have few alternatives. They can self-destruct through democratization—Nigeria has tried this once with quite disappointing results and is set to try again. Or they can do what most statist regimes decide to do—increase their coercive capacity, hoping to force policy implementation as well as maintaining the regime in power through the stifling of opposition and one-party rule (as Hyden describes in chapter 10). These factors, justified as requirements for development and as traditionally African in character, lead to regime insecurity and to suppression of opposition. Any attempts at coups, assassinations, or the arousal of popular opposition provide evidence to legitimize and magnify these fears among the leadership, which in turn accelerates the slide to suppression.

Once insecurity becomes part of the political culture of the statist regimes and the central government, countermeasures are bound to develop. In human rights terms, allowing people to aggregate their unfairness grievances is seen as a danger to national security and state/regime stability. Events all over Africa support this generalization. In Nigeria it is unlawful to criticize public officials openly. In many of the African states, incarceration without trial for "security" reasons is common practice. Freedom of expression is curtailed in manifold ways, again for reasons of security (Schatzberg 1988). It is as if African leaders see themselves as sitting on a powder keg. As Okoth-Ogendo and Nagan point out in chapters 3 and 4, respectively, rights then take second place to public order, and regime continuity and empowerment are justified in the cause of development. Given any kind of threat to state control (as in Kenya in 1982 and again in 1990 over popular demand for a multiparty system), then "emergency" conditions become the justification for a sudden magnification of state power curtailing citizen rights, the rule of law, and suppression or tight control of any opposition or public criticism. In the name of state security, personal security begins to constrict. And opposition to the regime or any activity defined as such, even satirical folksinging, can be declared dangerous to public order.

But when the lid goes on, the pot boils more easily. The foregoing argument indicates that statist regimes try to stifle those impulses inherent in human interaction out of which human rights emerge in a constant, insatiable flow. Thus it is no accident that rights are emerging as a widespread concern in Africa. The statist path to development has stimulated the constriction of rights in the name of social progress. Because humans cannot be programmed to accept social and cultural rules uncritically and cannot stop trying to increase their degrees of freedom to negotiate with one another, the attempt to constrict such activity increases the pressure to obtain more rights. It is rather like Boyle's law: the greater the constriction on a gas, the greater its pressure. Analogically, the greater the pressure applied to suppress personal security and the aggregation of unfairness judgments, the greater is the likelihood that the pressure to secure these rights will rise as a social force in the current events of the society. And this increased pressure leads ultimately to new kinds of questions and new kinds of goals—namely, determining what kind of society and culture not only fosters and sustains growth in material prosperity and its most equitable distribution but also fosters and protects the personal security of the citizenry and the right to assert and seek rights if and when these become relevant to citizens' own needs in the developing nation. It is the emergence into prominence of these issues and their place in the culture that I call matters of the civil society, and to these we must now turn.

Civil Society

The discussion of human rights and the empirical domains and factors that constrain and select for their enhancement assumes a normative goal—their enhancement in contemporary African societies. In effect I have been asking, what factors are predictive of greater human rights emergence and which are predictive of their suppression? The argument is deductive and hypothesis-generating but artificially analytic. Each set of conditions is in turn dependent on others, some of which are also theorized (rather artificially) to be independent variables on their own. This systemic quality in which causal arrows can be drawn every which way is difficult to conceptualize because of the interactive relations among determinants. Not surprisingly, the real world of rights is an evolving, fuzzy, kaleidoscopic intermingling of things I have so far taken to pieces.

To clarify the logic, it is necessary to raise the level of abstraction so that relationships discussed so far can be derived from a more general level of analysis. What we need is some kind of crucible in which these relations occur and a broader conceptualization that holistically represents our normative theory goal. For this purpose I have chosen a set of cultural-ideological conditions whose operation either weakens or strengthens all of the factors already listed and discussed.[13] I call this domain the *civil society*—a commitment to ways of doing things, to ideal goals, and to the quality of human interactions and their relations to power that fosters human rights concerns and practices in the society as a whole, indeed between societies in the international arena.

The civil society has a respectable history. As a notion it first surfaced with the Enlightenment to refer to the product of the contractarian covenant. Under Hegel it was reversed and represented a kind of collective id—the uncontrolled competitive and unruly realm that required ordering by the state to turn its potential savagery into something predictable and safe. Tocqueville and later Gramsci viewed it in terms closer to what I am reaching for. Tocqueville saw American society as wonderfully but dangerously individualistic (Bellah et al. 1985). It required a sense of the public good to survive, and he hoped that autonomous organizations and civic duty would develop sufficient strength in American habits to counteract the destructive force of libertarian self-seeking. Gramsci (1971) saw that the existence of autonomous organizations outside the direct control of the state—the civil society—was a safeguard against totalitarian statism, the hegemonic force that turns necessity into freedom: "[I]n Russia the State was everything; civil society was primordial and gelatinous. In the West, there was a proper relation between State and civil society, and when the State trembled a sturdy structure of civil society was at once revealed. The State was only an outer ditch behind which there stood a powerful system of fortresses and earthworks" (A. Gramsci, cited in Lewis 1989).

My own approach has emerged somewhat independently and inductively from my concern with human rights issues and the problem of statist development in Africa. After a series of interactions with colleagues at the University of Florida and with African colleagues, I began to define a cultural domain whose growth and incorporation into the behavior and character of peoples would safeguard human rights. This I have called the civil society—not because it is the other side of the coin to the "political" society, but because it embodies the concept of "civility," implying both culturally induced considerateness and behavior fitting to proper, moral citizenship. In this sense I am departing from traditional usage in order to imagine a political-cultural domain that generates theoretical questions (and, I hope, answers) about human rights.

In carrying this idea forward I have included three qualities. It must be stressed that these are simply heuristics, i.e., working ideas to get things started. I begin with the relations of the state to the citizenry. It is clear that human rights practices are deeply conditioned by the way in which people see and believe the state to be dealing with its citizenry. The just and fair outcomes of the state's everyday and long-term relations to the citizenry define the setting for the civil society. The measure of this is simply the way in which a majority of the members of constituent plural groupings and individuals feel when they wish to or must have dealings with government, including officials in bureaucratic agencies, elected representatives if such exist, law enforcement personnel, and the courts when disputes and charges against them are adjudicated. The greater the majority who believe that such actions are indeed fair, then the more auspicious is the environment for human rights safeguards and emergence.

Second, the civil society is measured by the degree to which the norms and values of the society propagate a concern for the public or common good. This involves a widespread ideology that everyone in all walks of life in the plural society has an obligation to contribute to the collective well-being. It is measured by the degree to which individuals and groups in the nongovernmental sector display a belief in the importance of the public good. The depth of concern over the quality and distribution of education, health care, and other public amenities not just for self but for the public at large is a specific indicator of this quality. The degree to which such matters are debated and claims made on their behalf for an entire public or for humankind as a whole, rather than for a more limited or parochial segment, is a measure of this feature in a particular sociocultural setting. This level of civil society is therefore cultural; it assumes that peoples vary in the degree to which their teachings and debate about duties to the public good are given prominence in everyday life.

Third, the civil society embodies a quality of civility in the everyday life of the modern plural society, in Africa as elsewhere. What I refer to here is a cultural feature that goes beyond duty to a personal involvement in the welfare of others. This is defined as the degree to which social, economic, and political—indeed all—interactions and negotiations are governed by culturally defined norms of sympathy and empathy for the welfare of other individuals or groups as opposed to benefits for self or one's own group, that is to say, by altruistic rather than aggressive, selfish, or parochial goals. Measures of such civility have been developed by those engaged in "altruism" or so-called prosocial research. These generally include measures of helping behavior and records of sympathy for the plight of other persons and groups at various degrees of social distance in a plural society. To this I would add the degree to which "good manners," i.e., cultural traditions of obligatory considerateness, are developed and practiced in everyday life in plural society settings. In this sense good manners are ritualized forms of thoughtfulness. Their scale and scope, the degree to which they are valued and used across all activities, are measures of the civility of interactions among persons and groups in a society.[14]

This is not the place to develop and explain a theory of the civil society. However, it is clear that the greater the civil society components that exist in the modern African setting, the greater will be all of the conditions that increase the probability of human rights recognition in the social and political life of the state. Factors that in turn determine a more civil society are qualities that form a research frontier. They include dual evolutionary (biological plus cultural) potential for altruistic behavior, governance features that promote accountability of public servants and government in general, socialization and education that stress both citizenship and the belief that personal and group fate is determined more by the exercise and protection of just outcomes than by membership in particular groups (ethnic, occupational, or class), protected legal processes that ensure the rule of law, and the degree to which public and private debate about rights issues occurs and is fostered as a protected and hallowed part of the national culture (Ackerman 1980).

As Hyden points out in chapter 10, public debate is a crucial factor. Such "rights talk," or dialogue, is a quality that must be sought after, enabled, and protected if civil society and human rights are to be selected for and retained in a society's development. What it refers to is the notion that a society values and promotes its sources of self-criticism. Intellectuals, religious leaders, the politically ambitious, the press and other media—all foster and responsibly contain the critical assessment of the society and its performance as a whole. By my definition rights are not reified things. They exist as personal security and the capacity to aggregate unfairness judgments in the social life of the state. Free and responsible dialogue about local and national issues is the fundamental condition required both for civility and for enabling all the other factors already discussed. Such assessments have to be responsible, i.e., sensitive to their effects, especially in Africa, where conflicts over access to resources can lead to the breaking of the dam of social order and a flood of conflict and violence. But those close to such situations and experienced in the local conflicts and frustrations know where the thresholds are. And governments can discover and regulate the (changing) conditions and thresholds of incitement as opposed to the healthy and necessary safeguarding of rights talk.

Conclusion

We have come as far as this present volume will allow. There is more, much more to be done, as the above section on civil society has shown. At the same time this introduction and the papers of the volume have opened a new chapter for African studies. So far we have asked questions, posed puzzles, and sought knowledge claims about the history, the meaning, and the development (primarily economic development) of the continent. It is now time to move on to issues of human welfare and critical appraisals. Our African colleagues are ahead of us in this regard. Leaders like Ogendo in Kenya (chapter 3), Eze (1984) in Nigeria, and other writers and artists of all kinds are well into "rights talk." Our task is to apply tools of social science and legal scholarship to aid in this task. Working with colleagues on the continent research is part of a wider quest for the expansion of human rights awareness and safeguards. As I have described it, this campaign is closely associated with the development of a more civil society that acts as Gramsci suggested—to buttress societies against tyranny and to build the foundations of a more decent and tolerant existence for Africans in their everyday lives. That is what we seek, that is what we hope for.

Notes

1. Thus one writer (Emerson 1975) posited an African "regression" from a previous state of comparatively greater political order and civil justice under colonial rule. And another (Falk 1981) views the problem as one of transition in the normative orientations of governments among Third World nations in which, it is hoped, they can develop greater reliance on consent rather than on statist coercion. All or most of this critique used Western ideology and contemporary practices as a standard of comparison. On the other hand, Howard (1983) has examined the criteria for comparison between colonial Africa, colonial times, and early and comparable conditions in Europe to indigenous African cultural values. She also uses what she defines as universalistic standards of rights behaviors. As with most fine-grained analyses, her results show African states to have a mixed and complex record in the human rights domain—neither all bad nor all good, once the details and their causes and correlates are gone into carefully. It is therefore important to acknowledge her contribution and to note that this present undertaking owes much to her pioneering efforts.

2. See the various Amnesty International reports on Kenya (1987, 1988), Zaire (1988), Sudan (1988), and Uganda (1989). They can be obtained from the National Office, 322 Eighth Avenue, New York, NY 10001.

3. Personhood is itself a controversial concept whose beginning and end are unclear. It is most consensually viewed within contemporary Western culture as a variable boundary between conception and second-term fetus on the one hand and brain-dead vegetative states through total heart failure on the other. Exact definitions for any particular case are variably determined by social debate, technology and its availability, professional ethics in medicine, plus the force and flexibility of religious values defining the nature of life (Jones 1990). In traditional African cultures there are tests applied to newborns whose full personhood is in doubt, to determine whether they should become fully recognized community members. In many instances, naming is delayed to see whether the newborn survives. Until that event, the neonate is not a full person and is generally deprived of the right to a proper burial.

4. It was easy to define forced labor, or wage labor, as an obligation that people had to perform as a duty to the state in return for privileges such as roads and administration. Some—for example, the Portuguese—simply stated that it was the duty of all adult African males to show through local records that they were not "idle," i.e., that they had performed specified forms of work, including corvée labor, during a calendar year (see Harris 1958).

5. At the 1988 workshop on human rights in Nairobi, F. Baldwin made the case for a finite and restricted set of means to protect human rights within the structure of the modern state.

6. Seighart (1986: x–xi) claims that discussions over what is and what is

not a human right are endless because there is no agreed-upon method of establishing consensus. He therefore abandons this goal and adopts a behaviorist position in which a human right exists when made manifest in some form of law that prescribes conduct and that once in force is disobeyed at peril to those who break it. The difficulty of this definition for research and theory is obvious. Once we go outside the working laws of a society or some internationally accepted codes, the topic is defined as outside our reach.

7. The ascribed rights of the aristocracy in medieval Europe or the race-based rights of whites in South Africa were seen by their protagonists as their "human rights," just as many of the peoples of the Muslim kingdoms of the savanna saw their non-Muslim neighbors as not having or deserving of human rights. As with many other racist or parochial views on human rights, these can be predicted to atrophy over time.

8. Fairness involves an assessment of equitableness in the acceptance of outcomes of interactions and the distribution of scarce values. As Hayek (1971) notes, all interactions are both rule-directed and the result of spontaneous negotiations in which bargains are constantly being struck within varying degrees of freedom for all parties concerned. In Rawlsian terms the bargained outcomes are fair and can be assessed as such if those receiving the less valued outcomes find them acceptable. The situation is then said to be fair or "just." But should a party deem outcomes unacceptable, that group will conclude that it has a grievance over the exchange/interaction. The situation is then assessed as unfair or "unjust." However, in some situations (e.g., abortion and right to life) there have to be winners and losers both of whom see their side as just, the other as unjust. Fairness then involves allowing those supporting the losing position a continuing voice to debate and foster their own assessment, i.e., an environment that protects their views.

9. Scale refers to the number of persons who accept and practice a tradition; scope is the degree to which a particular tradition is incorporated into the entire gamut of varied activities in a way of life. When asked, everyone in the United States claims to accept democracy and support it in practice. But this acceptance refers primarily to the political sphere and voluntary associations. There are many contexts, such as the workplace, where democratic practices are for the most part quite unwelcome.

10. For example, Grimm's fairy tales, with their emphasis on the lone individual who cannot even trust close kin, as well as the cowboy who remains moral by avoiding the Sodom and Gomorrah of the town. The biblical image is not accidental. In the West there is a tradition that collective life is compromising and therefore demoralizing, while lonely individualism is a condition of moral purity. The monk, the biblical prophet, and the cowboy refrigerate morality by staying away from town, the Sodom and Gomorrah these heroes avoid or only enter to set things right morally, then leave in order to remain pure through asceticism.

11. Bellah et al. (1985) cite Tocqueville and note that Western individualism, especially its American variety, stems out of a tradition of personal freedom that has a constant tendency toward isolation from the community. However, there are "countervailing tendencies that pull people back from their isolation into social communion. . . . The habits and practices of religion and democratic participation educate the citizen to a larger view than his private world would allow" (Bellah et al. 1985: 65). And it is only when self-interest has been transcended that both individualism and the society at large can succeed.

12. Research on social democracy in Scandinavia indicates that the greater and longer the welfare functions are absorbed by the state, the greater is the tendency for individuals to transfer their sense of individual responsibility to the state. In effect, the state becomes the legitimate and primary locus of moral initiative. This is associated with increased problems of social order, anomie, and, most especially, new and unintended constraints in the reproduction of morality down the generations (Wolf 1989).

13. In order to justify my choice paradigmatically, which is not important to me from an eclectic point of view (Cohen 1988: 26–27), I would have to argue the case for the fundamental causal origins—in this instance (certainly not always) of ideological and cultural phenomena over those of the material base or the social/political/economic structures. In the case of rights, the goal of expanding them in ideological terms is the engine driving an increase across all of the independent variables. As I will argue, this ideology has various causal forces determining its entitativity, and its scale and scope, but it also has causal force on its own. From the eclectic point of view, even though there is much validity in the ultimate causal significance of material factors, understanding of more immediate or proximal causality requires that we be open to causal influences from any and all sources.

14. I am aware that "good manners" have also been widely used historically to support and reflect inequality and respect between the more and the less powerful. However, such usages atrophy with democratization while ritualized consideration remains as the adaptive residue of traditions that (among others) structure altruistic acts.

References

Achebe, C. 1988. *Anthills of the Savanna*. New York: Anchor Press.
Ackerman, B. A. 1980. *Social Justice in the Liberal State*. New Haven: Yale University Press.
Baldwin, F. 1988. Universal Aspects of the American Constitution. Paper delivered at Nairobi workshop on human rights.
Bellah, R. H., et al. 1985. *Habits of the Heart*. New York: Harper and Row.

Cassese, A. 1990. *Human Rights in a Changing World*. Cambridge: Polity Press.
Cohen, R. 1970. "Traditional Society in Africa." In *The African Experience*, ed. J. N. Paden and E. W. Soja. Evanston, Ill.: Northwestern University Press.
———. 1978. "Ethnicity." *Annual Review of Anthropology*. Palo Alto: Annual Reviews.
———. 1981. "Evolutionary Epistemology and Human Values." *Current Anthropology* 22: 201–18.
———. 1988. "Introduction: Guidance and Misguidance in Africa's Food Production." In *Satisfying Africa's Food Needs*, ed. R. Cohen, pp. 26–27. Boulder, Colo.: Lynne Rienner.
———. 1991. "Altruism and the Evolution of Civil Society." In *Embracing the Other*, ed. P. M. Oliner et al., pp. 104–29. New York: New York University Press.
Cohen, R., and A. Schlegel. 1968. "The Tribe as a Socio-Cultural Unit: A Cross-cultural Examination." In *Essays on the Problem of the Tribe*, ed. J. Helm. Seattle: University of Washington Press (for the American Ethnological Society).
Cranston, M. 1977. "Human Rights, Real and Supposed." In *Political Theory and the Rights of Man*, ed. D. D. Raphael. London: Macmillan.
Donnelly, J. 1985. *The Concept of Human Rights*. New York: St. Martin's Press.
Emerson, R. 1975. "Faith of Human Rights in the Third World." *World Politics* 27: 1–17.
Eze, O. C. 1984. *Human Rights in Africa*. Lagos: Macmillan Nigeria.
Falk, R. 1981. *Human Rights and State Sovereignty*. New York: Holmes and Meier.
Gramsci, A. 1971. *Selections from the Prison Notebooks*. New York: International Publishers.
Harris, M. 1958. *Portugal's African Wards*. New York: American Committee on Africa.
Hayek, F. 1971. *Law, Legislation and Liberty*. Chicago: University of Chicago Press.
Howard, R. 1983. *Human Rights in Anglophone Africa*. Totowa, N.J.: Rowman and Littlefield.
Hyden, G. 1983. *No Shortcuts to Progress*. Berkeley: University of California Press.
Jones, M. L. 1990. "What Is the Difference between Humanness and Personhood?" Paper prepared for Civil Society Seminar, Dept. of Anthropology, University of Florida, Gainesville.
Lal, D. 1985. *The Poverty of "Development Economics."* Cambridge: Harvard University Press.
Legesse, A. 1980. "Human Rights in African Political Culture." In *The Moral Imperatives of Human Rights: A World Survey*, ed. K. W. Thompson. Washington, D.C.: University Press of America.

Lewis, Flora. 1989. "The Rise of Civil Society." *New York Times*, 25 June.
Marx, K. 1977. "On the Jewish Question." In *Karl Marx: Selected Writings*, ed. D. McLellan. Oxford: Oxford University Press.
Milne, A. J. M. 1986. *Human Rights and Human Diversity*. London: Macmillan.
Pressman, D., and A. Wildavsky. 1971. *Implementation*. Berkeley: University of California Press.
Richardson, J. 1853. *Narrative of a Mission to Central Africa*. Vol. 2. London: Chapman and Hall.
Schatzberg, M. G. 1988. *The Dialectics of Oppression in Zaire*. Bloomington: Indiana University Press.
Schermerhorn, R. A. 1970. *Comparative Ethnic Relations*. New York: Random House.
Seighart, P. 1986. *The Lawful Rights of Mankind*. Oxford: Oxford University Press.
Shue, H. 1980. *Basic Rights: Subsistence, Affluence, and U.S. Foreign Policy*. Princeton, N.J.: Princeton University Press.
Vincent, R. J. 1986. *Human Rights and International Relations*. Cambridge: Cambridge University Press.
Wolf, A. 1989. *Whose Keeper?* Berkeley: University of California Press.
Wunsch, James, and D. Olowu, eds. 1990. *The Failure of the Centralized State*. Boulder, Colo.: Westview Press.
Young, C. 1976. *The Politics of Cultural Pluralism*. Madison: University of Wisconsin Press.

2

Human Rights and Precolonial Africa

TIMOTHY FERNYHOUGH

Recent debate about rights in Africa has turned on a division between those who deny and those who affirm the existence of an indigenous human rights tradition. Ironically, both groups take as their starting point a precolonial Africa that they agree was precapitalist and predominantly agrarian, relatively decentralized politically, and characterized by communal social relations. Their argument over African human rights is fundamentally interpretive. Thus Donnelly (1985: 49-50) and Howard (1986b: 13-20) contend that in precolonial Africa, as in most non-Western and preindustrial societies, forms of social and political organization rendered the means to attain human dignity primarily through duties and obligations, often expressed in a communally oriented social idiom and realized within a redistributive economy. Yet both reject with unwarranted emphasis the notion that in the search for guarantees to uphold human life and dignity precolonial Africans ever formulated or correlated such claims to protection in terms of human rights (Donnelly 1982: 307-8; Howard 1986a: 17-18). For Donnelly and Howard, it is only Africa's relatively recent incorporation into the capitalist world economy, albeit in a subordinate role, that has created a new and individual "modern man and woman," physically removed from family and local community and reaching for protection, often in new urban contexts, beyond these primary effective and supportive ties to new concepts of human rights (Donnelly 1985: 82-84; Howard 1986a: 28-33).

By contrast, though also with precolonial Africa as their baseline, the proponents of a historically indigenous human rights tradition have tried to discern these rights in the continent's past. Mojekwu (1980: 85) has posited that concepts of human rights have been basic to Africa since antiquity. Adegbite (1968: 69) has moved a step further to assert that individuals in precolonial Africa may have enjoyed greater freedom than their modern counterparts. With scholars like Wai (1979), Marasinghe (1984), and Legesse (1980), both Mojekwu and Adegbite portray a pleasing, if not entirely credible, image of precolonial Africa. They highlight the contractual, co-optive, and consensual in politics; the redistributive in justice and economy; and the communitarian in ideology and forms of social organization.

In this attractive picture, which embraces a morally immaculate image of "Merrie Africa" (Hopkins 1973: 10), is rooted a whole communitarian tradition in African legal philosophy and political theory. Long in pedigree and articulated early by the first leaders of independent Africa, notably by Kaunda (1966: 22–28) and Nyerere (1968: 11–12), the communitarian idiom stresses the primary role of ascriptive corporate groupings from extended families to lineages and clans. By extension, it also affirms the importance of collective rights, as well as the reciprocal commitments Africans have to their communities in return for protection of their human dignity. In recent years this idealized view of precolonial Africa clearly moved those who drafted the African Charter on Human and Peoples' Rights (the Banjul Charter) to advance with their definition of individual rights incorporated from the Universal Declaration of Human Rights the concept of collective or "group" rights and the notion of duties owed by citizens to sovereign states.[1]

Hence, fairly similar views of precolonial Africa have led to very different conclusions. From one perspective the human rights tradition was quite foreign to Africa until Western, "modernizing" intrusions dislocated community and denied newly isolated individuals access to customary ways of protecting their lives and human dignity. Human rights were alien to Africa precisely because it was precapitalist, preindustrial, decentralized, and characterized by communal forms of social organization (Donnelly 1985: 82; Howard 1984a: 176). From the opposing viewpoint there is a fundamental rejection of this as a new, if rather subtle, imperialism, an explicit denial that human rights evolved only in Western political theory and practice, especially during the American and French revolutions, and not in Africa (Vincent 1986: 37–38). Behind this protest is the very plausible claim that human rights are not founded in Western values alone but may also have emerged from very different and distinctive African cultural milieus (Wai 1979: 116–18).

The primary aims of this analysis are two, a thematic division that is also reflected in the essay's structure. The intent of the first section is to depict a middle path between the two predominant and opposing views of human rights in Africa, though this course requires challenges to premises discrete and elemental to each perspective. The objective of the second part of the essay is to identify, characterize, and evaluate rights held and enjoyed in Africa before the coming of Europeans, and to move beyond this to determine which, if any, of these were claimed or perceived as specifically *human* rights. To date, virtually all Africanist scholars who have examined rights in precolonial Africa have generalized on the basis of scant historical evidence, a meager empirical base that is most often quite narrowly confined, both chronologically and geographically. Yet few have hesitated to make broad assertions about peculiarly African rights on the basis of cursory analysis.[2]

Perspectives on Human Rights in Africa

In the extant literature, Donnelly (1982, 1985), Vincent (1986), and Howard (1986b) offer analyses of human rights, and of non-Western conceptions of rights, unmatched in their theoretical sophistication. Howard's *Human Rights in Commonwealth Africa* (1986a) marks the most solid recent contribution to understanding rights in the African context, with a cogent argument for profound structural transitions as remedies for human rights abuses. The views of these three scholars are by no means identical and they diverge in matters of emphasis and specificity. Nevertheless, they share essentially common views about the sources and the nature of human rights. Because an extended analysis of these issues lies beyond the scope of this essay, suffice it to say that their notions of human rights include the following assumptions.

First, they assert that human rights derive directly from a person's humanity. Their source is the best side of man's moral nature (Donnelly 1985: 9, 31–37; Vincent 1986: 13–18). Rooted in this nature that all human beings share, human rights are by implication inalienable, relatively absolute, and universal in scope and application. Second, they argue that human rights uphold human dignity but that these are by no means synonymous, pace Pollis and Schwab (1979: 8–9; 1982: 10), who tend to equate the two. The difference between human rights and human dignity is quite clearly the difference between means and ultimate ends (Donnelly 1982: 313). By the same token, human rights are claimed rights or moral entitlements, not simply duties, reciprocal obligations, or benefits. Moreover, basic rights take prior claim, in Dworkin's sense (1978: xi–xii), as "trumps," or even as Donnelly's "honor cards" (1982: 306) with special status over other demands.

Third, Howard and Donnelly (1987: 6) assume the interdependence and equivalence of different kinds or "generations" of human rights.[3] However, Howard (1986a: 221–22) argues that the pursuit of civil and political rights cannot be postponed until the achievement of social and economic rights, or indeed of women's rights, rights to development, or group solidarity. Indeed, in her view equitable economic distribution may rest on the previous implementation of civil and political rights. Finally, Donnelly (1982: 305–6), Vincent (1986: 13–16), and Howard (1986a: 220) agree that because human rights derive from human nature, both moral and physical, they must inhere in individuals and in our mutual need to live meaningful lives. Donnelly (1985: 32–37) is at pains to stress that human rights are not merely defined by an individual's innate moral dignity. In fact, they are the product of an activist or "constructivist" interaction between individual claims to rights, social conditions, and political realities.

These assumptions are largely at odds with prevailing opinion about human rights in Africa. In the first instance, they force front stage the debate between those who view human rights as culturally relative and proponents of their universality. Working within the communitarian tradition, Legesse (1980: 129) and Marasinghe (1984: 32–34) affirm that for many African societies, which shared the Western experience not at all or only as the transitory dominance of European colonialism, moral precepts and values, including notions of rights, are inseparable from the cultures that validate them. Their view is clear. Human rights that are Western in origin and construct have only limited application in a culturally plural world (Pollis and Schwab 1979: 4, 8–14). Hence, proponents of universal rights advocate an insidious and pervasive Western ethnocentrism (Vincent 1986: 38).

Central to this culturally relative perspective is the by now familiar notion that human rights in Africa were founded in communal principle and practice, which favored groups over individuals. At root human dignity and justice rested on membership and ascribed status within a social unit, which gave meaning and substance to political, social, and economic rights (Mojekwu 1980: 86-87). Moreover, the group provided a normative system that upheld basic moral principles and patterns of behavior (Marasinghe 1984: 33). Incorporation within the social unit, whether clan, lineage, age grade, generation set, village, or family, validated in communal terms an individual's claim to human rights. Denied moral and material support by the community and deprived of protection under the law, the outcast in African society was a sorry and isolated figure, though provisions often existed to accommodate traders and the offspring of slaves (Miers and Kopytoff 1977: 3-49). From this perspective, exclusion eroded human dignity through a fundamental diminution of a person's humanity and a basic loss of rights (Mojekwu 1980: 85). Indeed, Marasinghe (1984: 36) regards the power to exclude the very element that made membership in community a human right in precolonial African societies. However extreme that assertion, by all these definitions the line between human dignity and human rights is effectively blurred.

Two further conditions frame the concepts of those who approach human rights in Africa from a communitarian perspective. As they posit the redistributive and equalizing function of the communal model, Legesse (1980: 125-27) and others stress that social and economic claims are as important as civil and political ones and may in fact take a higher place in the hierarchy of human rights. Though tempered subsequently, this was a view initially and most forcibly expressed by Nkrumah (Welch and Meltzer 1984: 25, 31). More recently, the provisions of the Banjul Charter assert specific entitlements to social and economic rights and to the right to development, the latter first articulated and argued by the Senegalese jurist M'Baye (1972: 505-34). In placing such rights at the very least on a par with the enjoyment of civil and political rights, those who drew up the Charter reflected the prior and often immediate concern of many African governments with problems of economic development (Vincent 1986: 40).

Nonetheless, as Nyerere's writings (1968: 106) suggest, there are many Africans who would argue that the primacy of economic rights in Africa is time-honored, far older indeed than the current debates about development and human rights. Reaching back before European rule, the communitarian perspective stresses the allegedly egalitarian composition of precolonial African societies, particularly the perceived absence of exploitative classes. Even where class structures existed, so this argument runs, they were tempered by reciprocal social and familial bonds (Nyerere 1968: 107–8).

The second condition also derives from the communal model. The Western approach to human rights stresses the point that they are vested in the individual, by virtue of a person's quintessential humanity. Human rights are held against other individuals and especially against society and state structures that are most likely to abuse them (Donnelly 1982: 306; Howard 1986a: 16–17). By contrast, the emphasis on collective rights in African philosophy and political theory reflects not only a preoccupation with the communitarian ideal but also a profound difference over where to locate human rights. Legesse (1980: 124) refutes explicitly the notion that for Africa "the ultimate repository of rights is the human person," while Mojekwu (1980: 92) is clear that neither the colonial nor the postindependence period successfully erased African notions of kinship and communal rights in favor of a universal principle of individual human rights. For Legesse (1980: 129), the idea that human rights inhere in each individual denies the primacy of collective or group rights. Unaware that the Soviets argued, unsuccessfully, for collective rights in the 1940s, he argues that had those who framed the Universal Declaration of Human Rights been African they might have couched their definitions in very different terms. For Mojekwu, the very suggestion that human rights communally expressed and guaranteed be somehow individualized implies yet another attempt to apply Western concepts in the African setting.

Distillation of a new human rights blend from the African mixture requires an attempt to move analysis beyond previous discussions of the origins and nature of rights, whether derived from a Western tradition looking back to Cicero, Aquinas, Locke, and Mill or from a nostalgic view of precolonial Africa. Simultaneously, the framing of a new way of thinking about rights in Africa also demands that this cannot consist merely of adding the extant approaches to human rights together or making long, cumulative lists of rights. Therein lies no solution. As Vincent (1986: 50) has suggested, the process of addition fails to mediate the difference between opposing views, nor does it distinguish adequately between the general and the particular. In the African case, for example, this approach offers no way to reconcile contending views of individual or collective precedence in the determination of human rights. Conversely, an effort to reduce the different human rights approaches to their lowest common denominator, to look for a universally shared set of core rights, flies in the face of our understanding of anthropological diversity and is fundamentally ahistorical (Vincent 1986: 49).

In reality, it is possible to work toward consensus and a new approach to human rights in Africa at one and the same time. Previous scholarship offers critical insights to interpreting African human rights that we cannot afford to discard, whatever the prevailing perspective. Thus the preface to discussion of a new paradigm necessarily requires a further definition of terms and a comment on context. In the former lies the kernel of my dissent with those who uphold a uniquely African concept of human rights, ultimately rooted in African kinship and community. From the latter emerges my dissatisfaction with those who assert the universality of human rights but then argue that they are "an artifact of modern Western civilization" (Donnelly 1982: 303).

My view is that Donnelly, Howard, and Vincent are far more consistent human rights theorists than Marasinghe (1984: 42–44) and others might allow. The strength of their argument is that they place the source of human rights exactly where it belongs, with the individual human, not the collective. Their derivation of human rights from man's moral nature is fundamental and not necessarily inimical to cultural diversity. A human rights theory founded on a moral view of human nature makes prerequisites of such elements as man's basic physical and psychological needs (see Bay 1968: 241–60; Bay 1981: 90–94) or, by other terms, his rights to certain "goods," notably security, liberty, and subsistence (Shue 1980: 18–20; Gewirth 1982: 5–10). Moreover, Donnelly's (1985: 32–35) emphasis on the dialectical relationship between human nature, human rights, and political society that works to shape and therefore to define all three has important implications for the development of an evolutionist approach to human rights in Africa.

The alternative, as many Africans believe, is to base human rights theory on the collective and not the individual. This poses both philosophical and practical problems. Together these detract from, if not invalidate, this particular tack. Assuming that a human rights theory needs grounding in an appeal to physical or moral needs, whether communal or personal, and is not merely derived from prevailing cultural traditions and practices or an arbitrary rationalization of the status quo, the initial issue is one of substantive definition. Defining human rights concepts in terms of a collective base requires us to accept analytical imprecision and to acknowledge that empirical testing is near impossible. Thus there are few who would try to ground a human rights theory in such notions as "great tradition" (Redfield 1956: 70–79), "moral economy" (Thompson 1971: 78–79), or the "economy of affection" (Hyden 1980: 18–19; Hyden 1983: 8–22). While these attempts to conceptualize the behavior of rural communities are vital to understanding *mentalités*, the evolution of political language, and the ideological bases of social institutions, they are too open-ended to substantiate human rights theory.

In this ambiguity lies our inability to define accurately a particular community's physical and moral needs and thereby establish a basis for concepts of human rights. What further compounds the situation in Africa is the perennial difficulty of establishing spatial boundaries for historically dynamic and ever-changing societies, a problem highlighted in recent years by the penetration of Western ideas and institutions. Defining the community and its universally held moral and material horizons becomes no more than a subjective judgment call. By contrast, because individual needs derive from human nature, they offer a foundation for rights that is manifest and empirically sound. Lacking a firm base, especially as a definitive moral posit, communally founded notions of human rights rest on very shaky theoretical ground. In these circumstances empirical testing is probably a futile exercise.

It is at the practical level that the essential contradiction between communally based group or "peoples'" rights and individual rights remains unresolved. In the real world the former impinge on the latter. Moreover, society's needs can easily be used to rationalize the derogation of human rights. In Donnelly's terms (1982: 312), it appears that the community permits the individual to enjoy human rights but has the prior right to deny that enjoyment. The community can always amend individual duties required for its own well-being, though this may detract from human rights. Loose terminology accentuates the problem, for in most instances community, group, or "people" really means the state and the ruling elites within it. Noting the failure to define "people" or "peoples' rights" in the Banjul Charter, Howard has argued with forceful logic that in Africa the assertion of "peoples' rights" is simply a means to favor the rights of states and their ruling classes over the interests and rights of individuals (Howard 1986a: 8, 16, 221).

Donnelly presents one of the most articulate explications of how to derive and formulate a theory of human rights. It is the internal cogency of his argument about the source and nature of such rights which convinces me that these are vested in the individual, not the elevation of the individual in Western political theory since the European Renaissance. Indeed, it is precisely for this reason that I believe that Donnelly, Vincent, and Howard are wrong in their conviction that *human* rights were "not the way of traditional Africa" (Donnelly 1982: 308). When scholars like Legesse, Marasinghe, Mojekwu, and Wai assert that human rights existed in precolonial Africa, they are correct, but not because human rights are necessarily held collectively or vested in community.

Almost alone among those engaged in the discussion about African rights, Eze and Asante have questioned the communal basis of human rights, though from different perspectives. As Shivji has remarked (1989: 13–14), Eze appears to argue "that Africa did have notions of human rights *qua* human rights." Eze explicitly rejects as "romantic" the usual communitarian emphasis on social harmony and redistributive justice (Eze 1984: 13). However, there is a frustrating hesitancy about his conclusion. He comments that Africans knew and practiced derogations from human rights, with slavery and human sacrifice as cases in point. He also highlights such individually based rights in Africa as those to life and freedom of expression (Eze 1984: 13). Yet Eze advances us little further with his final assertion that precolonial Africa witnessed only a limited "concern for human rights" (Eze 1984: 288). By contrast, Asante reminds us that human rights are essentially about protecting human dignity. He believes that human rights are "ultimately based on a regard for the intrinsic worth of the individual" (cited in Shivji 1989: 12 and n. 8). Asante thereby affirms the view that the philosophical basis of human rights is not culturally specific but a universal phenomenon.

Eze and Asante aside, there are few who even hint at an individual foundation for human rights in precolonial Africa outside the context of group identity. Unfortunately, those like Donnelly who do seek to define human rights in terms of *individual* claims and entitlements are explicit that the very notion of human rights is historically foreign to indigenous African societies. However, I would argue that Donnelly and Vincent in particular fail to apply their own definitions and philosophical concepts of human rights to precolonial Africa. Instead, and ironically like Mojekwu and proponents of the communal idiom, they accept that in the precapitalist, decentralized, predominantly rural Africa before European penetration, human dignity was upheld by extended family and community. Howard is considerably more sensitive to the existence of precolonial states and complex class societies (1986a: 20, 92). Nevertheless, in her argument that in a land-rich continent it was economic factors, not a communitarian ideal or individual claims, that underpinned the distribution of resources, she too dismisses an individual foundation for precolonial human rights in Africa (Howard 1986a: 20–22).

Scholars like Howard, Donnelly, and Vincent have deceived themselves about "Merrie Africa" as effectively as have proponents of precolonial communal harmony. Clearly there were differences between preindustrial societies in Europe and Africa. I would not question, for instance, Goody's argument (1980: 21–33) that across much of sub-Saharan Africa plentiful land, extensive agriculture, and low levels of technology, especially the lack of the plow, modified political structures and worked against the emergence of distinct social classes. However, Goody makes no automatic assumption that the African milieu required that economic factors therefore sustained political systems operating according to a redistributive ethos. Indeed, Goody has indicated that in political terms land surplus and low levels of agricultural productivity simply meant that chieftainship tended to be over people rather than land (Goody 1980: 30). In distinguishing between Europe and Africa Goody highlights differences in precolonial patterns of domination and subordination, not the absence of state structures or social differentiation, nor necessarily the equal allocation of economic resources. The medieval empires of the western Sudan, the interlacustrine states, and the savanna kingdoms of central Africa rested in varying degrees on control of long-distance trade, ideological and political domination through ritual, imposition of tribute and force, and finally, pace Goody, in certain instances through elite denial of commoners' access to land (see Botte 1974: 609–11; Vidal 1974: 53–62).

As Iliffe (1987) has revealed, the redistributive elements within precolonial African societies varied enormously. Far from guaranteeing individuals sufficient resources, including land, for adequate sustenance, as Howard suggests, many precolonial rulers used their power to deprive their subjects of economic autonomy. Plentiful land and a shortage of men to work it may have in fact and on occasion reinforced servitude (Fage 1974: 15–17). If it ever existed, Howard's "initial redistributive economy" should be confined to African prehistory. Even more misleading is her notion, again ironically shared with advocates of the communitarian tradition, that incorporation within the capitalist world economy since the fifteenth century caused the redistributive economy to fall apart. Because the Africa of plentiful economic resources, supportive social and familial bonds, and limited social and economic differentiation should be taken with a pinch of salt, the idea that Western penetration initiated profound class distinctions, economic inequity, and capitalist rationality and individuation belies the nature of much of Africa before Europeans arrived. By the same token and in contemporary context, I am not convinced by Howard's argument that articulation with the world economy and its attendant processes (rapid urban development, rural to urban migration, differentiation by function and class, provision of national education, exposure to the mass media, etc.) is as erosive of prior attachments and loyalties Africans have to extended families, local communities, time-honored values and patterns of behavior as she would have us believe. In fact, I find Howard's assessment of the new culture of modernity, like her new "modern" African, strangely unsophisticated and lacking in sensitivity. I am not sure how far we can measure individuation or judge changing worldviews by counting radios and cinemas.

The existence of substantial state complexes in precolonial Africa requires one further comment. In Donnelly's view, Wai and others have confused human rights with limited government (Donnelly 1985: 50). Donnelly refutes Wai's argument that in articulating rights against the "alleged necessities of state" (Wai 1979: 116), African belief systems and customary practices and institutions embodied a concern for specifically human rights. Donnelly is clear that governments may be limited in many ways. These can include human rights claims but may also encompass divine commandment, natural law, legal rights, and extralegal checks (Donnelly 1982: 308). However, I would argue that Donnelly is overly quick to dismiss Wai's views about the importance of examining restraints on government. Moreover, I believe he is wrong even by his own terms to assert that within a given society the existence of limitations on government says little about human rights. Donnelly has himself stressed that while human rights are universal, in practice they are held against society, and particularly against "society in the form of the state" (Donnelly 1982: 303). For Africa the critical issue here is whether the institutional and ideological restraints on government represented the entrenchment of human rights or derived from other foundations. Donnelly believes that in Africa the duties of rulers to uphold human dignity and justice are often muddled with human rights, while the personal rights precolonial Africans held against their rulers were vested not in an individual's essential humanity but in community and family. Once again, we return to the stereotyped view of preindustrial societies in Africa in which the individual is assumed to be politically inert, or at best passive, except for membership in a collectivity.

My view is that, just as in the West, the historical development of limitations on government in Africa was a function of the interaction between individuals and the state. Restraints on state action were worked out in the "space" between rulers and ruled. Indeed, it would be presumptuous to believe that somehow the precolonial context was so tied to communitarian tradition and practice and elites so proscribed by elaborate sets of duties to uphold human dignity that Africans failed to develop the profound view of human nature that informs human rights and that in turn delineates the scope of state authority. From this perspective it is quite valid to examine how precolonial African states were constrained by their subjects. Once we set aside the dismissive notion that Africans based their rights only on community and kin, there is no reason to distinguish between African and Western experiences. In both milieus human rights were derived from human nature, as defined so effectively by Donnelly, and were subsequently shaped historically within the political arena by individual action and state response, by challenges to the ideological and physical dominance of ruling groups. As Cohen states in chapter 1, an operational definition of human rights in Africa must embody the right of individuals and communities to feel secure from excesses of state power, though it is in the "social process," in the interface between the two, that these rights are forged.

This certainly accords with my own experience as a student of what Nieburg (1969: 104) calls the "great beast," "the people's capacity for outraged, uncontrollable, bitter and bloody violence," which for him underlies all norms of civil, legal, and institutional behavior. With Crummey (1986) and a long line of radical historians of popular culture and resistance in Europe (Hay et al. 1977; Hobsbawm 1959, 1981; Rude 1981, 1985; Thompson 1975), I believe that judgments about disorder and uncontrolled behavior reveal more about the class prejudices of observers than about the protestors.[4] Indeed, there are probably few scholars who would disagree with Crummey's view that there is "another beast altogether"—the violence of the state and ruling elites directed against common people, the state's claim to an exclusive and legitimate right to use force (Crummey 1986: 1).

It is in the intersection of ruling-elite violence and popular violence that we may see one of the focal points in which human rights are constructed, often at moments of social and political dysfunction, as in the France of 1789–94. These represent the moments when violations of established customs and patterns of behavior may have led to new claims against individuals, communities, or states. Thus I would posit that concepts of human rights often emerge from what Charles Tilly, in describing the twists and turns of French history, has called the "repertoires of contention" (Tilly 1986: 1–12; see also comment in Watts 1987: 128). My basic assumption is that in resorting to resistance, rebellion, brigandage, and even crime, individuals in Africa were rational about how and why they stepped outside the bounds of preexisting civil society and put their grievances, and often themselves, on the line. My sense is that the implication is very straightforward, that in Africa, as in most historical societies, common people had clear notions of individual (and collective) rights as human rights and responded when these were abused by elites or superordinate groups.

Howard, Donnelly, and Vincent have distracted our attention from the individual and moral basis of human rights in Africa just as effectively as have Mojekwu and scholars working within the communitarian tradition. Both groups have diverted us from the individual to the collective, and through their preconceived views of precolonial Africa they have made it difficult to discern claims to specifically human rights in the continent's past. Yet there is no doubt that across the precolonial continent claims to justice, economic resources, and political office were expressed in *both* individual and collective terms and that the value of the individual and of individual achievement was and still is no less in Africa than elsewhere. Individual identity and importance is not just a product of Africa's recent history, the corollary of intrusive Western capitalism. Following Gramsci, many of these scholars distinguish between individual "peasant intellectuals" who have social function and many others who merely engage in intellectual activity that lacks an individually creative dimension.

In recent years others have also begun to reinterpret rural societies, moving firmly away from structuralist analyses of community and kinship to place new emphases on modes of production, labor processes, commodity production, and environmental and ecological contexts.[5] As these approaches have in their turn failed to explain convincingly patterns of agrarian change and rural conflict, especially in a decade of drought and declining per capita food production, scholars have focused their attention on individual actors in the countryside (Isaacman

1989: 28–30). It is no surprise that in the 1980s Africanists looked especially to the recovery of oral testimonies and life histories (see Watts 1983: 31–38; Kanogo 1987: 1–6). As Isaacman (1989: 28) has remarked, these are "social texts with hidden, often multiple meanings." Nevertheless, in the elusive search for the "authentic voices" in African social history, analysis and interpretation of these subjective perceptions of daily life have revealed how rural Africans understood the opportunities and constraints before them. Such analysis and interpretation also disclose how rural producers thought as individuals about their rights and obligations within states and about concepts like justice, human dignity, and power. Agrarian scholarship, not least in the study of songs and oral narratives (Vail and White 1986: 197–222) and other forms of popular culture, has rediscovered that individual African farmers had few illusions about the power relations, class divisions, and gender and generational conflicts that governed their communities.

Thus the human experience in Africa was not necessarily informed by "subjective" or "false" consciousness (Isaacman 1989: 18; Fields 1985: 14–23, 270–74). Indeed, these are terms that Rude (1980: 9) suggests are of little relevance to preindustrial societies, a view I am disinclined to embrace entirely. However, it is evident that in Africa members of the subordinate classes adopted diverse forms of protest and resistance to challenge exploitation, forms that ranged from the overt to the "daily" and "hidden." As Scott (1985) has suggested, rural producers could always respond to individual oppression through subtlety and ingenuity. However humble the weapons and however submerged the mode of resistance, it is clear that close examination of popular culture, a domain often insulated though rarely isolated from political authority, offers fresh insights into the processes whereby human rights are first articulated and claimed. Rather more tentatively, I would suggest that the establishment of human rights in Africa, as elsewhere, derived not merely from resistance to that ideological dominance of ruling elites that Gramsci (Busi-Glucksmann 1982: 116–48; Hoffman 1984: 51–75) and Foucault (1979: 16–30, 293–308) have both argued, albeit in different ways, rested on consent as much as coercion (see also Feierman 1990: 21). Whether or not a pervasive moral hegemony existed, what may have promoted political consciousness in precolonial Africa was not just the open challenge to rulers but also the interplay in the rural community between the active and passive voices, the defiant and deferential, the radical and conformist. Rural populations in Africa were rarely homogeneous, as Isaacman (1989: 22–26) and others have demonstrated. Hence, rural producers might advance their interests by taking on class elites. Very often they also promoted those interests through intraclass conflict and local strategies that operated at community, family, and household levels (Isaacman 1989: 35; McCann 1987: 39–63).

Thus the establishment of rights historically was not only the product of challenges to hegemonic authority but also derived from the dialectical struggle within societies, even, as Gramsci perceived, from the conflicts that persist within individuals (Kolakowski 1982: 3: 234–35). It is in the vast area of the lives and consciousness of rural Africans that we find the contradictions that contributed to the creation of patterns of social, political, and economic behavior and particularly, but not exclusively, in the relations between rulers and ruled. These patterns were often embodied in customary law, which thereby generated respect for human dignity and upheld claims for specifically human rights. Even in acephalous societies, where the struggle to improve the human condition may have taken very different paths from resistance in societies where ruling elites were natural targets of antipathy, rights emerged from the claims of individuals on each other. Whether our interest is in centralized state formations or in communally organized societies, it is clear that oral documents will ultimately provide the critical insights to the worldviews of rural Africans, through which we may discern popular perceptions of rights.

Rights in Precolonial Africa

I now wish to focus on "popular rights"—a term I use advisedly, not in the sense of the "peoples'" or group rights of the Banjul Charter—but with particular reference to precolonial Africa. Under the rubric popular rights I include individual and collective rights, embracing specifically human rights, which African peoples enjoyed, shared, and molded and which gave meaning to their lives. These rights had particular importance for individuals in relation to overarching state structures. When denied, the result was outrage, resistance, and popular violence.

Any effort to illuminate human rights in the precolonial past encounters several major methodological problems. First and rather familiar is the problem of sources. For much of preliterate Africa oral traditions and testimonies are critical historical tools for gaining insights to rights perceptions and practices. However, the problem here is not just the usual difficulty of placing oral narratives in context and decoding effectively but also one of viewpoint. In West Africa griot recitations about the history of elites and dynasties offer only limited scope to measure popular perspectives of political authority and of rights claimed against abuse of power. Free-text traditions, such as those collected in the East African interior (see, for instance, Lamphear 1976: 17–60), touch the lives of ordinary people and their communities. In their focus on customs, rituals, changes in political and social structures or lineage organization, tribute and trade, they are promising material. Nevertheless, despite the importance of letting the actors, or their descendants, speak, historians will still have to rely heavily on written sources for the analysis of precolonial human rights perspectives, most obviously travelers' logs and diaries, chronicle sources, and in the early colonial period official and missionary accounts.

The second methodological problem is how to deal with the sheer scale and diversity of Africa. Without surrendering to the relativists, I must note that our knowledge to date of precolonial notions of human rights is so meager that this essay is best described as exploratory. Future research into precolonial rights will have to demonstrate sensitivity to the broad range of often contradictory beliefs and practices across the African continent. Several examples concerning women spring to mind. As El Naiem has argued (1984: 81), in much of North Africa the *sharia* denied women the right to exercise unilateral divorce, but in Christian Ethiopia, as in many other parts of Islamic Africa, either partner could initiate separation. Strict adherence to Islamic law implies that women could not acquire education or employment (El Naiem 1984: 82), except in the latter case for subsistence. Thus the historical expectations of women in the Sokoto caliphate were quite different from those of their counterparts in the coastal societies of West Africa, where women have long enjoyed considerable economic independence, marketing beer, dried fish, and other local produce. Indeed, in central Africa, most notably in Angola in the figure of Queen Njinga of Ndongo, there were examples of women serving as political leaders and chiefs (Thornton 1983: 7; Thornton 1991: 27–40; Hilton 1985: 110, 203). Even within the Islamic belt there was plenty of room for compromise with indigenous custom, as suggested by the condition of women in prejihad Hausaland (Watts 1983: 117).

The third methodological problem derives from previous discussion but emphasizes the historical dimension. If it is difficult to discern the extent to which Africans articulated claims to specifically human rights in the relatively recent past, it is far more problematic across a hundred, five hundred, even a thousand years. In many cases, all the historian can do is simply infer perceptions from patterns of behavior, though we may never be able to get at real intentions or judge the extent to which rights claims were founded on moral-nature considerations and traditions. The study of popular culture remains critical, but there are limits to its historical efficacy. Folklore performances, proverbs, and oral traditions by and large offer diminishing returns as societies become more remote in time. Moreover, projecting further and further back into the past accentuates the problem of subjectivity. Yet if there is anything the *histoire de mentalités* has revealed, it is that actors in the historical scene, both elite and subaltern, are rational beings capable of moral judgments.

Finally, the student of human rights in Africa has to locate a starting point, which is not as easy to do as it might appear. It would be bizarre to simply list basic rights in Western human rights conventions and try to match precolonial Africa against them. In the first instance it would be a very long list, which could include the rights to life, liberty, security of person, privacy, and property; freedom from slavery, torture, and arbitrary arrest; freedom of assembly, association, and movement; freedom of opinion, expression, thought, conscience, and religion; rights to an adequate standard of living, education, and so on. Moreover, to apply the list to precolonial Africa and use it as a measure is simply anachronistic. Scholars are hardly expected to find in precolonial Africa the right to join a trade union or to periodic holidays with pay! The best way to avoid these problems is to direct analysis to those mechanisms that upheld social equilibrium, examining the roles and voices of individuals and groups where possible. As previously suggested, it is in the area of social and political discourse that we may discern expectations of rights, particularly at points when these were abused.

In an effort to inform future research into human rights in Africa, it is important to stress that there are clear continuities between the rights claimed in the precolonial period and in the contemporary era. There is no definitive list, but precolonial Africans clearly recognized and claimed rights to life; to liberty (especially the right to resist oppression); to justice; to marry and have a family; to freedom of speech, conscience, and association; to participation in political process; and to freedom from poverty. Not all precolonial African societies claimed or observed these basic human rights. As one might expect, observance and expectations varied widely from village to village, from one ethnic group or political system to another. Nevertheless, respect for the human rights of others was typical, and far more directly pertinent to individuals than the overemphasis on communitarian tradition suggests.

What is striking about most precolonial African societies is a profound respect for the right to life, often worked out in a wide range of relationships within kinship boundaries, ethnic groups, or multiethnic state structures. In practical terms this often required mutual cooperation, or protection in return for services or tribute. The claim to a right to life could equally be seen as a right to defense.

Moreover, the right to life is itself contingent on rights to justice and basic economic resources. Despite the assumptions of scholars working within the communitarian tradition, these were not necessarily conceived or practiced within corporate groups. There is no clearer indication of the importance attached to the individual's right to life than the fact that in many precolonial African societies the power over life and death was reserved to a few individuals or groups of elders. These notables generally exercised that power only after elaborate judicial procedure, with appeals from one court to another, and often only in cases of murder or manslaughter. Thus, in such widely separated societies as those of the Swazi and Asante only chiefs could impose the death sentence, which in normal circumstances they did rarely (Beattie 1959: 104). Among the Bemba junior chiefs had to send murder cases to their ruler, the *Chitimukulu*, in the eighteenth and nineteenth centuries because he alone could impose capital penalties or mutilation, and only then in consultation with his councillors (Roberts 1973: 166). Indeed, among the Bemba there were specific sanctions against those who took the law into their own hands, exacting their own vengeance for murder. The penalty for summary avenging of a murder was usually payment of a slave. In Kuba society in Zaire local chiefs automatically referred all matters involving bloodshed and murder to the central judicial court at the capital (Vansina 1978: 150-51). The nine-member crown council, which included the king, handled appeals. Only the king could condemn a convicted murderer to death. In the Islamic area judges were the first to handle capital cases in Sokoto. However, the chief judge reviewed all such cases and referred them if necessary to the caliph. He in turn sought legal advice from his vizier, always distinguished by his learning, and from other councillors well versed in Koranic law (Last 1977: 181-82). Nor was this clear recognition of the right to life, as revealed by judicial process, confined to state societies. Among the Igbo of Nigeria the elders, or *oha*, sat to judge those accused of homicide. Those found innocent were discharged, but the *oha* expected an individual presumed guilty to conjure a spirit. If the accused survived the swearing of an oath on the spirit by a year, during which he was incarcerated, he then regained his freedom (Isichei 1978: 96).

Precolonial Africa did not always respect human life, especially in times of war. However, in peacetime civil societies there was a significant exception: the practice of human sacrifice. This is such a sensitive topic that until recently most Africanists have been loath to discuss it, not least because it contributes to unfavorable stereotypes of Africa that most scholars try to dispel. Nevertheless, human sacrifice was a feature of many precolonial societies, from the interlacustrine region to the West African coast (Austen 1977: 305–15; Vansina 1978: 165–68). It occurred for a variety of reasons, primarily religious. Both travelers' accounts and oral traditions concur that on the death of an Igbo elder as many as sixty human sacrifices might occur (Isichei 1978: 256). Among the Kuba and Asante similar sacrificial acts might follow the deaths of their leaders or eminent citizens. In Zaire those sacrificed were usually slaves (Vansina 1978: 180–81). Wilks has argued (1975: 592–99; 1988: 443–52) that in the Asante case most sacrificial victims were those found guilty of capital offenses. By contrast, Williams (1988: 438–49) posits that the Asante sacrificed slaves, prisoners of war, and criminals and, ironically, that after the British abolition of slaving in 1807 sacrifices of slaves on the Gold Coast increased because their price slumped.

Africans in the precolonial era also claimed and enjoyed rights to personal freedom, though not necessarily in Western terms. Miers and Kopytoff (1977: 17–18) have suggested that freedom in historical societies in Africa should be identified not in terms of withdrawal into "a meaningless and dangerous autonomy" but in attachment to kin group or, as in Rwanda, in patron-client relationships (Des Forges 1986: 316; Vidal 1974: 53–60). Thus, Mojekwu (1980: 86) is right to assert that in many instances it was actual "belonging" to a society or political unit that guaranteed rights. Often only adhesion to the unit could provide the individual with the protection that the law of the land could offer. This did not necessarily imply that rights were held communally, but it did mean that in many precolonial societies the outcast or stranger had no rights. Kikuyu society offers a good example (Leakey 1977: 1015–17; Muriuku 1974: 129–30). However, outsiders could negotiate rights through their hosts or acquire them through gradual incorporation, possibly over generations. In the nineteenth century Sherbra communities of coastal Sierra Leone accommodated large numbers of Mende and Temne peoples who were keen to exploit commercial opportunities. MacCormack has recorded a pertinent proverb: "You cannot sit alone and be a chief" (cited in Miers and Kopytoff 1977: 14). The saying captures the readiness of many African societies to incorporate strangers and reduce or absolve their marginality—that is, their lack of "freedom"—by recognizing their individual rights. Once recognized, these rights would then improve the legal status and raise the social and economic standing of the outsider.

So far, this discussion has addressed concepts of freedom in the abstract. However, extant work on the "great beast" demonstrates that in practice Africans from diverse parts of the continent reacted sharply when others abused their customary rights, whether these were held individually or collectively (Prochaska 1986: 233–45; Brantley 1986: 333–42). In state societies restraints on the abuse of political or judicial power were often institutionalized. They were embodied in coronation oaths, for example, which frequently acknowledged the subjects' claims against the ruler and emphasized that political power often rested on the chief's capacity to justify his actions to his people. At the installation of an *Asantehene*, the new ruler was admonished not to abuse his subjects or to disregard the advice of councillors. In Old Oyo in Nigeria the notables, the *Oyo Mesi*, might call on their ruler, the *Alafin*, to stand down or poison himself if he had lost the confidence of the people. The ceremonial act of deposition was the dispatch by the *Oyo Mesi* of a clutch of parrot eggs (Law 1971: 30–37). In Lesotho the nineteenth-century king Moshoeshoe created a new state, held together as a loose federation by ties within a ruling dynasty. However, Moshoeshoe's state also depended on the consent of chiefs and subjects. A resilient political system embodied a series of reciprocal duties, functions, and obligations shared by rulers and ruled. Within deliberative assemblies, *pitso*, chiefs and commoners could influence policy and approve major executive decisions, thereby reducing potential for rights abuses and internal conflicts. As a Sotho maxim had it, "A chief is a chief by the people; a people are a people through the chief" (Weisfeder 1977: 163; Potholm 1979: 25).

By contrast, in nineteenth-century Swaziland responsibility for protecting the rights of subjects and preventing abuses of royal power lay in the *liqoqo*, or council of chiefs, for popular assemblies convened rarely and were politically unwieldy. Nevertheless, religious and magical checks constrained arbitrary rule in Swaziland (Potholm 1977: 136–37). There is a curious parallel here with Buganda, that most centralized and hierarchical of precolonial states, where one of the few checks on royal absolutism was the *kabaka*'s inability to act as an intermediary with the spirit world and his lack of political influence within traditional religious cults, the *lubaale* (Young 1977: 203). As in Nupe in Nigeria (Beattie 1959: 104), priestly and popular refusal to cooperate in ritual and public ceremonies was an important device for frustrating overambitious or capricious leaders.

These curbs that common people placed on state and chiefly authority were not purely hypothetical or merely symbolic. Rulers who deviated from prescribed or accepted norms enshrined in customary law faced censure or overthrow by their councils. At worst they faced the specter of the "great beast": overt opposition and popular revolt. In Asante the queen mother and royal council, ever sensitive to popular disaffection, could destool and remove an errant *Asantehene* who failed to live up to his coronation oaths. This removal from office happened to Osei Kwame in late 1803, when his rule became increasingly sanguine (Wilks 1975: 253, 546). Even in highly autocratic Rwanda events in the late nineteenth and early twentieth centuries demonstrate that commoners could challenge their political masters in defense of customary rights and obligations owed to them by the state (Lemarchand 1977: 69–73). This is not to deny that the "drum" was greater than the "shout" (Des Forges 1986: 312)—that is, that the power of the state was greater than that of the people—but simply to note that in the circumstances of the Rwandan state's expansion northward in the nineteenth century the crown worked out varying arrangements with incorporated Hutu peoples. Usually the state offered royal protection in return for tribute and service, often backed up by the sanction of force. By the late nineteenth century the Rwandan ruler, Musinga, had come to rely heavily on his notables, agents, and new settlers to administer the north for him. It was these people who denied northerners their former access to the king, appropriated the best lands, and imposed unprecedented demands for tribute and labor services (Des Forges 1986: 313–16). These demands specifically denied northerners of their rights as *abagaba* (free men). The predictable result was an upsurge of resistance and banditry fomented by mediums of the spirit Nyabingi, pretenders to the kingship, and by enterprising brigands. These elements coalesced into overt rebellion in Rwanda in 1912. The underlying causes were very clearly the defense by northerners of rights against demands that were new, exploitative, and contrary to moral behavior. By failing to recognize the rights of his subjects, Musinga forfeited their loyalties, which they transferred very quickly to others (Des Forges 1986: 318–26).

I have dwelt on the Rwandan example because it is instructive and because it is fairly typical of precolonial Africa. Feierman (1974: 167, 183) has interpreted the hiving off of parts of the Shambaa kingdom in northeast Tanzania in the 1870s in similar terms. As Shambaa rulers began to engage in the slave trade, appreciating as they did that the demand for slaves in Pemba made cohorts of their people more valuable as marketable commodities than as tributaries, their people rebelled. The oral traditions describe the later Shambaa rulers as deviant and explicitly as violators of the mutual trust between ruler and ruled. They had broken the community of interest on which the kingdom was originally founded.

Perhaps the most obvious way in which precolonial African societies curtailed personal freedom was through the institution of slavery. Following their notion that across much of precolonial Africa individual freedom lay in attachment to community, lineage, or patron, Miers and Kopytoff (1977: 3–12) have defined slavery as fundamentally a way of denying outsiders full civil rights and privileges so they could be exploited for economic, social, and political purposes. They have also argued that we need to discard concepts of chattel slavery in analysis of servitude in Africa, though this may well be an error for Islamic contexts or Christian Ethiopia. Nonetheless, they claim that the African "slaves" can only be evaluated in the terms of the society to which they belonged, drawing analogies not to slavery outside Africa but to other institutions of dependency in African communities. These include clientage, pawnship, marriage, and concubinage. Miers and Kopytoff (1977: 22–24) also lay considerable stress on the extent to which succeeding generations of slaves could acquire individual rights and on how the relations of slavery could be redefined into those of quasi kinship and kinship.

The utility of these distinctions is clear. There are few who would now seek to apply Western definitions of slavery to Africa. However, like Meillassoux (1975: 15–25; 1986: 9–22) and Lovejoy (1983: 3), I think that in trying to define African slavery as culturally distinctive, Miers and Kopytoff have overlooked the economic imperatives and the physical act of deprivation of freedom. Almost always slavery in Africa was related to an act of violence, to warfare, raiding, or kidnapping, which reduced the victim from a condition of freedom and citizenship to one of servitude. Moreover, it is wrong to play down the extent to which slave status was inherited in many parts of sub-Saharan Africa, especially in the Islamic zone, although here, notably in the successive western Sudanic states of Mali and Songhay, slaves rose high in the ranks of government and in slave armies (Levtzion 1980: 112–13). Yet for most slaves the outlook was less rosy. Reality was subordination to a slave master, who controlled the slave's reproductive and productive capacities. In terms of the former, masters had sexual access to slave women, administered their marriages, and controlled their offspring. In the case of men, masters had ultimate control of their sexuality through castration. In terms of the latter, Lovejoy (1983) has highlighted how early historically and how extensively slaves were used in large-scale agricultural and industrial production in sub-Saharan Africa. They were to be found on estates in the Niger valley in the sixteenth and seventeenth centuries; in the gold mines of Bambuk and Bure and the Taghaza salt mines in the Sahara in the same period; on agricultural estates in Futa Jallon, Dar Fur, the Funj sultanate, and the Sokoto caliphate in the eighteenth and nineteenth centuries; and on the other side of the continent in the clove and coconut plantations of Zanzibar, Pemba, and the East African coast. Even outside the Muslim area the large-scale use of slaves was very common by the nineteenth century. Thousands worked on estates in the Lozi state on the inner floodplains of the Zambezi (Lovejoy 1983: 237) and on the lands of nobles in the Omotic polities of southwest Ethiopia (Fernyhough 1988: 106). Lovejoy argues that for the victim slavery was the great equalizer. However, it also reveals very dramatically the derogation of a fundamental human right, which Africans recognized, and a basic inequity of the precolonial milieu to which the communitarian tradition pays little heed.

Discussion of African perceptions of rights to life and liberty has indicated that many precolonial societies were distinguished by their respect for judicial and political procedure. Within such societies the precise recognition of rights in law reflected the common claim to a right to justice and due process. Indeed, what characterizes so much of Africa is a preoccupation with law, customary and written, and with legal procedure. Levine (1965: 23) has noted that in Ethiopia the Amhara have long regarded litigation as a pleasurable pastime, relishing the cross-examination of witnesses in a process analogous to that of Western courts. Particularly striking was the judicial structure of the precolonial Kuba state as it had developed by the late 1800s (Vansina 1978: 145–52). At the *Ibaanc*, the central court, panels of competent jurors assembled separately to hear cases, each one presided over by judges. As Vansina has commented (1978: 151), this marked a highly original development in Africa, again inviting comparison with Western practice.

Even where judicial structures and practices bore no such resemblances to Western models, there existed elaborate rules of procedure intended to protect the accused and provide fair trials. In the Tio kingdom north of modern Brazzaville, the courts not only provided for cross-examination of witnesses but also strictly excluded irrelevant testimony about the characters of interested parties or about other court cases in which the plaintiff and defendant might have been involved (Vansina 1973: 342–47). Here, as elsewhere in Africa, a strong tradition of jurisprudence existed, with specific rulings for penalties cited as precedents, such as levels of fines for adultery. In contrast to Western practice, the feel for justice often overrode legal strictures. Judges discouraged the use of loopholes, and they rarely occurred.

It hardly needs to be said that in areas of Islamic influence there was also a long and highly developed tradition of jurisprudence based on the Koran and the *hadith* and embodied in the *sharia*. This was certainly true of the Maraboutic states of the Maghreb and the Maghrebian empires of the eleventh and twelfth centuries—the Fatimids, Almoravids, and Almohads. Here, as in the Sokoto caliphate and most of West Africa, the Maliki school of jurisprudence prevailed. Indeed, in the nineteenth-century jihad states of the western Sudan, the position of the caliph was intertwined with maintaining Islamic law. As long as the caliph in Sokoto upheld the *sharia* his authority was unimpeachable. Last (1977: 232) has commented that while men grew less keen on jihad, they still recognized the basis of their ruler's power. He argues that in fact the *sharia* gave Sokoto the power it lacked militarily and the acknowledged right to call on subordinate emirs to fight the wars of Sokoto against unbelievers and rebels.

In diverse societies individuals in precolonial Africa claimed and enjoyed rights of free speech, conscience, and association. The extent to which they exercised these rights varied enormously. In Igboland all adult males and elder women could attend and speak at village meetings, and all men and women could express their views at meetings of their lineage (Isichei 1976: 21–22; Isichei 1978: 72–74). Village democracy rested on freedom of speech, opinion, and association, though people tended to defer to age and experience and, by the nineteenth century, to wealth also, often institutionalized in the purchase of titles. Nearby, in the historical kingdom of Benin, members of palace associations, representatives from towns, and hereditary chiefs all had rights to speak openly before the *oba* (Potholm 1979: 26). Eighteenth- and nineteenth-century Yoruba societies also regarded the freedom to speak and express an opinion as a common right, though it was clearly restrained by a hierarchy of respect for parents, heads of households, and elders (Marasinghe 1984: 37–39). Defamation of a chief could result in a civil action, where the offender's family had to mediate and negotiate a compensatory payment, comparable in certain ways to a fine for slander in the West. Similar constraints also surrounded the freedom to express religious and political beliefs, though not the personal freedom to believe. Far less inhibited were the women of Kom, in the Cameroon grasslands, who used their rights of free speech and association to exert extreme social pressure in the form of *anlu*, ostracizing and humiliating in public those (usually men) who had transgressed certain moral rules—for example, by acting incestuously, by insulting or injuring either parent, or by beating pregnant or elderly women (Ritzenthaler 1967: 98–101).

Not all precolonial African societies recognized such vocal claims to freedom of expression and opinion, particularly not in political process. In many state societies free speech, especially in a political context, was the prerogative of royal councillors and relatives, hereditary or appointed notables. In short, it was the preserve of elites, not commoners. In Swaziland only the king's mother, his agnatic kinsmen, and his council could criticize the king openly (Potholm 1977: 135–37; Potholm 1979: 25). In Buganda only the *kabaka*'s most senior and trusted officials could remonstrate with the king without fear of reprisal (Beattie 1959: 105). Within the political sphere what diminished free expression of opinion was probably not only deference and fear but also a sense of futility. In Nupe, for instance, peasants could approach their ruler over the heads of local chiefs, but requests for redress of grievances were rarely heeded (Beattie 1959: 112). Likewise, in the Kongo kingdom in the seventeenth century, villagers also claimed and exercised the right to criticize overbearing nobles in royal courts (Thornton 1983: 41). The aristocratic judges who listened to these complaints rarely ruled in their favor. In Kongo the "great beast" was never far from the surface. Let it be noted, however, that ordinary people in most state societies tempered deference with healthy defiance, a reaction embodied in a proverb from the strictly hierarchical society of highland Abyssinia: "The wise man bows low to the great lord and silently farts" (Hoben 1970: 212; see also Crummey 1989: 137).

A basic right in precolonial Africa was to enter into marriage and to have children. It is here that precolonial practice is at times at variance with patterns of behavior that have become increasingly common in contemporary Africa. Common customs in precolonial Africa, often reinforced by adherence to Islam, included polygyny, bridewealth, betrothal of children, and the inheritance of widows by members of the deceased husband's lineage. It is unnecessary to cite historical examples, because these practices were common to many societies. However, the material dispositions required of these transactions cemented alliances between families, lineages, even dynasties (Solanke 1982: 28-30). There is an interpretive problem here, which future students of precolonial rights will have to address. These practices were appropriate in preindustrial African societies (Welch and Meltzer 1984: 3, 13-17, 27-28). Polygyny, for instance, provided the man with status, economic resources in his wives' collective labor, and future material security for children. For the woman it offered companionship and allowed her to share responsibilities as a wife and in production and reproduction (Howard 1984b: 60). Likewise, bridewealth was a form of insurance against the death, incapacitation, or unreliability of the husband, while widow inheritance was eminently practical and rational in the precolonial context (Howard 1984b: 61-62; Marasinghe 1984: 39). It helped protect the bereaved wife and children and provided a form of social assistance unavailable elsewhere. Although contemporary Africans still hold many of these practices as quite legitimate, there are clear discontinuities here between historical and contemporary practice. In Nigerian law, for instance, widow inheritance is held to be contrary to "natural justice, equity, and good conscience" (Marasinghe 1984: 40). Tanzania's marriage laws do not reject polygyny, but they have subordinated a variety of customary practices, including Islamic ones. To cite but one example, the rights of children are now held to be paramount over all other considerations (see Howard 1984b: 59, and chapter 5 of this volume). We have moved some way from precolonial Africa.

Finally, Africanists interested in precolonial rights will have to consider the notion of a right to freedom from poverty. In Western terms this might be reformulated as a right to an adequate standard of living.

However it is expressed, it is a recurrent theme across diverse societies in precolonial Africa. Two factors have a bearing here. The first is simply that in an overwhelmingly agrarian continent, most Africans had some access to land. They may not have owned it, though private property was not unknown among peoples as different and remote from each other as the Kanuri of Nigeria (Cohen 1987: 92-95) and the Oromo of southern Ethiopia (Lewis 1965: 30; Hassan 1990: 121-22). Elsewhere, ruling elites may have tried to control access to land, with varying degrees of success. Nevertheless, across Africa there was a range of use rights, clearly delineated and often inherited. Most often the exercising of these rights was vested early in households, families, or descent groups, as among the Shona (Beach 1983: 247-48), or granted by ruling elites in return for tribute or labor, as in Burundi and the Uganda kingdoms (Botte 1982: 277-80; Steinhart 1967: 610-14; Steinhart 1977: 7-24; Beattie 1964: 28, 35). Occasionally use rights and obligations were duplicated. Among the Amhara fiefs overlapped lands were distributed according to rules of ambilineal descent (Hoben 1973: 1-28).

The second factor is that many historical African societies emphasized a basic concern with community welfare. Iliffe's (1987) recent work is a classic for study of this topic and very revealing both of attitudes toward poverty and the modes of relieving it. Thus in Ethiopia, where bilateral kinship provided relatively little support, generosity was a distinctive Christian act, and as such poor relief occurred through the charity of emperors, nobles, merchants, and secular and regular clergy (Iliffe 1987: 9-29). In the towns of the western Sudan the Islamic practice of almsgiving, including both the compulsory *zaqat* (the poor rate) and the voluntary *sadaka*, helped provide for the destitute. Those who could afford it gave to the poor, not only out of a sense of Islamic charity, but also as a source of social prestige and reward in heaven. Yet Iliffe (1987: 30-47) has remarked that in Muslim West Africa, as in Christian Ethiopia, provision for the poor depended on personal charity and generosity, including the generosity of rulers, but was rarely institutionalized as in other Islamic and Christian lands. By contrast, he shows how in the highly stratified savanna states of central Africa, in the Kongo, Lunda, Bemba, and Lozi kingdoms, provision for the poor rested on political authorities (Iliffe 1987: 48-64). They were expected to support the very young and the old and incapacitated, especially in times of want. In the interlacustrine region, where strong kings could but often failed to provide help, only the rulers of Rwanda claimed this role. Even here the rituals did not specifically mention provision for the poor, so the extent of relief depended on the ruler.

Despite Iliffe's caveats, the one theme that emerges from his study of African poverty is the degree to which states, extended families, and households provided for impoverished subjects and kinsmen, in very different societies. Central to much of Iliffe's thinking about poverty in Africa is the notion that the poor often had a right to assistance and also to improve their lot in life. In contemporary rights jargon, we might talk about rights to welfare and to development. It is, as Iliffe (1987: 7) comments, no surprise to find that in many African languages the word for "poor," as among the Chewa of Malawi, implies lack of kin and friends.

The foregoing reflections mark but a starting point, an invitation for substantive and focused research. However, they also point to pitfalls ahead. Close historical observation may lead us to identify human rights in precolonial Africa, but we should be wary of analysis where the evidence is inconclusive. Thus patterns of customary behavior may indicate the recognition and practice of individual rights, but equally they may not. Even where individual rights were protected by custom, legal codes, or judicial process, as in Islamic Africa, the assumption that these embodied a widely understood notion of specifically human rights may be very misleading. Much the same could be said of my previous remarks about precolonial rulers' obligations to consult their subjects or about the clear limitations on who should apply the death penalty. I have suggested that there is good reason to infer concepts of individual, even human rights, from such constraints, but it is not difficult to turn this premise on its head. From an alternative perspective, these customary practices may simply indicate accepted norms of government and civic life. While they might restrict those who ruled, they do not necessarily imply that the common people claimed individual rights or, still less, fundamental human rights.

These cautionary remarks are intended to highlight the interpretive complexities within the topic, not to deter future scholarship. Indeed, I hope the argument and evidence of these pages demonstrates the very richness and texture of rights held in the precolonial era. It may be very wrong to think that the majority of Africans were incapable of thinking in profound ways about human nature and rights derived from that nature. The task of those historians who choose to study rights in precolonial Africa further is clear. They must try to identify accurately human rights perceptions and practice in the continent's past and to see how these developed, especially at times of social and political dislocation, moments of *conjoncture*. Only when we have recaptured the voices, claims, and perceptions of the past will we start to hear and understand the voices of the present.

Notes

I would like to thank Ronald Cohen, Lovett Elango, Paul Goldsmith, and Peter Schmidt for encouraging me to write this essay and for their comments on its original presentation, "Human Rights and the 'Great Beast': A Diachronic Analysis of Popular Rights in Precolonial Africa" (Carter Lecture, April 1989). I am also indebted to Anna Fernyhough for her editorial assistance.

1. For the text of the Universal Declaration of Human Rights, see Howard and Donnelly (1987: 459-62); for the Banjul Charter, see Welch and Meltzer (1984: 317-29). See also two useful essays in the Welch and Meltzer volume: E. Kannyo, "The Banjul Charter on Human and Peoples' Rights: Genesis and Political Background" (pp. 128-51), and R. Gittleman, "The Banjul Charter on Human and Peoples' Rights: A Legal Analysis" (pp. 152-76).

2. Thus Mojekwu (1980) extends his analysis of his section of the Igbo to the whole of Africa; Marasinghe (1984) does likewise for the Yoruba. See also Howard (1986b).

3. See also Welch and Meltzer (1984: 25-26).

4. A comparable group for Africa might include, among others, Iris Berger, Cynthia Brantley, Karen Fields, Allen Isaacman, Terence Ranger, Edward Steinhart, and Charles Van Onselen. For discussion of their scholarship and of themes in protest and resistance studies, see Crummey (1986: 1-29).

5. For a comprehensive survey and critique of this literature, see Isaacman (1989: 14-26). Examples for modes of production analysis might include Crummey and Stewart (1981) and works by E. Terray, Claude Meillassoux, and Catherine Coquery-Vidrovitch. For a focus on commodity production and labor process, see, for example, Watts (1983), Hyden (1980), and Kanogo (1987). For the new sensitivity to ecological factors and environmental contexts, see, for instance, Thornton (1983) and Packard (1989).

References

Adegbite, L. O. 1968. "African Attitudes to the International Protection of Human Rights." In *International Protection of Human Rights: Proceedings of* the *Seventh Nobel Symposium, Oslo, September 25–27, 1967,* ed. A. Eide and A. Schou, pp. 69–81. Stockholm: Almqvist and Wiksell.

Austen, R. 1977. "Slavery among Coastal Middlemen: The Duala of Cameroon." In *Slavery in Africa: Historical and Anthropological Perspectives,* pp. 305–15. *See* Miers and Kopytoff 1977.

Bay, C. 1968. "Wants, Needs and Political Legitimacy." *Canadian Journal of Political Science* 1:241–60.

———. 1981. *Strategies of Political Emancipation.* Notre Dame and London: Notre Dame Press.

Beach, D. N. 1983. "The Zimbabwe Plateau and Its Peoples." In *History of Central Africa,* ed. D. Birmingham, pp. 245–77. London and New York.

Beattie, J. H. M. 1959. "Checks on the Abuse of Political Power in Some African States: A Preliminary Framework for Analysis." *Sociologus* 9 (2): 97–115.

———. 1964. "Bunyoro: An African Feudality?" *Journal of African History* 5 (1): 24–36.

Botte, R. 1974. "Processus de formation d'une classe sociale dans une societe africaine precapitaliste." *Cahiers d'etudes africaines* 14 (4): 605–26.

———. 1982. "Burundi de quoi vivait l'Etat." *Cahiers d'etudes africaines* 22 (3–4): 277–324.

Brantley, C. 1986. "Mekatili and the Role of Women in Giriama Resistance." In *Banditry, Rebellion and Social Protest in Africa,* pp. 333–47. *See* Crummey 1986.

Busi-Glucksmann, C. 1982. "Hegemony and Consent: A Political Strategy." In *Approaches to Gramsci,* ed. A. S. Sassoon. London: Writers and Readers Publishing Cooperative.

Clarence-Smith, W. G., ed. 1989. *The Economics of the Indian Ocean Slave Trade.* London: Frank Cass.

Cohen, R. 1987. *The Kanuri of Borno.* Prospect Heights, Ill.: Waveland.

Crummey, D., ed. 1986. *Banditry, Rebellion and Social Protest in Africa.* London: James Currey; Portsmouth, N.H.: Heinemann Educational Books.

———. 1989. "Abyssinian Feudalism." *Past and Present* 89:115–38.

Crummey, D., and C. C. Stewart, eds. 1981. *Modes of Production in Africa: The Precolonial Era.* Beverly Hills: Sage Publications.

Des Forges, A. L. 1986. "'The Drum Is Greater than the Shout': The 1912 Rebellion in Northern Rwanda." In *Banditry, Rebellion and Social Protest in Africa,* pp. 311–31. *See* Crummey, 1986.

Donnelly, J. 1982. "Human Rights and Human Dignity: An Analytic Critique of Non-Western Conceptions of Human Rights." *American Political Science Review* 76 (2): 303–16.

———. 1985. *The Concept of Human Rights.* London: Croom Helm.

Dworkin, R. 1978. *Taking Rights Seriously.* London: Duckworth.

El Naiem, Abdullahi Ahmed. 1984. "A Modern Approach to Human Rights in

Islam: Foundations and Implications for Africa." In *Human Rights and Development in Africa*, pp. 75-89. *See* Welch and Meltzer 1984.

Eze, O. C. 1984. *Human Rights in Africa: Some Selected Problems*. Lagos: Nigerian Institute of International Affairs.

Fage, J. D. 1974. *States and Subjects in Sub-Saharan African History*. Tenth Raymond Dart Lecture, 5 February 1973. Johannesburg: Witwatersrand University Press.

Feierman, S. 1974. *The Shambaa Kingdom: A History*. Madison: University of Wisconsin Press.

———. 1990. *Peasant Intellectuals: Anthropology and History in Northern Tanzania*. Madison: University of Wisconsin Press.

Fernyhough, T. 1988. "Slavery and the Slave Trade in Southern Ethiopia in the Nineteenth Century." *Slavery and Abolition* 9 (3).

Fields, K. E. 1985. *Revival and Rebellion in Colonial Central Africa*. Princeton, N.J.: Princeton University Press.

Foucault, M. 1979. *Discipline and Punish: The Birth of the Prison*. New York: Vintage Books, Random House.

Gewirth, A. 1982. *Human Rights: Essays on Justification and Applications*. Chicago: University of Chicago Press.

Gittleman, R. 1984. "The Banjul Charter on Human and Peoples' Rights: A Legal Analysis." In *Human Rights and Development in Africa*, pp. 152-76. *See* Welch and Meltzer 1984.

Goody, J. 1980. *Technology, Tradition and the State in Africa*. London: Hutchinson.

Hassan, M. 1990. *The Oromo of Ethiopia: A History, 1570-1860*. Cambridge: Cambridge University Press.

Hay, D., P. Linebaugh, J. G. Rule, E. P. Thompson, and C. Winslow. 1977. *Albion's Fatal Tree: Crime and Society in Eighteenth-Century England*. Harmondsworth: Penguin.

Hilton, A. 1985. *The Kingdom of Congo*. Oxford: Clarendon Press.

Hoben, A. 1970. "Social Stratification in Traditional Amhara Society." In *Social Stratification in Africa*, ed. A. Tuden and L. Plotnicov, pp. 187-224. New York: Free Press.

———. 1973. *Land Tenure among the Amhara of Ethiopia: The Dynamics of Cognatic Descent*. Chicago: University of Chicago Press.

Hobsbawm, E. J. 1959. *Primitive Rebels*. Manchester: Manchester University Press.

———. 1981. *Bandits*. New York: Pantheon.

Hoffman, J. 1984. *The Gramscian Challenge: Coercion and Consent in Marxist Political Theory*. Oxford: Blackwell Publishers.

Hopkins, A. G. 1973. *Economic History of West Africa*. New York: Columbia University Press.

Howard, R. E. 1984a. "Evaluating Human Rights in Africa: Some Problems of Implicit Comparisons." *Human Rights Quarterly* 6 (2): 160-79.

———. 1984b. "Women's Rights in English-Speaking, Sub-Saharan Africa." In *Human Rights and Development in Africa*, pp. 46–74. *See* Welch and Meltzer 1984.

———. 1986a. *Human Rights in Commonwealth Africa*. Totowa, N.J.: Rowman and Littlefield.

———. 1986b. "Is There an African Concept of Human Rights?" In *Foreign Policy and Human Rights*, ed. R. J. Vincent. Cambridge: Cambridge University Press.

Howard, R. H., and J. Donnelly, eds. 1987. *The International Handbook of Human Rights*. New York: Greenwood Press.

Hyden, G. 1980. *Beyond Ujamma in Tanzania: Underdevelopment and an Uncaptured Peasantry*. London: Heinemann.

———. 1983. *No Shortcuts to Progress: African Development Management in Perspective*. London: Heinemann.

Iliffe, J. 1987. *The African Poor: A History*. Cambridge: Cambridge University Press.

Isaacman, A. 1989. "Peasants and Rural Social Protest in Africa." Paper commissioned by the Joint ACLS-SSRC Africa Committee and presented at the annual meeting of the African Studies Association, Atlanta, November.

Isichei, E. 1976. *A History of the Igbo People*. London: Macmillan.

———. 1978. *Igbo Worlds: An Anthology of Oral Histories and Historical Descriptions*. London: Macmillan.

Kanogo, T. 1987. *Squatters and the Roots of Mau Mau*. Athens: Ohio University Press.

Kannyo, E. 1984. "The Banjul Charter on Human and Peoples' Rights: Genesis and Political Background." In *Human Rights and Development in Africa*, pp. 128–51. *See* Welch and Meltzer 1984.

Kaunda, K. 1966. *A Humanist in Africa*. London: Longman.

Kolakowski, L. 1982. *Main Currents of Marxism: Its Origins, Growth and Dissolution*. 3 vols. Oxford: Oxford University Press.

Lamphear, J. 1976. *The Traditional History of the Jie of Uganda*. Oxford: Clarendon Press.

Last, M. 1977. *The Sokoto Caliphate*. London: Longman.

Law, R. C. C. 1971. "The Constitutional Troubles of Oyo in the Eighteenth Century." *Journal of African History* 12 (1): 25–44.

Leakey, L. B. S. 1977. *The Southern Kikuyu before 1903*. London: Academic Press.

Legesse, A. 1980. "Human Rights in African Political Culture." In *The Moral Imperatives of Human Rights: A World Survey*, ed. K. W. Thompson, pp. 123–38. Washington, D.C.: University Press of America.

Lemarchand, R., ed. 1977. *African Kingships in Perspective: Political Change and Modernization in Monarchical Settings*. London: Frank Cass.

Levine, D. N. 1965. *Wax and Gold: Tradition and Innovation in Ethiopian Culture.* Chicago and London: University of Chicago Press.
Levtzion, N. 1980. *Ancient Ghana and Mali.* New York: Africana Publishing Company.
Lewis, H. S. 1965. *A Galla Monarchy: Jimma Abba Jifar, Ethiopia, 1831–1932.* Madison and Milwaukee: University of Wisconsin Press.
Lovejoy, P. 1983. *Transformations in Slavery: A History of Slavery in Africa.* Cambridge: Cambridge University Press.
McCann, J. 1987. *From Poverty to Famine in Northeast Ethiopia.* Philadelphia: University of Pennsylvania Press.
MacCormack, C. P. 1977. "Wono: Institutional Dependency in Sherbro Descent Groups (Sierra Leone)." In *Slavery in Africa: Historical and Anthropological Perspectives,* pp. 181–203. *See* Miers and Kopytoff 1977.
Marasinghe, L. 1984. "Traditional Conceptions of Human Rights in Africa." In *Human Rights and Development in Africa,* pp. 32–45. *See* Welch and Meltzer 1984.
M'Baye, K. 1972. "Le droit au developpement comme un droit de l'homme." *Revue des droits de l'homme* 5: 505–34.
Meillassoux, C. 1975. *L'Esclavage en Afrique precoloniale.* Paris: Maspero.
———. 1986. *Anthropologie de l'esclavage: Le ventre de fer et d'argent.* Paris: Presses Universitaires de France.
Miers, S., and I. Kopytoff, eds. 1977. *Slavery in Africa: Historical and Anthropological Perspectives.* Madison: University of Wisconsin Press.
Mojekwu, C. C. 1980. "International Human Rights: The African Perspective." In *International Human Rights: Contemporary Issues,* ed. J. L. Nelson and V. M. Green, pp. 85–95. New York: Human Rights Publishing Group.
Muriuku, G. 1974. *A History of the Kikuyu.* Nairobi and London: Oxford University Press.
Nieburg, H. L. 1969. *Political Violence: The Behavioural Process.* New York: St. Martin's Press.
Nyerere, J. 1968. *Ujamaa: Essays in Socialism.* London: Oxford University Press.
Packard, R. 1989. *White Plague, Black Labor: Tuberculosis and the Political Economy of Health and Disease in North Africa.* Berkeley: University of California Press.
Pollis, A., and P. Schwab, eds. 1979. *Human Rights: Cultural and Ideological Perspectives.* New York: Praeger.
———. eds. 1982. *Towards a Human Rights Framework.* New York: Praeger.
Potholm, C. P. 1977. "The Ngwanyama of Swaziland: The Dynamics of Political Adaptation." In *African Kingships in Perspective: Political Change and Modernization in Monarchical Settings,* pp. 129–59. *See* Lemarchand 1977.
———. 1979. *The Theory and Practice of African Politics.* Englewood Cliffs, N. J.: Prentice-Hall.

Prochaska, D. 1986. "Fire on the Mountain: Resisting Colonialism in Algeria." In *Banditry, Rebellion and Social Protest in Africa*, pp. 229–52. *See* Crummey 1986.
Redfield, P. 1956. *Peasant Society and Culture: An Anthropological Approach to Civilization*. Chicago: University of Chicago Press.
Ritzenthaler, E. 1967. *The Fon of Bafut*. London: Cassell.
Roberts, A. D. 1973. *A History of the Bemba*. Madison: University of Wisconsin Press.
Rude, G. 1980. *Ideology and Popular Protest*. New York: Pantheon.
———. 1981. *The Crowd in History: A Study of Popular Disturbances in France and England*. London: Lawrence and Wishart.
———. 1985. *Criminal and Victim: Crime and Society in Nineteenth-Century England*. Oxford: Clarendon.
Scott, J. 1985. *Weapons of the Weak: Everyday Forms of Peasant Resistance*. New Haven: Yale University Press.
Shivji, I. G. 1989. *The Concept of Human Rights in Africa*. London: CODESRIA.
Shue, H. 1980. *Basic Rights: Subsistence, Affluence and U.S. Foreign Policy*. Princeton, N.J.: Princeton University Press.
Solanke, J. 1982. "Traditional Social and Political Institutions." In *African History and Culture*, ed. R. Olaniyan. Lagos: Longman Nigeria.
Steinhart, E. I. 1967. "Vassal and Fief in Three Lacustrine Kingdoms." *Cahiers d'etudes africaines* 7: 606–23.
———. 1977. *Conflict and Collaboration: The Kingdoms of Western Uganda*. Princeton, N.J.: Princeton University Press.
Thompson, E. P. 1971. "The Moral Economy of the English Crowd in the Eighteenth Century." *Past and Present* 50 (February): 76–136.
———. 1975. *Whigs and Hunters: The Origins of the Black Act*. London: Allen Lane.
Thornton, J. K. 1983. *The Kingdom of Kongo: Civil War and Transition, 1641–1718*. Madison: University of Wisconsin Press.
———. 1991. "Legitimacy and Political Power: Queen Njinga, 1624–1663." *Journal of African History* 32 (1): 25–40.
Tilly, C. 1986. *The Contentious French*. London: Belknap Press.
Vail, L., and L. White. 1986. "Forms of Resistance: Songs and Perceptions of Power in Colonial Mozambique." In *Banditry, Rebellion and Social Protest*, pp. 193–227. *See* Crummey 1986.
Vansina, J. 1973. *The Tio Kingdom of the Middle Kongo: 1880–1892*. London, New York, and Toronto: Oxford University Press.
———. 1978. *The Children of Woot: A History of the Kuba Peoples*. Madison: University of Wisconsin Press.
Vidal, D. 1974. "Economie de la societe feodale rwandaise." *Cahiers d'etudes africaines* 14 (1): 52–74.

Vincent, R. J. 1986. *Human Rights and International Relations*. Cambridge: Cambridge University Press.
Wai, D. M. 1979. "Human Rights in Sub-Saharan Africa." In *Human Rights: Cultural and Ideological Perspectives*, pp. 115–44. *See* Pollis and Schwab 1979.
Watts, M. 1983. *Silent Violence: Food, Famine and Peasantry in Northern Nigeria*. Berkeley: University of California Press.
———. 1987. "Banditry, Rebellion, and Social Protest in Africa: A Review." *African Economic History* 12: 123–30.
Weisfeder, R. F. 1977. "The Basutho Monarche." In *African Kingships in Perspective: Political Change and Modernization in Monarchical Settings*, pp. 160–89. *See* Lemarchand 1977.
Welch, C. E., and R. I. Meltzer, eds. 1984. *Human Rights and Development in Africa*. Albany: State University of New York Press.
Wilks, I. 1975. *Asante in the Nineteenth Century: The Structure and Evolution of a Political Order*. Cambridge: Cambridge University Press.
———. 1988. "Asante: A Rejoinder." *International Journal of African Historical Studies* 21 (3): 443–52.
Williams, C. 1988. "Asante: Human Sacrifice or Capital Punishment? An Assessment of the Period 1807–1874." *International Journal of African Historical Studies* 21 (3): 438–49.
Young, C. 1977. "Buganda." In *African Kingships in Perspective: Political Change and Modernization in Monarchical Settings*, pp. 193–235. *See* Lemarchand 1977.

3

Human and Peoples' Rights: What Point Is Africa Trying to Make?

H. W. O. OKOTH-OGENDO

The objective of this chapter is to provide a better understanding of the process of institutionalizing human rights in Africa. Focusing on the African Charter on Human and Peoples' Rights, I analyze from an African perspective the constraints and opportunities related to strengthening official adherence to the notion that human rights—both individual and collective—matter in the contemporary context. The African Charter—also known as the Banjul Charter, from the name of the city where it was first proposed—has been the subject of excellent analysis by others, notably Okere (1984). My purpose here is not to review the Charter in detail but simply to understand what point Africans are trying to make in that document.

The Banjul Charter was adopted in June 1981, when heads of state and government met under the auspices of the Organization of African Unity (OAU) in Nairobi. The document was the result of many years of discussion followed by nearly two years of drafting (Elias 1987). As stipulated in Article 63:3 thereof, the Charter came into effect five years later, on 21 October 1986, after a simple majority of OAU members had ratified it.

The African Commission on Human and Peoples' Rights contemplated in Chapter 1 of Part II of that Charter has since been established and members of the Commission have been elected. These members are Ibrahim A. Badawi El-Sheikh (Egypt), Alioune Blondin Beye (Mali), Alexis Gabon (Congo), Mahmoud Abou Hadiya (Libya), Grace Stuart

Ibingira (Uganda), Sourahata B. Semega Janneh (The Gambia), Habesh Robert Kisanga (Tanzania), R. M. D. Mokoma (Botswana), C. L. C. Mubanga-Chipaya (Zambia), Youssoupha Ndiaye (Senegal), and Issa Nguema (Gabon). The inaugural meeting of the Commission was held in Addis Ababa, Ethiopia, on 2 November 1987 under the auspices of the secretary-general of the OAU. Issa Nguema of Gabon was elected chairman, with Badawi El-Sheikh of Egypt as his deputy.

The adoption and coming into force of the Banjul Charter and the subsequent establishment of the Commission have been seen in many quarters as a historic achievement for Africa. For example, commentators point to the fact that the Charter constitutes a fundamental departure from the basic principle on which the OAU itself was founded twenty-five years ago, namely, *the collective defence of the sovereignty (internal and external) of each member state* (Art. III, Secs. 1–5 of the OAU Charter). Commentators further note that those events have brought Africa abreast of Europe and the Americas at least with regard to developing the structures for an institutionalized promotion and protection of human rights.

What has intrigued and to some extent perplexed observers of the human rights scene in Africa, however, is not the Banjul Charter per se nor indeed the Commission that it has created. For these have become standard prescriptions in regional human rights thinking. What has intrigued and perplexed observers is the fact that in addition to the entrenchment of the traditional concepts, rights discourse and practice, the Banjul Charter is also a charter of peoples' rights and individual duties. Therefore, one point in respect of which some clarification has become necessary is the significance of those additions for Africa. What point is Africa trying to make? In this chapter I develop some answers to that question and indicate what prospects for the promotion and protection of human rights in Africa lie ahead through the Charter.

The Need for a Charter

The decision to prepare a preliminary draft of the African Charter on Human and Peoples' Rights was taken at the Sixteenth Assembly of Heads of State and Government of the OAU, held 17–20 July 1979 in Monrovia, Liberia. That decision was not taken because a juridical void existed with respect to the promotion and protection of human rights at the continental or domestic level. The OAU Charter itself, in Article II, affirms commitment to the United Nations Charter and the Universal Declaration of Human Rights. Being members of the United Nations, the vast majority of these states have also ratified the International Covenant on Economic, Social and Cultural Rights and the International Covenant on Civil and Political Rights, which, together with the Optional Protocol to the latter convenant and the Universal Declaration of Human Rights, make up the International Bill of Human Rights (UNCHR 1987).

Acceptance of responsibility for the commitment to the promotion and protection of human rights has always been part of the OAU mandate even if very little of it appears to have been exercised in its twenty-five-year history. The decision to prepare a specifically *African* document was taken for two main reasons. The first was the obvious point that despite international commitment to the promotion and protection of human rights, no machinery existed at the regional level for the institutional coordination, supervision, or implementation of efforts towards that goal. The rather intolerable frequency of political instability (both regional and domestic) and the fanaticism with which the OAU often defended the doctrine of internal sovereignty, compounded by the chronic underdevelopment of Africa, made the absence of a continental body all the more visible and worrisome.

The second and perhaps more important reason was the need to develop a scheme of human rights norms and principles founded on the historical traditions and values of African civilizations rather than simply reproduce and try to administer the norms and principles derived from the historical experiences of Europe and the Americas. For this reason the first meeting of African experts held in Dakar, Senegal, on 28 November–8 December 1979 was specifically instructed to draw up an instrument "based upon an African legal philosophy and responsive to African needs" (Gittleman 1982).

This second reason was particularly important to the OAU. Most of its member states had come to consider the fundamental principles and precepts underlying the International Bill of Rights peculiarly Western, hence not wholly reflective of the broad spectrum of political values to which Africa as a civilization subscribes. In particular, member states and a number of African scholars were beginning to wonder whether a uniquely African contribution to international human rights discourse was not possible and indeed desirable. Of particular concern was the absence in the International Bill of Rights of community and family values, norms, and power management processes that are the bedrock of African social organizations. Simply to have adopted the language, content, and mechanisms of human rights discourse and practice fashioned out of Western individualism appeared, at least in the contemporary African situation, to be a neglect of these important realities. So it was that the Banjul Charter on Human and Peoples' Rights was born.

An Analysis of the Banjul Charter Provisions

Excepting the Preamble, the Banjul Charter is divided into three parts: "Rights and Duties," "Measures of Safeguard," and "General Provisions." The first two of those parts, which contain the Charter's substantive provisions, concern us here. Chapter 1 of Part I identifies what are described as human and peoples' rights. Chapter 2 sets out the duties owned by the individual (*not* peoples) to the society at large and to the state in particular. Part II outlines the establishment and composition of the African Commission on Human and Peoples' Rights (Chapter 1) and describes its mandate (Chapter 2), procedure (Chapter 3), and operational principles (Chapter 4).

Although the Charter provides no conceptual guidance on how to distinguish between "human" and "peoples'" rights, a quick reading reveals that it regards what others refer to as first- and second-generation human rights—i.e., political/civil and economic/cultural/social rights—as forming the essential core of the former, and some modified form of the rights of the third generation—i.e., solidarity—as comprised in the latter. Thus, with regard to human rights Articles 3 through 18 of the Banjul Charter reproduce all the well-known rights and freedoms enshrined in the International Bill of Rights, namely, those relating to: equal protection of the law and free access to judicial organs; nondiscrimination; the life and integrity of the person; the liberty and security of the person; conscience and the free practice of religion; expression and dissemination of information; association and assembly; movement internally and transnationally, including asylum; political choice, including participation in the political process; property, subject to the exercise of the police power; and social and economic power—i.e., work, health, education, social security, and integrity of the family.

Given this listing, the observation that the Banjul Charter "does not really present an alternative to Western (or indeed Eastern) civilization" is well founded (Kane 1987). This is not in the least surprising, since there is broad agreement among human rights activists and scholars of all shades of opinion, ideologies, and cultures that this list constitutes the irreducible minimum in human rights discourse.

The list of peoples' rights is not so easy to discern. In general, it would appear from Articles 19 through 24 that these rights include at least the following: the rights to equality as a group; political and economic self-determination (both internally and externally); the rights to cultural independence and identity; the rights to peace and security; and the right to an environment favorable to development.

Human rights scholars are familiar with the persistent controversies surrounding the very notion of the existence of collective rights at any level in the international legal order (Alston 1987). However, whereas arguments based on the rather spurious jurisprudential thesis that rights are meaningless unless they are vested in individuals can be easily dismissed, those that query the practical significance of those rights in conditions of underdevelopment cannot. Indeed, the Banjul Charter throws no light whatsoever on the latter issue apart from the fact that there is little in the list that cannot be found among the plethora of international conventions and declarations that have been issued on collective rights (United Nations 1983). Nothing is said of the nature of obligations that the existence of those rights place on the OAU as an organization and on its member states internally. Indeed, the Banjul Charter is clearly conservative on this matter, as it omits important new and essentially collective human rights. Rights such as those to food, to a clean environment, and to development itself (and not simply to an environment favorable to it) and the responsibility to strive toward their achievement have already gained some international acceptability (Tomasevski 1987; ICJ 1981). The duties imposed on individuals by the Banjul Charter are to be found in Articles 27 through 29. These duties relate to the family, the society, and the state. They include the following: the duty to preserve the harmonious development of the family (including respect and maintenance of family); the duty to serve the community and the nation; the duty to preserve African values; the duty to defend the security of the state; and the duty to pay taxes.

This scheme of duties has been severely criticized on the grounds that, *inter alia,* it is little more than the formulation, entrenchment, and legitimation of state rights and privileges against individuals and peoples (Okere 1984). Further, scholars question the intrinsic value of including such a scheme in a multilateral treaty and point to the danger that states might seize on it to justify excessive violation of the Charter's own "human rights" provisions in their domestic jurisdictions. More specifically, critics note that because the so-called duties are of domestic import only, they are, *ex hypothesi*, essentially within the domain of state responsibility. In addition, the first three of those duties are embedded in the cultural fabric of African social organization and hence require no restatement.

There is much merit in these criticisms. That merit, however, does not lie in the theory that the state is the villain against which human rights law is the effective weapon and hence individuals should not be called upon to discharge any duties with respect to it. The state, it must be remembered, is also the single most important agency in the promotion and protection of human rights at individual and collective levels (Boli-Bennett 1981). Rather, the merit of the criticism lies in the fact that a scheme of *legal* duties is meaningless if its precise boundaries, content, and conditions of compliance are impossible to ascertain. Such is the case with Chapter 2 of the Banjul Charter.

The provisions relating to the establishment, composition, mandate, procedure, and operational principles of the Commission are to be found in Articles 30 through 63. These introduce nothing new in international human rights discourse. In fact, there are a number of respects in which these provisions fall short of the minimum standards accepted in other jurisdictions. Four of these may be identified. First, by establishing the Commission as an organ of the OAU (Article 30), it is more than likely that the not-too-satisfactory record of the latter with respect to "human" as opposed to "peoples'" rights issues will be passed on to the former. An important pointer to that possibility is the fact that the Council of Ministers, which met prior to the assembly at which the heads of state and government adopted the Charter. Their meeting was almost deadlocked on such issues as the presumed sanctity of state sovereignty, the need to reassert the duty of noninterference in the internal affairs of member states, and the fear that the establishment of the Commission might provide opportunity for the prosecution of irredentist claims.

Second, the mandate of the Commission is primarily promotion (documentation, dissemination, assistance with model legislation, interpretation, and cooperation). It is much weaker on protection (fact-finding, receipt and processing of interstate complaints for discussion by the Assembly of Heads of State and Government). Furthermore, it accepts individual complaints only if they are not insulting to a state and are fully authenticated, and only as long as local remedies are exhausted (Articles 45–59). All these conditions clearly reduce any substantial impact that the Commission's establishment might be expected to have. Experience in Europe and the Americas suggests that a state-centered process of human rights supervision and protection is of little use in contexts in which complaints relate basically to violation of basic individual rights. In the context of the Banjul Charter, where complaints may also relate to state inability to supply or neglect in the provisioning of collective needs and services, such a process might be especially meaningless.

Third, the absence of a truly judicial mandate for the Commission or of the existence of a body with the power to make authoritative determination of specific human and peoples' rights abuses is, as many a commentator has noted, a fundamental flaw. The point here is not that justiciability per se is an essential ingredient of human rights protection but that to allow the Assembly of Heads of State and Government to determine the final outcome of the Commission's work goes against elementary principles of natural justice.

Finally, there is the question of the resolution of possible conflicts between the Banjul and OAU Charters. Under the present design it is virtually certain that should any such conflict arise, the Assembly of Heads of State and Government, in which the exclusive power to interpret the latter instrument lies, will lean against the former.

In my view these shortfalls are not compensated for by the requirements that the Commission should draw inspiration from the general body of international law on human and peoples' rights (Article 60); that states undertake to legislate those rights and freedoms in their domestic legal regimes (Article 1); and that they must, in addition, submit biannual reports on progress made in respect thereof (Article 61). They are not even compensated for by the fact that states are under a general duty to promote and respect the rights and freedoms contained in the Charter (Article 25) and to guarantee the independence of their own domestic course (Article 26). As I argue later, these requirements, while being standard provisions in international treaty-making, will not be easy for the OAU to police or for its member states to fulfill.

The analysis so far is neither new nor by any means exhaustive (Cobbah and Hamalengwa 1986). But we must still confront the important question, what is unique about the Banjul Charter? A simple answer is that because the Charter is a regional instrument in the nature of a multilateral treaty, one must expect a greater level of commitment to its provisions than to similar instruments at the global level to which those same OAU members may be a party. In this respect, therefore, the very existence of the Charter is a contribution to the fulfillment of an important goal of the United Nations system, namely, the establishment of effective regional mechanisms for the management of international obligations. The more complex answer, however, is that although the categories of rights and duties set out in the Charter may not be new, what they say is of peculiar relevance to Africa.

First, the Banjul Charter sets the record straight with respect to the confusion caused by the argument, often heard on both sides of the Mediterranean, that only certain categories of "human" rights—namely, civil and political rights, as distinguished from economic, social, and cultural rights—are the proper subject of international or domestic concern. The Charter Preamble states that "it is . . . essential to pay a particular attention . . . [to the fact] that civil and political rights cannot be dissociated from economic, social and cultural rights . . . and that the satisfaction of economic, social and cultural rights is a guarantee for the enjoyment of civil and political rights." This statement recognizes the fact that the category of demands or entitlements encapsulated in the body of norms described as "human and peoples' rights" is indivisible. More importantly, it recognizes that the violation of one part of the category cannot justify fulfillment of the other. In this respect the Charter also rejects the argument that development entails an abridgment of civil and political rights.

Second, by suggesting even imprecisely that a people—i.e., families, lineages, communities, or nationalities—may also suffer abuse or violations of rights in their collective capacity, the Banjul Charter has captured an important feature of contemporary human rights issues in Africa. There have been numerous instances across the continent in which whole communities have been massacred because one or some of their members had fallen out of favor with elites in power at the time.

The predicament of the individual in Africa is and will continue to be linked to, and hence remain an important concern and business of, the community in which he or she lives. The character of the refugee problem in many parts of Africa cannot be fully appreciated without understanding this individual/community interrelationship (Okoth-Ogendo 1986a). It is a matter of some regret, therefore, that the so-called peoples' rights were not more carefully formulated to include some of the rights and freedoms that the Charter reserves exclusively for individuals.

Overall, the foregoing evaluation suggests that despite its many flaws, there is something new in the Banjul Charter, namely, its sensitivity to the contextual social, political, and economic realities of contemporary Africa. Its value as a continental charter, however, will ultimately turn on how that sensitivity is woven into the fabric of national political and developmental behavior. This assessment begs a final question, and the only one which really matters: what difference is the Charter likely to make to the human rights situation in Africa?

Implementation of the Banjul Charter

I do not believe that the adoption of the Banjul Charter was an act of continental chauvinism; nor do I agree with those who suggest that the OAU adopted the document merely to answer some of its more vocal and important critics from the North. I am convinced that by this act the OAU and its member states were conceding an important point, namely, that in Africa the condition of human rights (even in the Western sense) is anything but healthy. To assess the likely effects of the Charter, then it is important that this condition be carefully assessed and its primary causes explained.

Moreover, the assessment must go beyond what has become the stock-in-trade of Western human rights activism concerning Africa, namely, the endless recital of civil and political rights violations with very little appreciation of the material conditions under which these occur. To continue on this path will only perpetuate what has become a most unsatisfactory response from Africa, which is to plead harassment or poverty or both and to point a finger at similar abuses in other, much older political systems rather than to do something about local conditions. If we are to put the human rights situation in Africa in its proper perspective, it is important that rights violations be seen as indicators of a deeper and more basic malaise. Although part of that malaise is clearly political, or related to the problem of governance, its epicenter is developmental. From this more widespread malaise, best described in basic material terms, stems what many now regard as Africa's chronic inabilities to attain an acceptable level of performance in human rights demands broadly conceived.

Regarding that inability, an assessment made ten years ago by the United Nations Economic Commission for Africa (UNECA 1983) states: "[A] diagnosis of the African situation—social, political and economic—has been attempted on many occasions. . . . The assessment, in all cases, has been unanimous; the African region is most seriously affected by the burden of underdevelopment. In spite of its vast human and natural resources . . . the region is unable to boast of any significant achievement. . . . Mass poverty, unemployment, social unrest, disease, hunger and ignorance continue to plague the region. As a result Africa continues to resound with cries of distress." The assessment goes on to predict that if no dramatic turnaround is achieved quickly, African socioeconomic conditions at the turn of the century are likely to be characterized "by a degradation of the very essence of humanity." This is because Africa does not have the threshold capacity to accord its citizenry, whether as individuals or as collectivities, a full measure of social, economic, and cultural rights. Such conclusions have important implications for the conduct of state power and the state of constitutionalism in general in Africa.

Regarding the first of these, it is indisputable that for most of Africa the most visible symbol of power is the presidency and the primary mode of exercise of that power is discretionary. For reasons that need not concern us here, the effect of that situation is that the main preoccupation of contemporary power elites in Africa is no longer the search for economic development and social progress but the perfection of ways, means, and techniques of survival and the expansion of opportunities for private accumulations (Nwabueze 1974). As a result political arenas in many African countries have "shrunk" to a level that pales before the expectations of the broad majority of the citizenry. It is significant in this respect that power elites have tended to react most adversely and swiftly to internal criticism.

Elsewhere I have explained some of the historical conditions that have molded the shape of power and its exercise in Africa in this fashion (Okoth-Ogendo 1986b). I have suggested that in addition to the personal (or collective) proclivities of power elites, as indicated above, it is also the case that at independence the majority of African states received power arrangements that were not only unsuitable but also subversive of their national goals and aspirations as they saw them at the time.

That condition, in turn, has had important implications for the state of constitutionalism and constitutional government in Africa. For in an attempt to redesign those arrangements, to suit those goals and aspirations, power elites have produced a most intriguing constitutional paradox. They have ended up by accepting the need for constitutions only in the minimalist sense of constitutive instruments, not in the maximalist sense as bodies of norms governing the legitimacy, exercise, and distribution of state power. As a result, in almost every African state the constitution lost any claim to being the *basic law* of the land. This was associated with increased discretionary power by elites, especially in those areas dealing with public order, security, and licensing, producing enormously enhanced control over public affairs. In short, the development, acceptance, and operation of structures, practices, and conventions concerning the control, supervision, and accountability of state power has yet to occur in Africa.

Does this mean that the Banjul Charter is of little assistance to the African citizenry in their efforts to subject centralized power to the discipline of popular (or majoritarian) expectations or in getting governments to deliver even the most elementary and basic needs required for survival? I must confess with some trepidation that I believe this is likely to be the case well into the next century. Some of the reasons for this, such as the very weak scheme of promotion and protection procedures built into the mandate of the Commission, the inadvisability of making that body an organ of the OAU, and the fierce jealousy with which member states are likely to continue guarding their internal sovereignties, have already been noted. In fact, in his address at the Commission's inaugural meeting the OAU secretary-general made it plain that African states are unlikely to tolerate aggressive prosecution of human rights causes by the Commission.

Of greater worry is the fact that many African governments are unlikely to legislate into their national legal systems the rights and freedoms enshrined in the Charter or, if they do, will certainly not be in a hurry to fully promote or protect them. A number of them are likely to argue that these are already enshrined in their national constitutions and, in the case of specifically "peoples' rights," woven into the fabric of indigenous legal regimes. In fact, as much as two-fifths of the OAU membership has not even ratified the Charter, which matches the response to similar provisions in the UN-administered system (Okoth-Ogendo 1974). With the very large number of military or extraconstitutional regimes in Africa, the duty to legislate Charter provisions into national legal systems is not even a realistic option. So as has happened in the domain of constitutions and constitutionalism, to which reference has been made above, yet another paradox may well develop, namely, the acceptance of a structure for the promotion and protection of human rights at the regional level side by side with an implicit (if not explicit) rejection of the processes, national and regional, necessary for its efficacy.

I have attempted in this essay to explore the dimensions of human rights promotion and protection in Africa. I hope I have made it clear that those who are interested only in cataloging excesses, an exercise that by its very nature is concerned exclusively with damning Africa's leaders, have missed the point. The human rights condition in any country or region should not be thought healthy by reason only of the absence of tortures, detentions, arbitrary arrests, denial of press freedom, "unfair trials," electoral fraud, or similar aberrations.

The study of human rights is much more. It includes the need to understand both the underlying causes of rights violations and the constitutive processes whereby rights are institutionalized. In other words, with specific reference to Africa, we need to understand both the constraints and the opportunities surrounding the implementation of human rights legislation. That mandate goes beyond the specific task of this chapter. Still, I cannot help concluding with reference to two factors that no doubt will influence the interpretation and implementation of the Banjul Charter in the 1990s. The first is the continued economic crisis affecting the African continent. The second is the growing political openness witnessed in many countries in recent years. These may be contradictory forces, but both will no doubt shape scholarship in the human rights and governance field in the years to come.

References

Alston, P. 1987. "The Nature of International Human Rights Discourse: The Case of the New Human Rights." Working paper for a conference on human rights, Oxford, 29–31 May.

Boli-Bennett, J. 1981. "Human Rights or State Expansion? Cross-national Definitions of Constitutional Rights, 1870–1970." In *Global Human Rights: Public Policies, Comparative Measures and NGO Strategies*, ed. Ved P. Nanda et al. Boulder, Colo.: Westview Press.

Cobbah, J., and M. Hamalengwa. 1986. "The Human Rights Literature on Africa: A Bibliography." *Human Rights Quarterly* 8 (1): 115.

Elias, Judge T. O. 1987. "The Contribution of the OAU to the Protection of Human Rights in Africa." Address delivered on the occasion of the United Nations Human Rights Day Celebrations, 10 December.

Gittleman, R. 1982. Introductory note to the *Banjul Charter on Human and Peoples' Rights in International Legal Matters.*

International Commission of Jurists (ICJ). 1981. *Development, Human Rights and the Rule of Law.* Report of a conference held in The Hague, 27 April–1 May. Oxford: Pergamon.

Kane, Risa I. 1987. "The African Charter on Human Rights and Peoples' Rights and the Tanzania Constitution: Alternative Approaches to the Protection and Promotion of Human Rights in Africa." Mimeograph. Boston University.

Nwabueze, B. O. 1974. *Presidentialism in Commonwealth Africa.* London: Hurst and Company.

Okere, O. B. 1984. "The Protection of Human Rights in Africa and the African Charter on Peoples' Rights: A Comparative Analysis with European and American Systems." *Human Rights Quarterly* 6 (2): 141.

Okoth-Ogendo, H. W. O. 1974. "National Implementation of International Responsibility: Some Thought of Human Rights in Africa." *East African Law Journal* 10 (1): 1–16.

———. 1986a. Lecture presented at a seminar on the social and economic condition of refugees in Kenya and Tanzania, Nairobi. *The Standard.*

———. 1986b. "Constitutions without Constitutional Law: Some Reflections on an African Political Paradox." Paper presented at the Center for African Studies, University of Florida, Gainesville, 25 February.

Tomasevski, K. 1987. *The Right to Food: Guide through Applicable International Law.* Dordrecht: Martinus Nijhoff.

United Nations. 1983. *Human Rights: A Compilation of International Instruments.* New York.

United Nations Commission on Human Rights (UNCHR). 1987. *Human Rights: Status of International Instruments.* Geneva: Palais des Nations.

United Nations Economic Commission for Africa (UNECA). 1983. *ECA and Africa's Development 1983–2008: A Preliminary Perspective Study.* Addis Ababa.

4

The African Human Rights Process: A Contextual Policy-Oriented Approach

WINSTON P. NAGAN

Of the many foci or vantage points we work with to understand and promote human rights, the perspectives of observers and participants loom large. This chapter reflects both of these perspectives. First, as a member (and former chair) of Amnesty International (USA), I actively promote human rights. Second, the human rights focus has long been an important element of my professional life as an academic lawyer.

I suspect that to disentangle these avocations would be a difficult undertaking in the best of circumstances. I have been a human rights activist for longer than I have been an academic. In primary school I ran messages for my teacher, who was a prominent member of a teacher antiapartheid organization, the Teachers League of South Africa. In high school I came under the influence of human rights workers like Dennis Brutus, founder of the South African Non-Racial Olympic Committee, and John Sutherland, editor of the *Evening Post* and staunch antiapartheid newspaper man. My university training at the University of Fort Hare (South Africa) in the early 1960s coincided with efforts to crush black resistance by extinguishing, inter alia, the intelligentsia. Today I work on a daily basis with urgent-action petitions, prisoners of conscience, the problems of torture, extrajudicial and judicially sanctioned executions, disappearances, the global issues of fair and prompt trials, and other issues of due process.

The original direction of my academic work was far afield from my active interest and concern for human rights (McDougal and Reisman 1985). During the early 1970s I came under the influence of Harold Lasswell, Myres McDougal, Michael Reisman, and Lung Chu Chen. These were the pioneers of a radically new and novel idea of law, international law, and international human rights. The core theoretical and methodological elements of their approach were presented in a seminar called "Law, Science, and Policy." Members of that seminar made up an international fraternity, including such African scholars as Francis Deng (Sudan), Medart Rwelemira (Tanzania), and Peter Nanenya (Uganda).

A happy coincidence of a deep intellectual interest on the part of McDougal and my own activist inclinations enabled me to persuade an already committed McDougal to offer a seminar in human rights. This was my initial baptism into the academic world of human rights. When I came to the University of Florida, I persuaded appropriate law school committees and authorities to approve the addition of a course called "Human Rights, Law, and Policy" as a regular part of the law school curriculum. The course has been taught at the University of Florida since the latter part of the 1970s.

Unfortunately, my academic interests in human rights do not necessarily complement my activist concerns. Occasionally the two roles meet, perhaps even collide, but they remain in some degree unintegrated. I mention these concerns because human rights theory is to some degree a luxury for the Amnesty activist. Indeed, although Amnesty International does have its share of relatively esoteric and academic concerns, even this discussion is viewed with the characteristic impatience of an activist organization whose immediate practical concern must be for the elimination of human rights violations and abuses.

My remarks in this essay will focus in some measure on human rights theory rather than immediate practicality. I begin by showing the importance of theory in this arena, then hive off some material to demonstrate the scope of the human rights problem in Africa. Next I argue for a decision-making approach to theory and discuss the broader issues of human rights as they are manifest in the problem of the so-called third generation of rights that has emerged from the Banjul Charter as a major controversy among those concerned with human rights. I end by returning to a consideration of the utility of a decision-making approach to these problems.

The Importance of Human Rights Theory

Even the most pragmatically minded persons have at least an "implicit" human rights theory. Nevertheless, theory counts. The implicit human rights perspective we hold affects how we discharge our human rights obligations. And invalid theory generally leads to bad practical results.

Amnesty International recently hosted an off-the-record colloquium for members of the African diplomatic corps in Washington, D.C. Most of the African ambassadors accredited to Washington assumed economic and cultural rights to be an essential precondition for civil and political rights. One of the possible implications of such a perspective is that gross violations of civil and political rights may be tolerable and predictable in Africa. By the same token, a view of human rights as essentially the product of the liberal state with attendant commitments to the rule of law promulgates a theory that distorts actual conditions when we remain insensitive to the economic, social, and cultural aspects of civil society. In other words, theory clearly affects the beliefs and practices of those who condition the delivery or nondelivery of human rights.

Only carefully designed research can grapple effectively with issues of theory. For now it is important to realize that such contradictory theories condition human rights policies and discussion in the international arena. These varying theoretical perspectives raise important issues. First, how should a theorist review past efforts at developing a theory about human rights? The immediate problem here is that academically we deal with a problem of multidisciplinary dimensions often requiring more skills than most academics possess. Second, the topic has a Kantian or universalist side in a multicultural world leading to problems of relativism and its place or validity in the creation of "universal" human rights. This in turn leads to the frequently heard complaint that human rights are a product of Western culture and are therefore of limited relevance to Africa. Third, it is important to understand just how and why human rights are prescribed and applied, invoked and promoted, terminated or appraised and what "intelligence" informs such a process. The conception of human rights as a Western artifact begs the question of ongoing intellectual and practical importance about what human rights are and how we get them. For example, there are theorists who argue that human rights are a form of positive morality, divine prescription, or law and that they are validated by custom, intuitive insight, postulation, theories of social contract, theories of justice, etc. In my view, both African theory and Western-oriented theory have some but not all of the answers, and each needs looking into as African scholars move toward increased awareness of, and research into, the rights problems of the continent.

The thrust here, then, will be a critique of some dominant theories and conceptions of African human rights.[1] Parts of the critique will, however, be relevant to more conventional or "First World" theory concerning human rights.

The Human Rights Problem in Africa

Human rights theory is still in its beginnings. Nomothetic and idiographic domains are still very unclear. Thus contexts as shown by specific example are a proper place to begin. The Sudan is a convenient starting point. The UN estimates that some 500,000 people have been killed in the southern Sudan since 1983—250,000 of these from 1988 onward. These deaths are attributable to the ongoing civil war and famine conditions associated with it. Amnesty International reports that tens of thousands of these deaths were "the deliberate killings of civilians by the militia, members of the armed forces and the SPLA" (*Amnesty International: 1990 Annual Report Summary, Africa*, July 11, 1990). The most consistent feature is extrajudicial executions of detainees by the armed forces during counterinsurgency operations. The military coup of 1989 exacerbated the situation. For example, in December 1989 Dr. Maamun Mohamed Hussein was accused of organizing a meeting to discuss strike action. Tried before a "special court," notable for its obvious unfairness, he was sentenced to death. This sentence was later commuted after worldwide protests. But the impact of the coup on the human rights of the Sudanese people was disastrous. Major political figures were arrested. The Bar Association was banned, and lawyers who protested were arrested. Opposition by judges and prosecutors led to their dismissal. Reports of torture are widespread (*Amnesty International: 1990 Annual Report*). Clearly, personal security is a serious issue in the Sudan. But starvation is no less severe. In effect, the Sudan illustrates how closely tied are basic needs and social, cultural, and economic rights to civil and political safeguards.

In South Africa statements by President F. W. de Klerk concerning the abandonment of apartheid and the unbanning of the ANC and other liberation groups coincided with confessions of death squad operations by former security force personnel. Even more alarming has been the emergence of South Africa's version of the killing fields in the province of Natal near Pietermaritzburg and now an extension of that same level of violence to the Transvaal province. Opinions differ on the causes; those blamed for the violence include members of the Inkatha (Zulu) organization, the ANC, and a shadowy "third force." What is not disputed is the scale and ferocity of the violence involving the wanton killing of innocent civilians, including women and children.[2]

The human rights vista of the African continent is a disheartening panorama of one violation after another: torture, executions, unfair or nonexistent legal procedures for imprisonment, detention, or killing.[3] The list of countries implicated involves every part of the continent (*Amnesty International: 1990 Annual Report*). Perhaps the poignancy and horror are best illustrated by the fate of Diallo Telli, former secretary-general of the OAU. On the orders of President Sekou Toure of Guinea, Telli was starved to death in prison.[4] And President Museveni of Uganda, addressing the OAU summit in 1986, condemned the silence of the world, including Africa, concerning Amin's depredations: "While Uganda perished . . . the rest of the world kept largely silent. . . . Ugandans . . . felt a deep sense of betrayal that most of Africa kept silent. . . . Tyranny is color-blind and should be no less reprehensible because it is perpetrated by our own kind."[5] Distinguished African intellectuals now talk openly of the regional variety of fascism—African fascism—when framing the discourse on African human rights or the problem of human rights abuse from a continentwide perspective (Ake 1987).

The problem of human rights in Africa mandates consideration of three domains:

1. The background of colonial rule, which has produced a legacy of effects on the political cultures of Africa.
2. In the latter part of the twentieth century, the state has concentrated power in the hands of new elites in ways even more complete than in colonial days. This has led to the marshaling of coercion to secure and maintain internal, most often undemocratic, control.
3. The organization of the international (external) environment makes nation building more complex because structural inequalities of a political, economic, and strategic-military character

are an omnipresent feature of the global war system, the global framework of economic allocation, and the global framework of politics. Even though this view is widely challenged by both Marxist and non-Marxist scholars (Warren 1980), it is obvious that no serious work on the African perspective on human rights can ignore this view because of its underlying impact on human rights discourse by African scholars and diplomats. Simply put, these premises reflect what African scholars regard as the proximate factors behind many of the human rights issues in Africa.

The OAU's concern for human rights in Africa is generally regarded as a poor one, if one excludes its concerns for the liberation of southern Africa. The birth of an African human rights document was a long and agonizing enterprise. It is unclear whether the drafters of the Banjul Charter have succeeded in articulating a culture-specific Africanist concept of human rights. A brief review of the Charter seems to indicate that its provisions are not exceptional, although the addition of the conception of peoples' rights is distinctive. The latter include "the right of equality to other peoples; the rights of existence and self-determination; the rights of disposal of wealth and national resources; the right to economic, social and cultural development; the right to peace; the right to a satisfactory environment." Peoples' rights are expressed as group rights and collective rights rather than as the individual political rights Westerners customarily associate with human rights issues.

Distinguished African scholars such as Claude Ake argue that the Western notion of human rights may be irrelevant in Africa. "There is much concern [in the West] with the right of peaceful assembly, free speech, thought, fair trial, etc. . . . They appeal to people with a full stomach who can afford to pursue the more esoteric aspects of self-fulfillment. The vast majority of our people are not in this position. They are facing the struggle for existence in its brutal immediacy. Theirs is a totally consuming struggle" (Ake 1987: 1–2). Ake argues that in Africa the struggle is fundamentally political, since leadership, offered the choice of democracy or repression of the masses, has largely opted for the latter. And this choice reflects the emergence of African fascism. Ake (1987) sees the state as more often than not the opponent of an African human rights agenda. Given the state as the problem, solutions lie in nonstate groups. As to content, Ake agrees with many African scholars that human rights must include collective human rights. In other words, as many have noted, peoples' rights, in a sense solidarity rights, are said to be an African human rights priority.

There are also positive developments. Although the responses of governments to African human rights crises have been disappointing, developments in nongovernmental circles, such as the work of ordinary persons, the African Bar Association, Africa Watch, Amnesty International, and the concern by intellectuals and opinion leaders, have led to widely distributed statements that theoretical excuses do not justify gross human rights violations in Africa. More specifically, examples like the commitment of SWAPO in Namibia to a human rights–conditioned constitutional future and, even more importantly, the constitutional guidelines and Bill of Rights recommendations of the ANC of South Africa illustrate a rising concern for human rights.[6]

Rights and Decisions

How we look at and think about human rights in Africa affects inquiry, observation, and theorizing. The approach taken here is informed by my assumption that decision making is a key to the understanding of how and why rights emerge, are suppressed, and may reemerge. The notion of decision implies choice. In our context there are choices about human rights or the deprivation of human rights—more precisely, choices about the delivery or nondelivery of human dignity. Decision or choice making about social process and the conceptions of public order implied within it suggest interventions whose purpose in a general sense is the allocation of the good and bad things in life (the allocation of the weal and the woe)—the allocation of values, so to speak. In effect, I am suggesting that for a theory about human rights to be practical, as well as providing a framework that explains what human rights are and how they may improve the public order, it must have as one component of the framework the element of decision making. Such a theory focuses on the processes of decision making that condition or undermine the human rights aspects of the public order. The scholar's role in the human rights arena is important, for scholarly critiques are interventions into decision making about human rights. But the scholar's role is only one of many such critical roles. We are all moral agents who are responsible for what we do or do not do. And ultimately rights and dignity depend on how all of us react to decisions that foster and restrain human rights locally, nationally, or globally.

There is spirited debate in academic circles about the content of the human dignity principle and how it may be objectively justified. For my part, I am willing to "postulate" rather than "justify" this precept. That is to say, this principle is a statement of my own value position and therefore influences my position accordingly. In short, I prefer a public order that optimizes the production and distribution, the shaping and sharing, of all scarce and elastic values: power, wealth, respect, affection, well-being and health, rectitude or belief-system values, enlightenment or education-system values (McDougal and Reisman 1985). The human rights problem may be simply stated as the disparity between, on the one hand, the rising common demands of all people all over the world that their essential dignity as human beings be honored and, on the other, the operational code that in practice frequently delivers the exact opposite.

Let me attempt to explain my conception of what human rights are. There are two dominant views: a narrow definition that holds that there are very few, if any, general human rights; and a comprehensive perspective in which human rights are seen as implicit in all human interactions and are therefore a practical issue.

The first view narrows the focus. If human rights are universal, then there must be very few of them because true universals can admit no exceptions. Thus the right to life cannot be universal, because it must give way to the right of self-defense and possibly even capital punishment. Similarly, the right to property must be limited by the right to tax. Freedom of movement and association gives way to the tyranny of passports and special visas. Taken to its extreme, the narrow view, with its legalistic a priori definition of human rights postulates, finds through the processes of logical, syntactical derivation that there are *no* universal human rights and therefore there are no human rights (Cranston 1983). This logic is intuitively disconfirmed in the face of summary executions and massacres in Guatemala or by the depredations of Amin's Uganda or the People's Republic of China.

The second view acknowledges the existence of a global social process, a global power process, and a global system of public and constitutive order in which values are shaped and shared in complex patterns of interdependence. In this kind of context, choice making is a ubiquitous outcome. The core value honored in the comprehensive perspective of human rights is that of respect—the principle of mutual deference conditioning decisions among human beings. This implies reciprocal deference to each other's freedom of choice to participate in and benefit from all the complex value processes in society. It means a public order committed to the widest sharing and production of the greatest abundance of all values; it means the right not to be coerced; it means the reciprocal freedom of choice for all. In short, the comprehensive perspective involves a contextual, problem-oriented, goal-guided, value-conditioned, dynamic conception of human rights. Some call it revolutionary!

I have sought to articulate provisionally a theory for inquiry about human rights, and I have suggested that such a theory would be given greatest operative effect by a focus on decision making. For an older generation of legal scholars, the legal realists, and a newer generation of scholars led by the late Harold Lasswell and Myres McDougal, such a focus makes human rights perspectives a key element in legal theory. In this approach law is a process of authoritative control through decisions whereby members of the community seek to clarify and implement their common interests. This means that theory about law must generate enlightenment about the decision process itself (observational) for the purpose of realizing more assuredly and expeditiously the common interest all share in the dignity of our species (interventionary). I leave open for the moment the complex and important question of how one "justifies" human rights and the human dignity principle. But I ask you to note that this question poses one of the central problems of both moral philosophy and legal theory, namely, how we derive and objectively justify values implied by the concept of human dignity. As Cohen notes in the introduction to this volume, the issue surfaces in cross-cultural contexts where human rights may conflict with local traditions. For example, if human rights are viewed as a culture-specific outcome of the Western tradition with its history of colonialism and imperialism, then are human rights not in some sense subversive of Islamic values, or African values, or non-Western values? I suspect that this problem is not simply one of cultural relativism "trumping" human rights, but a deeper one, that of the validation of human rights and human dignity in a cross-cultural world. Raising the problem in terms of Western ethnocentricism forces us to ask how specific human rights claims should be validated. Clearly, the place to begin is with the personal values of researchers themselves. Ideally, these should be clearly stated so we may judge how they affect observations and conclusions. Practically speaking, this may prove difficult if researchers are either unaware of their biases or intent on using research to support values they hold dear. The challenge to the social sciences is well stated by the theorist Moses Moskowitz:

> International human rights is still waiting for its theoretician to systematize the thoughts and speculations on the subject and to define desirable goals. Intelligent truisms do not necessarily add up to a theory. No one has yet arisen to draw together into a positive synthesis the facts and fancies which emerge daily from events of bewildering complexity and to carry on an authentic debate. International concern with human rights is still very much a theme begging for a writer. And the scholar has not yet appeared to redress the distortions through a calm and systematic application of facts, to ground abstractions in the specific, and to define the limits of discourse. In the absence of a definite body of doctrine, as well as of deeply rooted convictions, international human rights have been dealt with on the basis of the shifts and vagaries of daily affairs and of evocations of daily events. There is a great need for technical resources and ability to channel the facts to greater effect. Human rights as a matter of international concern is an untrodden area of systematic research. But a still greater need is for superlative virtuosity to deal with international human rights in their multiple human dimensions. (Moskowitz 1968: 88–89)

A Critique of Human Rights Theory

The critique of human rights by Third World scholars frequently assumes a coherent paradigm of human rights influenced by Western values. The paradigm takes for granted that "Western" human rights are clear and unproblematic and that, while good for the West, the "model" is of limited relevance to the rest of humankind. Such a view also seems to imply that there is some material or ideological "cause" that will ultimately produce a more universalistic, culture-free human rights consciousness for humankind as a whole. Unfortunately, experience shows that neither progress nor regress is inevitable. Whether we achieve progress in terms of an ultimately worldwide agreement about human dignity is in my view primarily a matter of choice rather than one of underlying deterministic causes.

From an Africanist perspective human rights can be classified into an evolutionary set of "generations." Third-generation (solidarity) rights require not abstention from but intervention in social processes. These rights are codified in Article 28 of the Universal Declaration of Human

Rights. They focus on such issues as self-determination in the broad sense, the right to development, the right to peace, the integrity of the environment, etc. Solidarity rights are said to meet the "basic need" of subsistence and to challenge the ethnocentricity of Western liberal values while incorporating African values of collectivism. As Ake points out, "It is necessary to extend the idea of human rights to include collective human rights for corporate social groups such as the family, the lineage, the ethnic group. Our people still think largely in terms of collective rights and express their commitment to it constantly in their behavior" (Ake 1987:7).

The problem Ake poses is not unique to Africa. All humans give up some autonomy to derive the benefits and protections of collective existence. Drawing the line between the individual's appropriate space and that of the collective is an age-old problem of law, power, and politics. What human-rights-as-a-process presents is a rational, operational decision-making process that reproduces and changes the protection and rights accorded to each domain.

Recently the ANC of South Africa and the de Klerk government produced two versions of a bill of rights. The official version (de Klerk's) modeled itself on the Western juridical paradigm (Nagan 1990). It resembles our Bill of Rights. The ANC version was broader, tracking the International Bill of Rights. De Klerk viewed a bill of rights as codifying only juridical Western forms of "legalistic" rights as seen through the lens of legal process. In contrast, the ANC argued that a bill of rights should not make an invidious choice between freedom and bread. It also suggested that a bill of rights should create, through constitutive design, regulative institutions other than courts of law that specialize in the implementation of economic, cultural, and social rights as part of the governance of society.

The ANC suggestions are in part affirmed by Item 11(B) of the agenda of the Forty-seventh Session of the Commission on Human Rights dealing with national institutions for the promotion and protection of human rights. The development of such institutions has in fact received increasing international attention by the Commission and the UN generally. A good concrete example of constitutive innovation is the Australian body known as the Human Rights and Equal Opportunity Commission (HREOC), which builds on the idea that law as authoritative decision, rather than as a priori "rules," more appropriately defines spheres of intervention to secure and enhance human rights.

The Liberal-Legalistic Paradigm

A number of African and Third World scholars attack human rights as a culture-bound enterprise used for ideological purposes to support the modern bourgeois state. Ideally, the bourgeois political culture posits the rule of law as an indispensable juridical expectation if individual "bourgeois" rights, including civil and human rights, are to be protected. The liberal model of human rights, or so goes the critique, is an offshoot of the rule of law writ large for the international community.

The older (1960s) and widely accepted liberal model of law (before the writings of liberal theorists such as Ackerman [1980]) and human rights conceived of these elements as a code of "rules" (Hart 1961). Rules are concrete prescriptive devices that define the reach of governmental authority and correspondingly limit its power. Under this set of assumptions legal rules are indispensable means for the protection of valued freedoms because they define the reach of state power and defend privatized freedoms. This limits the state's authority to abuse power and explains the notion that fundamental rights in the liberal state are "negative" rights because they limit the power of governance. It also explains why liberal theory is unable to accept the notion of a right to development as a juridical idea. In effect, then, the classic liberal state has always enjoyed an uneasy coexistence with the administrative state and its wide array of Keynesian developmental entitlements, regarded by many in Western societies as basic or fundamental. The notion of negative rights justifies a particular form of legalism; therefore it is not helpful in an inquiry about what rights are or how they can be explained.

Leaving aside ideological assumptions that accompany the liberal model—assumptions about individualism, egoism, autonomy as the key motor of social organization—the liberal-legalistic model presupposes the following technical matters:

1. A code or multiple codes.
2. Specialists to interpret the code.
3. A technique for interpreting the code, i.e., independent judicial processes.
4. The technique owes much to the presumed neutrality of legalism (i.e., judges and juries).
5. The technique used in judicial process is that of logical, syntactical derivation.

Because human rights codes—even those reduced to treatylike form—come with so many reservations, understandings, and cautions even where they are ratified, one can say that they exist, if this is the right word, in the twilight zone between morality-of-some-sort and law-of-some-sort—not quite law, not quite morality.

Unlike rights as entitlements, human rights are said to be claims until backed up by law (Seighart 1986). One solution to this problem is to use empirical rather than legalistic concepts. Operationalizing human rights in terms of "expectations" allows us to specify empirically verifiable anticipations in terms of what is a person's due owed simply because he or she exists (Vincent 1986).

Let us get back to the Banjul Charter. That code is the direct result of both continentwide and global agitation. The Charter is itself simply part of a process that may in the future map the contours of African human rights and give greater empirical specification and detailed elaboration of those rights. To paraphrase Churchill, the Charter may simply be the end of the beginning of the process of formulating, specifying, and implementing a human rights perspective in Africa. The term "human rights" symbolizes the processes of norm generation and application as well as appraisal and termination. It also symbolizes a deeper process of decision making operating at all levels of society.

Ideological Problems and African Human Rights

Because African theorists still tend to view human rights as a colonial or neocolonial artifact, it should be pointed out that the immediate precursor to the Universal Declaration of Human Rights was the Atlantic Charter and its famous "four freedoms." The Atlantic Charter's principles are also written into the ANC's Freedom Charter, and ANC leaders view the instrument as an internationally sanctioned basis for their freedom struggle. I mention this because black South Africans fought in North Africa and other theaters of war in the Allied cause and, as they saw it, in their own cause for liberation.

With this caveat, we may consider the collectivist and generational perspective. Ake's (1987) critique of human rights takes the widespread African view that much of the content of these rights is bourgeois and incompatible with African reality, because of Western individualism and African collectivism. Many with this perspective accept the widely used notion of first, second, and third generations of rights development in which collective rights are seen as the latest phase after earlier ones that emerged in the West. This view and that of Ake (1987) are concerned with the problem that in the West human rights center on civil and political matters, while economic and social rights are relegated to matters of national and international policy. Ake uses African poverty to brush aside the relevance of first- and second-generation rights. Since a starving man cares only about the next meal, how important are civil and political rights to Africa? And since the economic game plan of the world community is rigged in any event, structural inequality is endemic to the system, with Africans and others on the short end. This means that to speak the language of human rights in any Western sense here is cruel. The logic of Ake's argument poses questions like the following: Does a starving man care about being tortured and brutalized to boot? Does he care about voting? About litigating and suing his torturers? In any event, are these his choices?

There are two problems with Ake's view. First, the dependency/world-system theory implied in the argument has been seriously challenged for more than a decade. Africans have many more degrees of freedom and are now viewed as more responsible and accountable for their conditions than this theory allows. And human dignity demands that we and the Africans see them as able to choose to live in either more or less civil societies, as Cohen defines that term in chapter 1. Second, not every African is starving and mute, but many are without effective political participation in the political processes of their own countries. In general, this approach seeks to minimize the importance of civil and political rights in Africa, arguing that solidarity rights are the relevant ones for our time.

Implicit in this formulation is a method for ranking human rights priorities. The method is partly historical and partly analytical. Historically, it assumes an illusory notion of progress. As an analytical tool, it rests on the unproven conclusion that solidarity or third-generation rights are more important than all other rights in the African context. This blanket denial of the relevance of first- and second-generation rights, stated clearly by Ake (1987) as well, avoids a number of concrete issues, such as under what circumstances are rights known and protected in the West to be abrogated in Africa because Africa is both "different" and poor. Moreover, this view gives no detailed understanding of the deprivations of rights that follow if we accept the priority of solidarity rights over all others.

In essence the artificially separated sets of rights categorized into a sequence of generations are in fact a complex system of interdependent expectations about the scope, relevance, and importance of human rights in the global system of public and civil order. Hopefully, this awareness is part and parcel of the democracy movement now emerging in the political cultures in Africa, making this view a part of yesterday's argument, not tomorrow's.

The Banjul Charter deals with "human and peoples' rights." The collective rights in the Charter coalesce around solidarity rights to self-determination over political, economic, social, and cultural matters; the absence of foreign economic exploitation; the termination of economic dependence; and rights over the natural wealth and resources of these "groups." Finally, reference is made to the provision of an "adequate standard of living" and food security. To a large extent these collective rights have an economic dimension, and it may be important to examine the human rights components in the now much-tarnished idea of a new international economic order.

Second-generation and to some extent third-generation human rights pose the technical question of their appropriate juridical character. The Western skepticism of a "right" to development was most recently stated by Ambassador Morris Abraham at the Forty-seventh Session of the UN Commission on Human Rights (11 February 1991, Item 8, Right to Development): "Development is not a right but an economic goal whose achievement depends on respect for individual rights and civil liberties. . . . Unlike Political and Civil Rights, the right to development defies not only precise definition, but immediate or ultimate realization. It is little more than a dangerous incitement because it implies that fundamental freedoms can not be fully realized until all people enjoy the right to development." This is not a view shared by the developing nations, especially those in Africa.

In the same session, Ambassador E. A. Azikiwe of Nigeria described the right to development as "fundamental and inalienable," adding that it was "central and indispensable for the full realization and enjoyment of all human rights." He also noted that the opposition to discussing the right to development as a human right had "virtually diminished" in the Commission. The "New Economic Order" that figured so high on the African human rights agenda had its roots in part in the New Deal, whose ideas found their way into the Atlantic Charter and the Universal Declaration. They also found expression in Latin American–inspired international instruments such as the Economic Charter of the Americas, the Charter for Women and Children, and the Declaration of Social Principles of the Americas. Perhaps we will not all agree with the content and scope of the [Declaration of Principles of the Economic Charter.] Still, the evident optimism is based on the implications of the Atlantic Charter and the notion that the war effort was to provide not simply for the defeat of Nazi fascism but for a better world order—one free from fear and from want. The American Economic Charter speaks of "rising standards of living"; equality of access to markets, resources, and trading systems; international commercial policies that lower trade barriers, investment barriers, and currency speculation; prescriptions against restrictive trade practices of cartels and oligopolies; the limitation of economic nationalism; just and equitable treatment of foreign enterprise and capital; the problems of international surpluses of commodity overproduction and a rationalized system of distribution; a commitment in the Americas to private enterprise; and an enlightened regime of labor relations informed by the Labor Declaration of Philadelphia.

The Declaration of Social Principles of the Americas focuses on a host of entitlements characteristic of advanced welfare states today. These principles include minimum living wage, maximum working hours, industrial safety, prevention of occupational risks, workers' compensation systems, social security, and rights of workers to organize, bargain, and strike.

These and other documents led to the Declaration on the Establishment of a New Economic Order (NEO; 1974), the immediate precursor of the Charter of Economic Rights and Duties of States (1975). And in 1987 the UN General Assembly adopted the Declaration on the Right to Development. The objectives of the NEO are ones designed to protect the new and weaker states—hence the language of sovereign equality, self-determination, nonadministration of acquisition of territory by force, territorial integrity, and noninterference with domestic state issues. The counterpoint is the broadest level of cooperation by all members of the international community.

The problem of multiple ideological systems of economic organizations is handled by the expedient that this is an aspect of self-determination, and a state should not be "subjected to discrimination as a result of its ideological choice." The NEO codifies the right of permanent sovereignty over natural resources and the right to nationalize property. The NEO also focuses on the problems of neocolonialism, including a practical concern over the prices of raw materials and commodities and those of capital goods and equipment all of which constrain the development of the global economy. Other salient features of the NEO include such issues as technology transfer and easier access to capital for development purposes.

The NEO came packaged with a program of action focusing on such matters as raw materials, food, trade, transport and insurance, industrialization, technology transfers, transnational corporations, international fiscal matters, and so on. The NEO also strongly mandated the urgent adoption of the Charter of Economic Rights and Duties of States.

The problem these instruments address may be simply stated as follows: What principles or goals should inform the global economic system; that is to say, how (and by what criteria) do we obtain the rights to allocate the goods, services, resources, technology, managerial and technical skills, and know-how of the world community? And what strategies must be devised to secure sufficient power to achieve effective implementation?

The Charter of Economic Rights and Duties of States focuses on the exclusive powers of states themselves over economic matters, plus powers over international economic relations. This also includes all multilateral and universal organizations that constitute the realm of international transactions of all kinds. In other words, the Charter seeks to "order" all multinational and transnational economic relations toward more equitable outcomes for all concerned.

The principles of normative guidance embodied in the Charter of Economic Rights emerge in part from the International Bill of Rights and are given sharper focus by the Banjul Charter. It seems almost absurd to juxtapose the framework of international economic "soft" law—as Western writers call it—with such issues as

1. the debt crisis (a crisis that has paralyzed development in many Third World countries);
2. the accelerating patterns of population expansion and shrinking national resources that constitute a threat to new democracies and to the political gains that democracies have made in the Third World;
3. the debt crisis that has arrested the processes of technology transfer, further retarding development;
4. the problems of domestic clientelism, corruption, and a substitution of community policy for special interests of the corrupt few; and

5. the statal power and economic inequalities are matched by the fact that the GNP of many cosmocorps is higher than that of many states, making Third World states mere "bit" players in the world economic processes.

In the arenas of practical decision and statecraft the right to development, which I take to be an aspect of second- and third-generation rights, has received a significant measure of affirmation by the UN-inspired Global Consultation on the Right to Development as a Human Right.[7] Rights are expectations and claims leading, through a process of decision making, to entitlements. The expectations encompass individuals as well as individuals-in-groups. The fear in the Western tradition is that when a conflict occurs between the individual and the group, the group usually wins. The Western tradition involves the claims and entitlements whose effects dictate that the group (the collective or the people) ought not always to win.

This problem has been a ubiquitous part of Western political theory and jurisprudence and comes in many forms: the dualism between state and individual, society and personhood, the collective and the individual, the group and the person. Problems emerge over corporate entities when groups are personified and given the rights of persons. Thus for some the state is not a multi-individual phenomenon, but a superindividual.

A group is an organization of power. Intrinsically groups are neither good nor bad: their main function is protection and, in smaller aggregates, protection of interests important to the individual. Because groups are power institutions, they can be dangerous. They both protect individuals and place them at risk. So how do we protect the dignity of individuals in Africa, with its emphasis on collectivism? Sometimes it must be through groups; sometimes groups are the problem.

The way out is simply to reject the fictional cleavage between individual and group. I recommend a configurative mode of thinking, one that involves both contemplative skills and manipulative skills (Lasswell 1963). To break out of the older mode of thinking, we must substitute a decision-oriented approach. Because both human rights and change involve problems of combining the "is" and the "ought," operating over time, we need an organizing framework that can both describe and condition how we look at and intervene in social process, emphasizing the interrelationships between human rights and everyday decisions, and the nature of the public order in Africa. This kind of focus will, of course, emphasize both the perspectives and the operations of all relevant agents of political decision making whose interventions may generate decisions that secure or undermine human rights.

This means that change must be looked at as a process rather than as sets of abstract, formalistic, scientific definitions. The focus of such an inquiry is phenomenological. It centers on the power outcomes of social processes, in terms of identifying who the key factors are; their demands and expectations; the bases of power at their disposal; the situational contexts in which they are operating (geographic, institutional, temporal, or in conditions of crisis); the strategies at their disposal (military, diplomatic, economic, propaganda); and the short- and long-term consequences for public order. The inquiry would then seek to articulate all the claims for change or no change that emerge from the power-conditioned actors in social process or, more precisely, that discrete aspect of social process we call the "power process."

This approach might be described as the important empirical task of both understanding and expressing the problem of change in a relevant sociopolitical context. In the most general sense we might view this as a claim for extraconstitutional change or, in the parlance of modern international law, claims for self-determination and/or independence that frequently implicate extraconstitutional change as a demand.

Observing processes of claiming leads us to the first and most central problem-solving task: the issue of goal clarification or, more generally, the relevance of normative thinking. This, according to policy-science analysis, is the first of several crucial interrelated intellectual tasks that enable us both to understand and to be involved in the social process of human rights claiming and protection. We must clarify rights claiming in light of both the normative guidance of the traditions of constitutive processes as well as contemporary human rights standards. These are reflected in the UN Charter, the Universal Declaration, the International Covenant on Civil and Political Rights, and other important expressions of human rights expectations, and they demonstrate a logical and ultimate congruence with the value of human dignity.

We would examine trends in the processes of power and change as they move in the direction of, or recede from, clarified values. And we must study the conditions of decision making in relation to outcomes to determine why particular consequences occur that are relevant to human rights concerns. Here the relevance of prediction or forecasting should be self-evident. Where will we be at some future date without any decisional intervention? Forecasting may require that we model possible futures for the same constellation of trends and conditions. The challenge to "alternative" or creative decisional thinking may be formulated as follows: What kinds of decisional interventions may be employed to reach the "optimistic" predictive future at the least cost to humanitarian values (i.e., the principle of human dignity)? Or, more positively, to the extent that the desired "optimistic" future is a causal and normative possibility, what theories or challenges for creative decision making should be employed to secure that end?

It is obvious that my analysis borrows heavily from the literature of the policy sciences. It may not be obvious, however, that the elucidation and understanding of revolution as a process requires thinking that is both contemplative and, in some degree, interventionary—manipulative, if you will. The approach is contextual, problem-directed, goal-guided, and multidisciplinary with a heavy emphasis on decision making at all relevant levels of social, economic, and political organization. In a general sense there is an affinity with John Dewey's ambitious effort to state succinctly the processes of "how we think." As Lasswell put it:

> Any problem-solving approach to human affairs poses five intellectual tasks, which we designate by five terms familiar to political scientists—goal, trend, conditions, projection, and alternative. The first question, relating to goal, raises the traditional problem of clarifying the legitimate aims of a body politic. After goals are provisionally clarified, the historical question arises. In the broadest context, the principal issue is whether the trend of events in America or throughout the world community has been toward or away from the realization of preferred events. The next question goes beyond the simple inventories of change and asks which factors condition one another and determine history. When trend and factor knowledge is at hand, it is possible to project the course of future developments on the preliminary assumption that we do not ourselves influence the future. Finally, what policy alternatives promise to bring all preferred goals to optimal fulfillment? (Lasswell 1963: 78)

When put into a decision context, some problems enable us to identify appropriate decision institutions: the courts, etc. Others permit only generalized responses expressed in generalized policies, which require time to crystallize into rights. The identification of decision agencies is itself an important task because we deal with formal and informal inputs. But such a focus enables us to bring together abstract ideas and the particular claims, issues, and persons in a search for solutions.

The central question that scholars can ask in Africa and elsewhere is this: What kind of constitutional order, public order, and civil society does the system of governance, culture, and law promote and defend? The human rights challenge answers thusly: One that defends and promotes the dignity and respect of all.

The interplay of social, political, economic, and cultural rights represents a face of humanity—a profile of the measure of human dignity. If we accept this, then Africa has posed a challenge for global solidarity in that it confronts us with an integrated rather than partial view of humankind.

Notes

I am grateful to Ronald Cohen for helpful suggestions and editorial "interventions." All matters of opinion, fact, and theory are, however, my responsibility.

1. For background information from the perspective of the Pretoria authorities, see *South Africa: The Events of February 1990* and *President F. W. de Klerk's Visit to the United States of America, September 1990*. Both are publications of the South African Embassy, Washington, D.C. (1990). For more recent developments, see letter to Winston Nagan from Peter Goosen, First Secretary, S.A. Embassy, 19 February 1991. On the death squads issue, see *South Africa: Political Killings by Security Force 'Death Squads'*, Amnesty International Doc. AFR 53/01/90 (January 1990). See also "Spotlight Veers Back onto Continued Operations of Police and Military Hit-Squads," *South Scan* 5, no. 37–38 (5 October 1990): 281.

2. For documentation, see Michael Clough, "Brutal Power Struggle, Not Tribalism, Is at Root of Violence in South Africa," *Atlanta Journal and Constitution*, 16 September 1990, G3, col. 2; on the black-on-black violence in South Africa, see "Natal/KwaZulu, Buthelezi and the ANC: What's Behind the Violence?" *Background Paper*, November 1990; David Ottaway, "Five Zulus Arrested in South Africa Train Massacre," *Washington Post*, 9 November 1990, reprinted in AF Press Clips 25, no. 44, p. 3; and "Township Mirrors South Africa's Problems," *Independent*, 8 December 1990, p. 15, col. 1.

3. For a recent overview of the human rights situation in Africa from the perspective of Amnesty International, see *Amnesty International: 1990 Annual Report Summary, Africa* (11 July 1990), AI Index: POL 10/05/90. See also *The*

People's Republic of Congo: Unlawful Political Detentions and Amnesty International's Concern about Unfair Trials, Amnesty International Summary (30 May 1990), AI Index: AFR 22/02/89; and *Somalia: The Extrajudicial Executions and the July 1989 Jezira Beach Massacre, Amnesty International Summary* (June 1990), AI Index: AFR 52/25/90.

4. See Amnesty International *Newsletter* 20, no. 7 (July 1990) pp. 3-6.

5. See Amnesty International *Newsletter* 20, no. 7 (July 1990).

6. See Michael A. Hiltzik, "Ferment at Ballot Box in Africa," *Los Angeles Times*, 25 October 1990, A1, col. 1; and Scott Kraft, "South Africa Panel Proposes Black Vote, White Rights," *Los Angeles Times*, 25 October 1990, A15, col. 1. The pressures to democratize the continent emerge from the grassroots level as well as from the much-abused African intelligentsia. Further pressures have emerged from the interdependencies that condition the international environment. See Robert I. Rotberg, *Christian Science Monitor*, 29 October 1990, reprinted in AF Press Clips 25, no. 43, p. 15; "Prospects for Democracy in Africa: Approaches from Below and from Above," *Africa Today* 37, no. 3 (1990); "The Human Condition and Structural Adjustment in Africa," *Africa Today* 37, no. 4 (1990).

7. See "Question of Realization of the Right to Development as a Human Right," E/C N. 4/1990/9/ Rev 1.

References

Ackerman, B. A. 1980. *Social Justice in the Liberal State*. New Haven: Yale University Press.
Ake, Claude. 1987. *Africa Today* 1-2: 5-12.
Amnesty International: 1990 Annual Report. 1990.
Amnesty International. 1990. *Newsletter*.
Cranston, M. 1983. *What Are Human Rights?* New York: Taplinger.
Hart, H. L. A. 1961. *The Concept of Law*. Oxford: Clarendon Press.
Lasswell, H. 1963. *The Future of Political Science*. New York: Atherton Press.
McDougal, M., and M. Reisman, eds. 1985. *Power and Policy in Quest of Law*. Boston: Martinus Nijhoff.
Moskowitz, Moses. 1968. *The Politics and Dynamics of Human Rights*. Dobbs Ferry, N.Y.: Oceana Publications.
Nagan, W. 1990. "South Africa in Transition, Human Rights, Ethnicity and Law in the 1990s." *Villanova Law Review*.
Seighart, P. 1986. *The Lawful Rights of Mankind*. Oxford: Oxford University Press.
Vincent, R. J. 1986. *Human Rights and International Relations*. Cambridge: Cambridge University Press.
Warren, B. 1980. *Imperialism: Pioneer of Capitalism*. London: Villiers.

PART II

Substantive Issues

5

Women's Rights and the Right to Development

RHODA E. HOWARD

Women's rights and development are not necessarily compatible. The long-run social changes that will result ostensibly in development in sub-Saharan Africa are undermining and will continue to undermine the status of African women. The changes in modes of production from pastoralism and peasant agriculture to peripheral capitalism will put control of the national economy into elite male hands and control of the family into the hands of its male members.

Women as a social category are almost everywhere subordinate to men, although the degree of their subordination varies. The subordination of women predates the development of the cash economy, peasant agriculture, and more developed trade and industrial systems. While many analyses of the subordination of women focus on their economic roles, their subordination is also evident at the political and especially at the ideological level, where it is reflected in symbol systems that connect female/male with left/right, dirt/cleanliness, evil/good, and other such world-ordering dichotomies. Thus women's rights cannot be expected to emerge without changes in the political and ideological as well as in the economic sphere. Recent preoccupation with the economic dimension of African women's status (Robertson 1987: 102) deflects analytical attention from these other crucial realms.

If women are to achieve rights in Africa, it will be through their own organization and through pressures both on the family/kinship group and on the state for acknowledgment of their equal status. The task of achieving women's rights is therefore not the same as the task of "integrating women into development"; the latter requires more efficient use of female labor power, while the former requires political empowerment of women. There is some prospect for the foreign aid establishment in the Western world to assist African women in the pursuit of their rights. But both development and rights are primarily results of internal social change, not of foreign aid efforts, however benignly intended or appropriately organized. Moreover, foreign aid directed at the empowerment of women to obtain their rights is not necessarily compatible with foreign aid directed at economic development.

"Women in Development"

The preoccupation with "women in development" (WID) is an outgrowth of the feminist movement in North America and Western Europe that achieved significant public influence by the mid-1970s. As more women scholars entered the field of development, they began to study both the effects of development policies on women (Boserup 1970) and the treatment of women in the development establishment (Barbara Rogers 1980). There is now a large body of substantive literature on the relationship between women and development in Africa (Robertson 1987). Further, there has been feminist pressure on aid establishments in the Western world to acknowledge the often detrimental effects of development projects on women in aid-recipient countries and to include special projects for women, and special assessments about the impact on women, in aid programming. It is now recognized that women "[act] upon the success or failure, productivity, and efficiency of the development process" (Staudt 1989: 5; see also Guyer 1986b: 405). Thus all projects now proposed by the Canadian International Development Agency (CIDA) must go through an impact-on-women "filter" before final approval for implementation. In the United States, as a result of intense lobbying by U.S. women's groups (Staudt 1985: 32), a tenth of U.S. AID projects have "integrated" women since 1973, although agency resources devoted to women only increased from 2 percent (in 1973) to 4 percent (in 1987) of the total budget (Staudt 1989: 160).

Although the original WID focus was not generated inside the aid-recipient countries, it is not correct to dismiss it, as some critics do, as merely an outgrowth of Western liberal modernization theory (Bandarage 1984; see also the reply by Staudt 1986b) or as merely a preoccupation of the Westernized African elite. Many African women scholars are now involved in studying the impact of development and development projects on women. While most of these scholars are by origin or achievement members of the elite, recognition of their status does not obviate their arguments. Arguments for social change are frequently articulated, and movements for social change are frequently led, by middle-class actors; and in Africa, where illiteracy rates among women are still high and where tertiary education is still almost exclusively a male preserve, the argument that "ordinary" African women are not represented in the articulation of demands for women's rights falls particularly flat. The debates on women's rights in Africa and their relation to development must be addressed on a scholarly level and not deflected by *ad hominem* (or *ad feminam*) accusations about the geographic or class origins of the participants.

Women's Rights

Women have the same human rights as men. The international consensus on human rights is represented by the International Bill of Rights, a set of United Nations documents that includes the Universal Declaration of Human Rights (1948) and the two 1966 International Covenants on Civil and Political Rights and on Economic, Social and Cultural Rights. Most African states have agreed in principle to this set of human rights documents, and many African constitutions make specific reference to it. The rights are too numerous to be listed here, but they include protections against state abuses of a citizen's physical integrity and personal freedom; guarantees of substantive and procedural justice; the right to participate in one's government; guarantees of the right to food, livelihood, and an adequate standard of living; and the right to participate in the cultural life of a community. The Preamble to the Universal Declaration of 1948 and Article 2 of the two 1966 Covenants specify that rights are due to all persons regardless of sex (United Nations 1978).

Women's rights have also been addressed in the United Nations through a variety of supplementary documents, including conventions on the abolition of slavery and the traffic in women, on voluntary marriages and minimum ages for marriage, on political rights for women, and on the nationality of married women (Howard 1986: 184–85). In 1979 the United Nations proclaimed the Convention on the Elimination of All Forms of Discrimination against Women (United Nations

1980). This Convention specifically addresses the rights of women in development, and in particular the rights of rural women, acknowledging "the significant roles which rural women play in the economic survival of their families, including their work in the non-monetarized sectors of the economy" (Article 14:1). As a result of this acknowledgment, women are promised, inter alia, the right "to have access to agricultural credit and loans, marketing facilities, appropriate technology and equal treatment in land and agrarian reform as well as in land resettlement schemes" (Article 14: g). These concerns reflect the issues raised in the 1970s by scholars working on the effects of development on women—in Africa, these include loss of land (Okeyo 1980), differential access to credit (Staudt 1978), and discrimination in land resettlement schemes (Brain 1976). The Convention Declaration on the Elimination of All Forms of Discrimination against Women entered into force in 1981 and by 31 December 1990 had been ratified or signed by thirty-four African governments (United Nations 1991: 165–66).

The establishment of these rights for women is predominantly a normative exercise. As normative statements, United Nations declarations are not necessarily enforceable in international or national law; nevertheless, they do provide a standard of comparison by which activists—African as well as Western—who favor rights for women can assess their governments, especially when governments have ratified these documents or included reference to them in their own constitutions.

Finally, it should be noted that the African Charter on Human and Peoples' Rights was adopted by the Organization of African Unity in 1981. (The Charter is included in Hamalengwa, Flinterman, and Dankwa [1988: 5–19] and Welch and Meltzer [1984: 317–29].) Women's rights are addressed ambiguously in this Charter. Article 2 guarantees rights without discrimination on the basis of sex, but Article 18 stresses the family as the "natural unit and basis of society," and Article 17: 3 mandates that the state should protect "morals and traditional values recognized by the community." Traditional values frequently reflect deeply held ideological beliefs that include an entrenched notion of the moral inferiority of women to men and of the need to subordinate women to men's familial and political authority—that is, to patriarchy in both its narrower and its broader sense. Nevertheless, the formal recognition of the equality of women in this Charter provides African women activists with a stronger normative standard than mere reference to international documents and also suggests a possible normative commitment by some elite males in Africa to women's rights.

The Right to Development

In general in the academic literature on Africa, the notion of economic development as pure growth has been rejected. In principle, development is now usually taken to mean some combination of growth, self-reliance, and equal or equitable distribution of resources to all citizens; frequently political participation or citizen "empowerment" is also included as an ingredient of development. This change in conceptualization in the academic community has been reflected in the United Nations. The right to development is one that the United Nations as an institution has generated and promoted, in large part as a result of pressures by its newer Third World members. The 1974 Declaration on the Establishment of a New International Economic Order is the first major statement asserting the obligation of the wealthy states to assist development elsewhere, even at the cost of their own material abundance (United Nations 1974). In 1986 the United Nations approved a Declaration on the Right to Development. In this document development was somewhat redundantly defined as the right of "every human person and all peoples . . . to participate in, contribute to and enjoy economic, social, cultural and political development, in which all human rights and fundamental freedoms can be fully realized" (United Nations 1986: 366).

But despite this broader conceptualization of development, it can be argued that from the point of view both of African governments and of aid donors, the primary criterion of success is still pure growth (Howard 1989). There is a practical reason for this: while in the 1970s growth without development was criticized, in the 1980s and 1990s development without growth has come under even more severe attack. Informed observers in both the academic (Hyden 1983) and the institutional community (World Bank 1989) have pointed out that a country cannot sustain equality or self-reliance in a stagnant economy or one with negative growth rates, as was tragically the case in some African countries in the 1980s.

Given that in practice the primary criterion of success is still growth, why then is so much effort devoted to promotion of the right to development? This effort is part of the larger enterprise of ideological legitimation in which both weak African states and their donor countries are engaged. For African governments, promotion of the right to development indicates concern for the basic needs of ordinary citizens. Such promotion can also be used as justification for ignoring basic civil and political rights in the name of the higher goal of economic progress (Howard 1983; Howard 1986: chaps. 3, 6, and 7; see also Donnelly 1985: 505). For donor countries, publicly articulated political concern with development helps to mask the more pragmatic reasons for aid, such as trade promotion, employment generation, and political influence in the recipient countries (on Canada, see Freeman 1985).

Thus development and the right to it, both originally proposed as radical counterparts to the preoccupation with growth, have now been incorporated into statist ideologies. Women's rights, like civil and political rights, are in danger of being subordinated to a new development ideology, whose very absorption of all other rights implies their irrelevance.

WID and the Ideology of Development

Despite the statist takeover of the notion of development, the ideal of an equitable, self-reliant model of growth responsive to citizen concerns still holds currency among many academics, activists, and international and national officials. Proponents of this ideal often do not recognize that in practice development is a political, frequently a coercive, activity. The international development community of the late twentieth century views development as planned, nonpolitical social change. But human rights are necessary precisely because nonpolitical social change is impossible. Women are one among many social groups that frequently suffer severe economic and social dislocation as a result of development plans and projects.

"Women in development" was originally a critical idea sponsored by women academics and activists concerned with the effect on women—especially, in Africa, rural peasant women—of technocratic, growth-oriented development projects. But increasingly WID is now part of the depoliticized, planned social change that the development establishment in general espouses. The co-optation of WID ideology can be viewed as part of the effort by Western states to satisfy mainstream liberal feminist demands for formal equality with men without addressing either structures of inequality or the deep ideological causes of the subordination of women. This is not to say that the adverse effects on women of individual development projects are not noted or that remedies are not attempted; for example, CIDA's internal literature on WID clearly notes such problems. It is to say that the assumption of planned, nonpolitical social change still obtains and that the systemic material, political, and ideological biases against women cannot be addressed by project-oriented models of development. "Women-in-development" has become an efficiency-oriented goal, as it is now acknowledged that the "integration" of women as producers implies "mobilization of maximum human resources" (Kenyatta 1985: 284). It is recognized that to ignore, for example, women's role in rice production in The Gambia is less efficient than to acknowledge it in groundnut production in Senegal (Robertson 1987: 118; Lewis 1984: 181-84). In short, integration of women into development projects now fits nicely into state-centric plans for economic growth. But it is not necessarily true, as the U.S. legislation on including women in U.S. AID projects assumed, that integrating women into development projects improves their overall status (Staudt 1985: 34).

It is not only the statist ideology of donors and recipients that is responsible for the absorption of the originally critical notion of women in development into an ideology that justifies confining social change to economic planning. A combination of certain strands of feminism and of dependency ideology also encourages this absorption.

Dependency theory was originally a critical notion pointing out the historical and contemporary roots of African poverty in its dependent integration into the world capitalist system. It is now, however, sometimes used as an excuse to externalize the causes of economic and political abuses in Africa—for example, in the 1980 Lagos Plan of Action for economic development in Africa (Organization of African Unity 1981: 7, clause 6; Ravenhill 1986: 88-89). In this ideological version of dependency theory, Africa is a blameless victim of imperialism. This approach accords well with some strands of the newer literature on human rights, in which Africa is presented as a morally superior continent, holding on to the values of individual dignity, commitment to the community, equitable distribution of resources, and consensual decision making in the face of the individualism, lack of commitment, selfish acquisitiveness, and abusive politics imported from the West (see especially Mojekwu 1980; Legesse 1980; and Cobbah 1987; for a critical discussion of this viewpoint, see Howard 1986: chap. 2; and Howard 1990). Similarly, in certain strands of feminist thought women are presented not only as the blameless victims of male power and authority but also as morally superior persons. This new version of the maternal feminism of the nineteenth century poses women as essentially different from men; they are supposed to be more cooperative, more committed to the family/community, less acquisitive, and less interested in power than are men. In this new ideology of innocence, both Africa and women are the innocent victims of Western male acquisitiveness and aggression.

Such essentialist beliefs about differences between men and women fit nicely into the male-dominated African ideology of the role of women in the community as guardians of the family and the indigenous culture. Specific grievances of African women against both the African state and African men are lost. African women, like Africa in general, become the innocent victims of Western imperialism, and, as with Africa in general, their primary rights claim is for the right to development. Thus we come full circle: the rights of women *in* development become the right of women *to* development, defined not by them but by the development establishment, both inside and outside their own country.

To break this circle requires assertion of women's rights, separate from development, possibly against the development establishment, and not necessarily compatible with the development enterprise. The political empowerment of women implies confrontation with men over some issues. As Guyer notes with regard to women's bureaus in Africa, "political action . . . such as advocacy of a women's perspective within the [development] organization as a whole, lobbying for more funding for women's projects, or the maintenance of links to other women's groups, demands . . . a somewhat more confrontational collective stance" (Guyer 1986b: 416). "Development" in practice has frequently meant economic growth that deprives women of their precapitalist access to and control of land, use values, and indigenous marketing systems. "The development process reduces women's power, decreasing their access to resources and often increasing their responsibilities . . . [New] life is breathed into the traditional values that discriminate against women, even as societies experience rapid economic and cultural change" (Jaquette 1988: 229). This process is facilitated by men's political, ideological, and familial dominance of women, in Africa as elsewhere. Yet within the development establishment there is little, if any, concern with these noneconomic dimensions of male control over women. Indeed, because one of the important latent objectives of development is to depoliticize social change, there is hardly going to be interest in the politicization of gender relations that women's rights implies. The agenda of women's rights intersects, but is not synonymous with, the agenda of development.

Women and Development in the African Context

In most of sub-Saharan Africa, development means a change in modes of production from subsistence agriculture and pastoralism, through peasant agriculture, to peripheral capitalism. Many Africans now face a situation comparable to that faced by the peasantry of Europe in the early stages of industrialization. But there are two significant differences from the European situation.

One difference is that in most of Africa (except Ethiopia and the west African states of the sahel) a system of status rankings and extraction of agricultural surplus similar to that of feudalism never evolved. Thus before colonialism the gendered division of labor in the rural areas of Africa had not undergone the period of conversion into corvée or wage labor that undermined the contribution of European women's use-value production to the family (Hamilton 1978: chap. 2; Middleton 1979). This change in Europe was reinforced by a hegemonic state religion, Roman Catholicism, that contained profoundly misogynistic strands and clearly declared women to be not only lesser beings but also temptresses who could lead innocent men into evil (Bullough 1973: chap. 5; Daly 1978: chap. 6). It may be possible for African women who have not undergone the same extent of economic and ideological subordination relative to men as have European women to use the modern ideology of human rights to demand continuation of the relatively more egalitarian status they enjoyed in prepeasant societies.

But a second difference between Africa today and Europe in its early capitalist phase bodes ill for African women. During its period of industrialization Europe was the world's dominant economic power. Its newly landless proletariat could enter industrial employment or migrate to the Americas and Australia. By contrast, sub-Saharan Africa today is the weakest of the world's continental economic actors, and there are very few opportunities for emigration. Thus African women who are presently undergoing the period of transition to peripheral capitalism are in a weaker economic position than were their European predecessors.

The role of women in contemporary African economies is well

known. Rural women work in both subsistence and cash-crop agriculture, yet men are frequently considered the legal owners of both the land and the income it generates. Women's use rights to land have been undermined by its conversion into a salable commodity. Urban and industrial jobs are very rarely available for women, and when they are, women are paid far less than men. Most women in the cities earn their living through petty trade or the offer of sexual or other domestic services.

The pattern of women's participation in peripheral capitalism in Africa resembles women's role in early capitalist England. Mid-nineteenth-century London was full of women engaged in petty trade and many women also sold sexual services (Alexander 1976: 100, 109). But by the early twentieth century British trade unions were sufficiently strong to demand a family wage for male workers, permitting women to withdraw to the home, where domestic labor was a full-time job. In Africa, the family wage system is not likely to emerge in the near future. African women will be increasingly subject to removal from their land with few other economic options to support themselves and their children and with very little chance that they will be able to marry a man who can support them.

Thus the material stakes are high in Africa, and conflict over resources and jobs between men and women can be expected to intensify. The respect reputedly accorded to women in traditional African societies may not be enough to counterbalance the intensification of the two strands of patriarchy—male control of both familial and national resources—that have accompanied the rise of capitalism worldwide.

The development establishment has now recognized the difficulties experienced by African women in the present transition to peripheral capitalism. But this recognition will not necessarily result in women's rights. The needs of women are rarely considered in macroeconomic planning, as opposed to microeconomic projects. In its important 1981 report on Africa, the World Bank made little or no reference to women and disregarded the highly detrimental effects on women and children of its recommendations to cut back on social welfare expenditures such as food-price subsidies and national health care schemes (Green and Allison 1986: 74–77). If one considers that in practice development still means economic growth, then development is more likely to occur at the expense of women than to their benefit. The development establishment appears to be more willing to incorporate women's special needs when such incorporation can increase overall efficiency than when it puts extra demands on the national economy and polity.

In any case, the Western development establishment is constrained in its activities by the policies of the sovereign states that are its aid recipients. Although women have not had to struggle for the vote in Africa and some governments have a few women members, national states in Africa are almost uniformly controlled by men. These men are influenced by, inter alia, their traditional cultural beliefs about the proper role of women in society. Thus, to understand why development may not be compatible with women's rights in Africa, one must also analyze the ideological dimension of women's subordinate status.

The Ideological Dimensions of Women's Subordination

Many women scholars have noted the lack of attention to the ideological and political dimensions of women's status in Africa. Staudt (1986b: 330) discusses the need to go beyond policy studies to studies of gender ideologies and the role of the state in perpetuating the subordination of women. Susan Rogers (1982: 26) has written of Tanzania that "the failure of various development efforts to substantially improve the conditions of rural women's lives can be traced to a refusal to confront the basic structure of gender relations. . . . [T]he object of analysis . . . must be relations between women and men."

It was suggested at the beginning of this section that African women, never having been subordinated to the authority of a hegemonic, misogynistic state church, may have enjoyed more respect and prestige in their precapitalist societies than did European women under feudalism. Such a comparatively enhanced status may be the key to protection of women's rights in modern African societies. Nevertheless there is a significant ideological component to women's subordination in sub-Saharan Africa that predates the entry of the colonial powers.

The subordination of women, pace Engels (1972), is not originally a product of the emergence of capitalism or even of feudal, slave-owning, or other earlier forms of caste/class-stratified societies. It is rooted in the norms of appropriate gender-specific behavior that emerged in much earlier social formations. These norms in their turn appear to depend on world-ordering dichotomizing concepts that characterize all religions. "In many African societies, there are ideological oppositions associating women with left rather than right, crooked rather than straight, and a whole host of negative, inferior qualities" (Robertson

1987: 112). Among the Mbum of Chad, the right hand, which is used for handling food, is connected with men, while the left hand, which is foul, is connected with women (O'Laughlin 1974: 315).

Puberty rituals in Africa frequently taught, and still teach, females to defer to men (Strobel 1982: 127). A girl growing up in the Rufiji valley in Tanzania was taught that "on going to her husband she must remain quiet and bear her lot; she must not use words or behavior that would offend him; she must not be stubborn; . . . and [she must] in all ways conduct herself as an obedient subservient wife" (Swantz 1985: 34). For their part boys are taught to spurn, denigrate, and separate themselves from women. According to Andreski (1970: 62), in precolonial times male members of secret societies in Ibibioland would kill women found outside their homes during certain important male rituals. Andreski refers to this custom as terrorism.

Women's fertility arouses very ambiguous emotions, in Africa as elsewhere. "Women . . . are anomalous creatures—intimately associated with the well-being of society through their life-giving attributes and deeply threatening to life through their polluting qualities" (Kilson 1976: 136). Women's capacity to bear children is connected with the capacity of the land to provide food or to bear crops, yet the fact that they bleed monthly without death is a matter of mystery. Fertile women are honored, yet in eight of the thirteen indigenous religions surveyed by Kilson, menstruating and pregnant women were considered to be religiously impure (Kilson 1976: 136). Among the Luguru of Tanzania, pubescent girls were confined to dark huts for one to three years, during which they were considered sacred but unclean (Brain 1978: 180). Similar attitudes to women's bodily changes are found among converts to Islam (Callaway 1984: 437). Childless women are humiliated: barrenness is grounds for divorce, and barren women are often considered to be victims of witchcraft (Knipp and Cohen 1981: 12).

Despite such ambiguous social reactions to female fertility, it appears that the connection of women with evil and chaos is weaker in Africa than in other parts of the world. In a cross-cultural survey of 156 societies, Sanday concluded that in fertile agricultural areas ("benign" environments), religious symbolism would include goddesses, goddesses of fertility would be especially honored, and women's status would be relatively high. In "hostile" environments, gods would replace goddesses and women's status would be concomitantly lower because female fertility would be perceived to have failed to enhance adequately the fertility of the land (Sanday 1981). One reason for the relatively higher status of women in Africa than in other continents at similar levels of economic development may be that, until the twentieth century, the environment in much of Africa was relatively benign. In land-extensive, labor-intensive ecosystems female contributions to production were important and acknowledged. Yet despite this weaker connection of women to evil and chaos in indigenous African religions than in the religions of other areas, some indigenous belief systems have deeply misogynistic bases. For example, a myth that men took power through a revolution that replaced unjust women rulers exists among both the Kikuyu and the Ibibio (Strobel 1984: 87; Andreski 1970: 58).

Factors other than world-ordering belief systems also militate in favor of an ideology that subordinates women. Political society is frequently characterized by the subordination of women even when it is stateless. Meillassoux has suggested that political society is in fact rooted in the exchange of women. Such exchange ensures social relations among groups of males who would otherwise be autonomous. It also impels travel and political negotiation by the men who do the exchanging and the rise of elders who control the supply of women and younger males' access to them (Meillassoux 1981). This analysis implies that male reification of women and subjugation of women to male authority occurs at a very early stage of human history. Such reification of women helps to explain, for example, the African custom of inheritance of widows. Among the Beti, widows were "the most valuable form of inheritable property. . . . [W]omen represented capital and labour, political alliance, military strength, and trading partnership, as well as domestic service and biological reproduction" (Hay 1989: 33 n. 20, citing Guyer 1986a).

In state societies, the subordination of women is universal. Patriarchal control over the reproductive and productive activities of the females of the family (wives, sisters, daughters, and female slaves) is entrenched by law as one of the earliest forms of property. With the institution of formal legal systems and systems of caste stratification, the ideological division of "good" (wives and free) and "bad" (prostitutes and slave) women is entrenched, as the formal and economic status of women is mediated through their sexual ties (see Lerner 1986: 8–10). Where such belief systems do not already exist, state societies tend to develop universalist, formal religions in which gods replace goddesses and women are ritually denigrated. Kilson found that African supreme beings were invariably male (Kilson 1976: 134).

The Baganda are an example of an indigenous, precapitalist "class" society in Africa in which women's status appears to have been significantly lower than in other, nonclass societies (Sacks 1975).

Thus in contemporary Africa an ideology of fear and hatred of women can still be found. This sort of ideology is readily evident, such as in popular songs. In Ghana, songs include such lyrics as "[O]bey your husband in all respects . . . the glory of a home lies in the woman, and the glory of a woman lies in the husband" (Asante-Darko and van der Geest 1983: 249). Misogynistic slogans are devised by Ghana's mammy lorry drivers: "I will rather play with the snake / Than fool around with a woman / Yes, I say / Fear woman / And play with snake" (Kyei and Schreckenbach 1976: 58). In Tanzania popular songs and short stories about women contain themes of "prostitutes preventing men from fulfilling their kinship obligations back home . . . unfaithful wives . . . wayward girls . . . unfortunate and nasty wives who dare to question their husbands' rule over household and checkbook; mean women, ambitious women, deceitful women, women who suffer and cause trouble until they learn what they really need/want most is to get married" (Susan Rogers 1982: 39 n. 5).

Women in Africa, as elsewhere, are clearly divided into "good" and "bad." This division is reflected in the belief that all single, unattached women in the cities are prostitutes; in the frequent attempts by governments to expel single women to their rural areas, sometimes with orders to get married; and in the physical attacks on urban women (Howard 1986: 194). Among the Baganda, "all independent single women . . . are indiscriminately referred to as *malaya* [prostitutes]" (Obbo 1976: 379). Touring Yoruba theater companies in Nigeria have five predominant roles for town women, "the prostitute, the co-wife, the witch, the half human/half animal, and the transvestite" (Strobel 1984: 99). Successful Yoruba businesswomen are often regarded as witches who possess strong psychic powers with which to attack men (Robertson 1987: 112). Such views are reminiscent of earlier practices such as forcing widows to undergo trial by ordeal to prove that they did not poison their husbands (Andreski 1970: 63).

Misogyny extends to the indigenous division of labor. It is extremely humiliating for men to do "women's work," even when they have no work of their own; thus one finds the village phenomenon of depressed, unemployed men lazing about while their wives collect wood, fetch water, care for children, and engage in subsistence cultivation. (This is clearly reflected in the Senegalese film *Selbe: One among Many* by Safi

Faye.) Among the Mbum, "Men who live alone without wives sometimes prepare their own meals, but because of the shame of doing women's work they cook only inside the house" (O'Laughlin 1974: 305). Dumont (1966: 232) reports of a society of fishermen-hunters that the men despise agricultural work because "they consider it essentially a woman's job, unworthy of truly virile men." In Tanzania, "women are apt to assume many jobs once considered to be men's but few men will undertake chores considered women's work" (Mbilinyi 1972: 373).

Where belief systems include the notion that women are untrustworthy and must be subordinate to men, the integration of women into development is a difficult task. Such beliefs characterize both ordinary male householders and elite male decision makers in Africa, as they do elsewhere. But because it is intellectually and ideologically illegitimate for academics and politicians on the world stage to oppose women's rights, members of the elite frequently mask their beliefs. In the African(ist) debate on human rights, this masking is often done either by accusing Western women scholars of ideological imperialism or by asserting the necessity of defense of African culture. Women are bound up, in many male Africans' eyes, with home, family, and community. It is the woman, as Obbo (1980: 143) has pointed out, who is expected to preserve culture and tradition while men migrate, move outward, and increasingly assert their individuality. Insofar as there appears to be far more fear that women will abandon their culturally prescribed roles than that men will, discriminatory ideologies of the proper place of the two sexes appear to be influencing the debate.

Women's rights require cultural change in all societies. The concern for respect for cultural differences should not obscure the fact that in most cultures women are subordinate to men. If African women are to organize in defense of their own rights, they may well articulate their struggle in ways that differ from those of Western feminists. But African women, like Western women before them, will have to confront the ideological and political as well as the material basis of their subordination before they can obtain equal rights with men.

Must History Repeat Itself?

The analysis above suggests a rather bleak future for African women in the short or even medium term. They are likely to become more economically subordinated in the future than they were in the past and to have fewer new opportunities either for employment or for dependence on a male breadwinner than did their predecessors in early capitalist Europe. While in the indigenous ideological systems there may be less misogyny than there was in Europe at a similar stage of economic change, there is nevertheless a substantial ideological predisposition in most African societies to regard women as inferior to men.

Moreover, Africa has been subject to several centuries of Islamic conversions and European ideological intervention, both of which have particularly affected those elite women who might be expected to be leaders of movements for social change. Christian and Islamic traditions both preach the subservient role of women, and the domestic ideal of the dependent wife hidden from the outside world has especially affected converts. Wealthy Muslim women in Nigeria, for example, retreat into purdah as a symbol of their husbands' success. This practice is increasingly spreading to the poor as well; in Kano, 95 percent of married women are in purdah, and a common Hausa Muslim saying claims "Every woman is inferior to a man" (Callaway 1984: 431, 435). Elite women in coastal Tanzania also stay at home, "enjoying prestige but condemned to silence in the presence of their male superiors and living a life circumscribed by rules and deprived of personal rights" (Swantz 1985: 37).

In politics as in personal life, colonialism undermined the roles of women. Women had ritualized representation—what Sudarkasa (1986: 98) calls "parallel chieftaincies"—in many precolonial African consultative assemblies. A famous case is the reassertion of women's rights in Aba, Nigeria, in 1929 against British colonial authorities. The Aba "Women's War" protested both the taxes imposed on women traders and the removal of women judges from traditional courts (Van Allen 1975). But there has been a tendency in the Africanist literature both to idealize women's precolonial political representation and to generalize from such cases as the Aba women's struggle. In other societies in Nigeria (Afonja 1986: 90) and Kenya, male gerontocracy was firmly entrenched. Staudt (1986a: 204) reports that in the society she studied in western Kenya, "community leadership was exclusively male, and women had no right to speak in mixed public groups."

Thus, in the present day, those elite and professional African women who might, as in the feminist movement in the West, be leaders in the assertion of women's rights must free themselves from Christian and Islamic socialization patterns. They must also free themselves from indigenous political heritages that were frequently discriminatory and from European modes of governance that reinforced or introduced male exclusivism in African politics. The cultural inheritance of precolonial patterns of women's authority, and the economic independence of many African women both in subsistence agriculture and in trade, may assist African women to gain equality in politics, but this inheritance should not be exaggerated.

It might be argued that African feminists have certain advantages over their early Western counterparts. One of the earliest demands of nineteenth-century Western women was for the right to custody of their children. In Africa, indigenous matrilineal descent structures frequently allocate children to the mother's kinship group. However, there are also societies in which children "belong" to the father, especially after the age of seven (Donegan 1972: 73). Mbilinyi maintains that in neither patrilineal nor matrilineal societies in Tanzania did women have any real rights to their children; rather, children "belonged" either to the husband or to the maternal uncle: "Up to the present time [before changes in Tanzania's marriage laws], if a husband died or if they were divorced, *the wife had no basic rights* . . . not even to her children" (Mbilinyi 1972: 374; emphasis in original). In Islamic societies, the father has custody of children both during the marriage and after divorce; if he dies, a male relative, not the mother, takes custody (Eze 1984: 151). Among modernized Africans it is likely that, as in the West until the late nineteenth century, custody struggles will be resolved in the father's favor.

The other early struggle in the Western world was over the right of women to control their own property and wages. African women are sometimes thought to have considerably more economic independence than did nineteenth- or early twentieth-century Western women. There is, however, some evidence to suggest that African husbands do take their wives' earnings. Women in Mitero, Kenya, channel their earnings from cash crops into self-help organizations in order to prevent "appropriation of their product by their husbands" (Stamp 1986: 40). Some women adopt Islam or Christianity because these religions give them (unequal) rights to inheritable or conjugal property where previously they had none (Strobel 1982: 122).

Such evidence modifies the perception that contemporary African women's status is radically different from the status of Western women during the early period of industrialization. Nevertheless African women do have one advantage, a heritage of the liberal constitutional models negotiated at independence: unlike Western women, they have not had to struggle to obtain the vote and the right to participate in politics. The existence of military regimes and personalist dictatorships, however, frequently obviates women's (and most men's) political participation in practice.

These slight advantages that African women have with regard to rights may help them to attain equality. For example, Nigerian women lawyers are already suing for equal inheritance rights for women in Yorubaland so that widows and daughters can retain control over land (Leigh-Williams 1988). Even the domestication of upper-class Christian and Muslim women could be stood on its head. Many nineteenth-century elite Western women were involved in voluntary activities that were frequently concerned with poor women and young girls in particular and sometimes were the forerunners of state social welfare schemes. In Kenya, Strobel has documented how Muslim women in purdah formed organizations to promote day nurseries and girls' education. These organizations then became interested in women's equality, and rudimentary attempts were made to press for increasing women's rights in the cultural and political arenas (Strobel 1976).

There are very few voluntary organizations in Africa concerned with human rights, and even fewer concerned specifically with women's rights. However the potential for a rights focus is evident in women's organizations that do exist. These include age-grade societies, secret societies of various sorts, market-women's organizations, occupational societies such as prostitutes' organizations, savings and credit societies, church groups, communal labor groups, and female members of "hometown" or ethnic associations (Wipper 1984). Such organizations ought not to be romanticized; they are subject to the same fissiparous splits as is any Western women's organization. In particular savings and credit societies frequently benefit wealthier women, who moreover prefer, when possible, to withdraw from them and use more impersonal private banking services (Lewis 1976). Furthermore, women's rights will hardly be the priority of most of these organizations at the moment; at most, they will engage in welfarist activities that tend to benefit women and children. This is the pattern that was followed in the West.

Moreover, many African women who engage in politics will not be interested in women's rights. Many will be interested in their own family, clan, or ethnic claims or in safeguarding their own economic privilege. For example, in the 1970s elite women used Kenya's Maendeleo Wa Wanawake organization to further their own political or status-oriented goals (Wipper 1975). In Tanzania, "wives of important government officials" profited from retail cloth shops purportedly set up by the national women's organization to assist local members (Susan Rogers 1982: 30). Such examples suggest the need for women's organizations that are independent of the ruling party, especially in one-party states.

In the struggle to organize themselves for political change African women do have one strong advantage over their earlier Western counterparts, namely, the existence of an international feminist movement and an influential ideology of women's rights. As Staudt argues (1986a: 213), the "new gender ideology [disseminated through United Nations organizations] supplements and potentially undermines the dominant ideology" of male supremacy. The international feminist movement will assist in the articulation of specifically feminist demands in Africa. To say this is not to prescribe that African women ought now to be making feminist demands on the state, development agencies, or male members of their own families. They may well have more pressing concerns. But these concerns may evolve into an indigenously articulated African feminism as the gender-based economic, ideological, and political blocks to women's participation in the direction of their countries' futures are more clearly identified.

Thus it may not be necessary for history to repeat itself in Africa. Despite the current economic crisis in that continent, African women may be able to obtain and defend their rights without going through a prior period of intensified subordination, as did women in Europe from feudal times until the recent past. But if historical repetition is to be avoided, social action in defense of their rights will have to be undertaken by African women themselves. And this will require an agenda separate from that of "development."

Foreign Aid and Women's Rights

Social change in the direction of a more rights-protective society comes about as the result of the collective but uncoordinated activities of many different private (nonstate) special-interest groups. These groups form, or change their focus, in reaction to political or economic stress. While they usually do not articulate their demands on the state in the terminology of human rights, a concern with what the international consensus calls rights can frequently be identified.

Among the disparate social actors who strive to attain rights in state societies, women are one of the weakest groups. The constraints that make it difficult for women to organize are well known: their child- and husband-care responsibilities, added to their responsibilities for subsistence agriculture, trade, or formal wage labor, mean that they simply do not have the time for political activity. Further, politicized gender consciousness in women is hampered by their personal relations with men. Finally, women are not an undifferentiated social category; they are divided by ethnicity, caste, class, and many other variables.

There is little hope in Africa, then, that foreign aid can greatly assist in realizing women's rights. Women's rights, like men's rights, must be wrested from below and are primarily a matter of internal social change. Even if Africa's position in the world economy were to improve, women would not necessarily benefit. Rather, gendered economic stratification would probably intensify. Even a development effort aimed in principle at redistribution of wealth could redistribute it to male heads of households, not to the women dependent on them. There is nothing inherent to the development process that impels a parallel promotion and protection of women's rights. Women's rights must be viewed as an objective separate from, and not necessarily compatible with, development.

Given this difficulty, is there any role for foreign aid in promoting women's rights in Africa at the broad societal level, as opposed to a project-oriented approach that attempts to "integrate" women where appropriate? There is such a role *if* the aid is clearly intended for rights and if it is accepted that such aid might not have any demonstrable "development" (growth) effect, at least in the short to medium run.

In November 1987 the Canadian government announced that it intended to establish an International Institute for Human Rights and Democratic Development. From a human rights perspective, this type of institute, set up by a nonimperial small or middle-range power, might be lauded. But unfortunately, none of the public or government discussion in Canada on the institute has focused on women's rights. In the several reports dealing with redirections in Canadian foreign aid produced between 1985 and 1988, women are still confined to a page or two on "women in development," while "human" rights are discussed elsewhere (see Winegard 1987).

But if African women are to protect themselves from the intensified gender inequality that "development" usually entails, then the main focus of aid directed to women's rights in Africa must be to assist African women in organizing themselves to become effective actors in national politics, especially through the exercise of freedom of speech, press, and association. Such participation is necessary to ensure that the development enterprise is also a gender-equal redistributive enterprise and that the ideological and political, as well as the economic, bases of women's subordination are addressed. These participatory freedoms are in their turn dependent on their judicial protection and on a reasonably high degree of education necessary so that women can articulate their rights claims both on male members of their own families and on the state. In all five of these areas—education, law and judiciary, speech, press, and association (Donnelly and Howard 1988)—there are roles that foreign aid could play in empowering African women.

The principle that foreign aid should have an educational and training component is relatively unproblematic. Unfortunately, however, there is a tendency to focus only on the technical and scientific educational needs of African countries. Even commentators very critical of development policies in general tend to assume that such a focus is a good idea and that Africa needs fewer general liberal arts graduates, male or female (O'Barr 1984: 152). But from the point of view of women's rights, what is needed are more African women trained in the humanities, social sciences, and law (Guyer 1986b: 415) whose primary object of study is gender relations. The Canadian aid program is to be geared to labor-market criteria for scholarships (CIDA 1987: 46). But there is not likely to be a labor market for African women who think critically about "women's issues." Rather, because of their democratic and their antipatriarchal preoccupations, such women are unlikely to be encouraged by the state or by their own male-dominated universities. Knowledge is power; African women need to be empowered by better access to knowledge about gender relations in their own societies. Further, certain social issues key to the abolition of patriarchy—such as violence against women—are now routinely discussed in Western universities, whereas in Africa the dominant ideology often still denies that such violence either exists at all or, if it exists, is illegitimate (Howard 1986: 201–2).

Aside from education, a rights-focused aid package could help women press for changes in law in Africa. Laws do not change social structure, especially when they are improperly enforced or subject to the executive control of the state, but they do have a normative, standard-setting impact. They can also provide some assistance to elite women capable of availing themselves of the system—for example, in matters such as child custody, maintenance, or inheritance. Finally, rights-protective legal aid in general assists women; female political prisoners as well as male need protection from torture, access to fair courts, and the other basic civil liberties.

With regard to the key political rights of freedom of the press and association, there is also room for foreign assistance. Supplies could be purchased and journalists trained to set up or sustain women's newsletters and networks (see Guyer 1986b: 414.) The Canadian government has already agreed in principle to consult women's organizations in underdeveloped countries to determine their needs (CIDA 1987: 44). If such agreement were guided by the principle that organizations specifically interested in acquiring civil and political rights or in struggling for equality with men would be as eligible for assistance as more "development"-oriented (economic) organizations such as women's agricultural cooperatives, then the mandate to promote human rights in general would be more adequately fulfilled.

All of the above suggestions are offered to indicate that foreign aid in the area of women's rights is possible, but it should be expected to have very limited impact on development in the short to medium run. Women's newsletters, for example, might focus more on family violence or on misogynistic religious beliefs than on development projects. Moreover, in the short to medium run immediate beneficiaries would more likely be upper- or middle-class African women than poor women. But in the long run, rights established in principle for the more privileged can be claimed by the less privileged too. And in the long run, a politically empowered female peasantry or proletariat, like its empowered male counterpart, will have a better chance of successfully making rights claims—including claims for economic equity and redistribution—than will its politically quiescent predecessors.

It could be argued that to allocate scarce foreign aid dollars to projects specifically concerned with women's rights is not a sensible strategy, because women are not unanimous in their views of their needs. In Africa as elsewhere, women are influenced by far more than their own gender-based subordination and associations of women who favor traditional ideologies and family-based roles may well emerge. To note these internal disagreements is not, however, to refute the claim that in the long run human rights, and women's rights, benefit even those ostensibly opposed to them. Most conservative North American women would be horrified to return to mid-nineteenth-century practice and lose rights to their own property, wages, and children. A focus on human rights implies acceptance that rights as enunciated in the international United Nations consensus are valid for all human beings regardless of their own stated political or normative preferences. In practice, of course, both Western aid establishments and Western feminist organizations should be guided in their activities in Africa by requests for assistance made by African actors themselves, oriented to projects that African women deem to be a priority.

The foreign aid measures proposed above may seem idealistic. They are indeed so, insofar as they do not accord with standard notions of economic development. But that is precisely the point of making them. Protection of women's rights is a separate matter from development. Women's rights are not necessarily a path to what development actually means in practice—that is, statecentric economic growth. Nor is such statecentric economic growth—however benignly camouflaged as concern for self-reliance and equitable distribution—necessarily a path to women's rights.

The ideological pacification of the originally critical feminist concern with women in development has obscured the need for specifically gender-based rights claims against the family, the kin group, and the state. Women, like men, need civil and political rights in order to make these claims. Democratic action by a free citizenry is the best path to both development and rights; but the absorption of women's rights into the "women-in-development" ideology may well hinder, not help, the eventual emergence of such democratic actions.

References

For their comments on an earlier draft of this paper, I am most grateful to Ronald Cohen, Jack Donnelly, and Sara Heller Mendelson.

Afonja, Simi. 1986. "Land Control—a Critical Factor in Yoruba Gender Stratification." In *Women and Class in Africa*, ed. Claire Robertson and Iris Berger, pp. 78–91. New York: Africana.

Alexander, Sally. 1976. "Women's Work in Nineteenth-Century London: A Study of the Years 1820–50." In *The Rights and Wrongs of Women*, ed. Juliet Mitchell and Ann Oakley, pp. 59–111. Harmondsworth: Penguin.

Andreski, Iris. 1970. *Old Wives' Tales: Life-Stories from Ibibioland*. New York: Schocken Books.

Asante-Darko, Nimrod, and Sjaak van der Geest. 1983. "Male Chauvinism: Men and Women in Ghanaian Highlife Songs." In *Female and Male in West Africa*, ed. Christine Oppong, pp. 242–55. London: George Allen and Unwin.

Bandarage, Asoka. 1984. "Women in Development: Liberalism, Marxism and Marxist-Feminism." *Development and Change* 15 (4): 485–515.

Boserup, Ester. 1970. *Woman's Role in Economic Development*. New York: St. Martin's Press.

Brain, James L. 1976. "Less than Second-Class: Women in Rural Settlement Schemes in Tanzania." In *Women in Africa: Studies in Social and Economic Change*, ed. Nancy J. Hafkin and Edna G. Bay, pp. 265–82. Stanford: Stanford University Press.

———. 1978. "Symbolic Rebirth: The *Mwali* Rite among the Luguru of Eastern Tanzania." *Africa* 48 (2): 176–88.

Bullough, Vern L. 1973. *The Subordinate Sex: A History of Attitudes toward Women*. Urbana: University of Illinois Press.

Callaway, Barbara J. 1984. "Ambiguous Consequences of the Socialisation and Seclusion of Hausa Women." *Journal of Modern African Studies* 22 (3): 429–50.

Canadian International Development Agency (CIDA). 1987 (September). *Canadian International Development Assistance: To Benefit a Better World*. Response of the Government of Canada to the Report by the Standing Committee on External Affairs and International Trade. [*See* Winegard 1987.]

Cobbah, Josiah A. M. 1987. "African Values and the Human Rights Debate: An African Perspective." *Human Rights Quarterly* 9 (3): 309–31.

Daly, Mary. 1978. *Gyn/Ecology: The Metaethics of Radical Feminism*. Boston: Beacon Press.

Donegan, C. E. 1972. "Marriage and Divorce Law in Sierra Leone: A Microcosm of African Legal Problems." *Cornell International Law Journal* 5 (1): 70–84.

Donnelly, Jack. 1985. "In Search of the Unicorn: The Jurisprudence and Politics of the Right to Development." *California Western International Law Journal* 15 (3): 473–509.

Donnelly, Jack, and Rhoda E. Howard. 1988. "Assessing National Human Rights Performance: A Theoretical Framework." *Human Rights Quarterly* 10 (2): 214–48.

Dumont, Rene. 1966. *False Start in Africa*. London: Andre Deutsch.

Engels, Frederick. 1972. *The Origin of the Family, Private Property and the State*. New York: Pathfinder Press.

Eze, Osita C. 1984. *Human Rights in Africa—Some Selected Problems*. Lagos: Nigerian Institute of International Affairs.

Freeman, Linda. 1985. "The Effect of the World Crisis on Canada's Involvement in Africa." *Studies in Political Economy* 17: 107–39.

Green, Reginald Herbold, and Caroline Allison. 1986. "The World Bank's Agenda for Accelerated Development: Dialectics, Doubts and Dialogues."

In *Africa in Economic Crisis*, ed. John Ravenhill, pp. 60–84. New York: Columbia University Press.

Guyer, Jane I. 1986a. "Beti Widow Inheritance and Marriage Law: A Social History." In *Widows in African Societies: Choices and Constraints*, ed. Betty Potash. Stanford: Stanford University Press.

———. 1986b. "Women's Role in Development." In *Strategies for African Development*, ed. Robert I. Berg and Jennifer Seymour Whitaker, pp. 393–421. Berkeley: University of California Press.

Hamalengwa, M., C. Flinterman, and E. V. O. Dankwa. 1988. *The International Law of Human Rights in Africa: Basic Documents and Annotated Bibliography*. Boston: Martinus Nijhoff Publishers and United Nations Institute for Training and Research.

Hamilton, Roberta. 1978. *The Liberation of Women: A Study of Patriarchy and Capitalism*. London: George Allen and Unwin.

Hay, Margaret Jean. 1989. "Queens, Prostitutes and Peasants: Historical Perspectives on African Women, 1971–1986." *Canadian Journal of African Studies* 22 (3): 21–38.

Howard, Rhoda E. 1983. "The 'Full-Belly' Thesis: Should Economic Rights Take Priority over Civil and Political Rights? Evidence from Sub-Saharan Africa." *Human Rights Quarterly* 5 (4): 467–90.

———. 1986. *Human Rights in Commonwealth Africa*. Totowa, N.J.: Rowman and Littlefield.

———. 1989. "Economic Rights and Foreign Policy." In *Human Rights and Development: International Views*, ed. David P. Forsythe. London: Macmillan.

———. 1990. "Group versus Individual Identity in the African Debate on Human Rights." In *Human Rights in Africa: Cross-cultural Perspectives*, ed. Abdullahi A. An-Na'im and Francis Deng. Washington, D.C.: Brookings Institution.

Hyden, Goran. 1983. *No Shortcuts to Progress: African Development Management in Perspective*. Berkeley: University of California Press.

Jaquette, Jane S. 1988. Book Review. *Signs* 14 (1): 229–34.

Kenyatta, Margaret W. 1985. "Women—Equality, Development and Peace." *Public Enterprise* 5 (3): 283–85.

Kilson, Marion. 1976. "Women in African Traditional Religions." *Journal of Religion in Africa* 8 (2): 133–43.

Knipp, Margaret M., and Ronald Cohen. 1981. "Women and Change in West Africa: A Synthesis." *Southern Association of Africanists' Bulletin* 9: 7–18.

Kyei, Koja Gyinaye, and Hannah Schreckenbach. 1976. *No Time to Die*. Accra: Catholic Press.

Legesse, Asmarom. 1980. "Human Rights in African Political Culture." In *The Moral Imperatives of Human Rights: A World Survey*, ed. Kenneth W. Thompson, pp. 123–37. Washington, D.C. : University Press of America.

Leigh-Williams, Stella. 1988. Oral statement at a conference on African Women and Development, York University (Ontario), 19 May.

Lerner, Gerda. 1986. *The Creation of Patriarchy*. New York: Oxford University Press.

Lewis, Barbara C. 1976. "The Limitations of Group Action among Entrepreneurs: The Market Women of Abidjan, Ivory Coast." In *Women in Africa: Studies in Social and Economic Change*, ed. Nancy J. Hafkin and Edna C. Bay, pp. 135–56. Stanford: Stanford University Press.

———. 1984. "The Impact of Development Policies on Women." In *African Women South of the Sahara*, ed. Margaret Jean Hay and Sharon Stichter, pp. 170–87. New York: Longman.

Mbilinyi, Marjorie J. 1972. "The State of Women in Tanzania." *Canadian Journal of African Studies* 6 (2): 371–77.

Meillassoux, Claude. 1981. *Maidens, Meal and Money: Capitalism and the Domestic Community*. New York: Cambridge University Press.

Middleton, Christopher. 1979. "The Sexual Division of Labour in Feudal England." *New Left Review* 18/12: 113–14, 147–68.

Mojekwu, Chris C. 1980. "International Human Rights: The African Perspective." In *International Human Rights: Contemporary Issues*, ed. Jack L. Nelson and Vera M. Green, pp. 85–95. Stanfordville, N.Y.: Human Rights Publishing Group.

O'Barr, Jean. 1984. "African Women in Politics." In *African Women South of the Sahara*, ed. Margaret Jean Hay and Sharon Stichter, pp. 140–55. New York: Longman.

Obbo, Christine. 1976. "Dominant Male Ideology and Female Options: Three East African Case Studies." *Africa* 46 (4): 371–89.

———. 1980. *African Women: Their Struggle for Economic Independence*. London: Zed Press.

Okeyo, Achola Pala. 1980. "Daughters of the Lakes and Rivers: Colonization and the Land Rights of Luo Women." In *Women and Colonization: Anthropological Perspectives*, ed. Mona Etienne and Eleanor Leacock, pp. 186–213. New York: Praeger.

O'Laughlin, Bridget. 1974. "Mediation of Contradiction: Why Mbum Women Do Not Eat Chicken." In *Woman, Culture and Society*, ed. Michelle Zimbalist Rosaldo and Louise Lamphere, pp. 301–18. Stanford: Stanford University Press.

Organization of African Unity (OAU). 1981. *Lagos Plan of Action for the Economic Development of Africa, 1980–2000*. Geneva: International Institute for Labour Studies.

Ravenhill, John. 1986. "Collective Self-Reliance or Collective Self-Delusion: Is the Lagos Plan a Viable Alternative?" In *Africa in Economic Crisis*, ed. John Ravenhill, pp. 85–107. New York: Columbia University Press.

Robertson, Claire. 1987. "Developing Economic Awareness: Changing Per-

spectives in Studies of African Women, 1976–1985." *Feminist Studies* 13 (1): 97–135.
Rogers, Barbara. 1980. *The Domestication of Women: Discrimination in Developing Societies.* New York: Tavistock.
Rogers, Susan G. 1982. "Efforts towards Women's Development in Tanzania: Gender Rhetoric vs. Gender Realities." *Women and Politics* 2 (4): 23–41.
Sacks, Karen. 1975. "Engels Revisited: Women, the Organization of Production, and Private Property." In *Toward an Anthropology of Women*, ed. Rayna R. Reiter, pp. 211–34. New York: Monthly Review Press.
Sanday, Peggy Reeves. 1981. *Female Power and Male Dominance: On the Origins of Sexual Inequality.* New York: Cambridge University Press.
Stamp, Patricia. 1986. "Kikuyu Women's Self-Help Groups: Toward an Understanding of the Relation between Sex-Gender System and Mode of Production in Africa." In *Women and Class in Africa*, ed. Claire Robertson and Iris Berger, pp. 27–46. New York: Africana.
Staudt, Kathleen. 1978. "Administrative Resources, Political Patrons and Redressing Sex Inequalities: A Case from Western Kenya." *Journal of Developing Areas* 12: 399–414.
———. 1985. *Women, Foreign Assistance, and Advocacy Administration.* New York: Praeger.
———. 1986a. "Stratification: Implications for Women's Politics." In *Women and Class in Africa*, ed. Claire Robertson and Iris Berger, pp. 197–215. New York: Africana.
———. 1986b. "Women, Development and the State: On the Theoretical Impasse." *Development and Change* 17 (2): 325–33.
———. 1988. "Women Farmers in Africa: Research and Institutional Action 1972–1987." *Canadian Journal of African Studies* 23 (2): 567–82.
———. 1989. *Women and the State in Africa.* Boulder: Lynne Rienner Publishers.
Strobel, Margaret. 1976. "From *Lelemama* to Lobbying: Women's Associations in Mombasa, Kenya." In *Women in Africa: Studies in Social and Economic Change*, ed. Nancy J. Hafkin and Edna C. Bay, pp. 183–212. Stanford: Stanford University Press.
———. 1982. "African Women." *Signs* 8 (1): 109–31.
———. 1984. "Women in Religion and in Secular Ideology." In *African Women South of the Sahara*, ed. Margaret Jean Hay and Sharon Stichter, pp. 87–101. New York: Longman.
Sudarkasa, Niara. 1986. "The Status of Women in Indigenous African Societies." *Feminist Studies* 12 (1): 91–103.
Swantz, Marta-Liisa. 1985. *Women in Development: A Creative Role Denied. The Case of Tanzania.* New York: St. Martin's Press.
United Nations. 1974. "Declaration on the Establishment of a New International Economic Order." General Assembly Resolution 3201 (S-IV) (1 May), in United Nations *Resolutions* (1972–74), vol. 14, pp. 27–29.

———. 1978. *The International Bill of Human Rights.* New York: United Nations Office of Public Information.

———. 1980. Doc. 34/180. "Convention on the Elimination of All Forms of Discrimination against Women: Resolutions and Decisions Adopted by the General Assembly during the Thirty-fourth Session, 18 September 1979–7 January 1980." Supp. No. 46 (A/34/46). New York: United Nations.

———. 1987. *Resolutions and Decisions Adopted by the General Assembly during the First Part of Its Forty-first Session, from 16 September to 19 December 1986.* New York: United Nations Press Section, Department of Information, Press Release GA/7463, 12 January 1987, 366.

———. 1991. *Multilateral Treaties Deposited with the Secretary-General. Status as of 31 December 1990.* New York: United Nations.

Van Allen, Judith. 1975. "Aba Riots or the Igbo Women's War? Ideology, Stratification and the Invisibility of Women." *Ufahamu* 6 (1): 125–41.

Welch, Claude E., Jr., and Robert I. Meltzer, eds. 1984. *Human Rights and Development in Africa.* Albany: State University of New York Press.

Winegard, William. 1987 (May). *For Whose Benefit? Report on Canada's Official Development Assistance Policies and Programs.* Ottawa: House of Commons Canada, Standing Committee on External Affairs and International Trade.

Wipper, Audrey. 1975. "The Maendeleo Wa Wanawake Organization: The Co-optation of Leadership." *African Studies Review* 18 (3): 99–120.

———. 1984. "Women's Voluntary Associations." In *African Women South of the Sahara,* ed. Margaret Jean Hay and Sharon Stichter, pp. 69–85. New York: Longman.

World Bank. 1981. *Accelerated Development in Sub-Saharan Africa: Agenda for Action.* Washington, D.C.: World Bank.

———. 1989. *Sub-Saharan Africa: From Crisis to Sustainable Growth.* Washington, D.C.: World Bank.

6

African Refugees: Defining and Defending Their Human Rights

ART HANSEN

The first decades of independence in Africa were marked by widespread abuses of human rights, continuing political instability, interminable civil warfare often compounded by the involvement of non-African powers, widespread military coups, the failure of many economic development programs, increasing indebtedness, intermittent famines, and the forced migrations of millions of Africans as refugees. Indeed, success stories in Africa over the past three decades have been few, horror stories common. After 1984, as famine crises threatened entire regions and the inability of African countries to feed themselves became widely known, the sentiments of many Africans and foreign observers became as negative and pessimistic as they were once positive.

There are no simple explanations for the abuses, problems, and failures. A mere indictment of African regimes is too easy an answer. The incompetence, ambition, greed, and shortsightedness of many African rulers, elites, and policies certainly deserve some of the blame, but many of the problems of African countries have been caused by their initial poverty, the instability and disruptions that always accompany major political changes such as state creation, superpower rivalries, the disadvantages of new agriculturally based states attempting to establish themselves in an already structured and hierarchical global economy, the global recession and higher oil prices of the 1970s, and below-normal rainfall. Another cause of problems has been the adoption and continued use by African states and leaders of political forms and precedents that grew from, and were organically related to, the European experience. Those of us who have been concerned about Africa and the well-being of the African people must also assume part of the blame because our advice has not always been appropriate; far too often, our expertise has helped to create problems rather than solutions.

This context of multiple crises and shared responsibilities is particularly appropriate for the subject of this chapter—the human rights of refugees. Although there have been important and progressive developments in the definition and defense of human rights since World War II, the recurrent creation, long-term displacement, and deplorable living conditions of millions of refugees demonstrate the repeated failure to recognize and satisfy fundamental human rights.

Many discussions of the expansion of human rights legislation and awareness seem to imply an uninterrupted and easy development. This is misleading for at least three reasons. First, it shows historical amnesia. The evolution of human rights has been complex, convoluted, and bitterly resisted. Though many people when they think of human rights think only of the past few decades since World War II, the struggle to define and protect human rights has lasted for centuries. Wars have been fought, people tortured and murdered in the struggle for these rights and laws. Each right represents prior bitter experience (or "aggregated grievances," as Cohen calls them in chapter 1) with what happened in the absence of that right's legitimacy.

Second, there are significant differences between the ideal (or, in this instance, the legal) and the real—that is, between human rights as defined in law and treaty and as practiced in the streets, barracks, countryside, and frontier areas. All too often, governmental and private prejudices, vested and conflicting interests, and simple brutality intercede between law and practice. Universal standards of moral behavior have been debated and agreed on in many state and international laws, declarations, and covenants, but we are still forced to witness every year the systematic and widespread abuse around the world of these agreed-on human rights. The progressive development of legal rights is beneficial because they provide standards, goals, and a moral persuasion and pressure, but the struggle must be fought on other fronts as well.

Third, the development of human rights has by and large bypassed the millions of refugees in the world. In essence, none of the human rights legislation applies to refugees, who, by their flight, have apparently abrogated many rights generally assumed to be "human." Refugees express the abuses of human rights in their countries of origin and, although less frequently recognized, their continued presence and deprivation indicates a complementary abuse of human rights in the host countries that have received them. Refugees are among the most vulnerable to abuse, yet they are not protected by the human rights that apply to others. As Milne notes: "If the adjective 'human' is taken seriously, the idea of human rights must be the idea that there are certain rights which . . . belong to all human beings at all times and in all places. These are the rights which they have solely in virtue of being human, irrespective of nationality, religion, sex, social status, occupation, wealth, property, or any other differentiating ethnic, cultural or social characteristic" (Milne 1986: 1).

I propose a simple, though radical, universal extension of the concept of humanness (and thus human rights) to cover refugees. Within that broad proposal, I deal at some length with a few rights of particular interest to refugees, such as the rights to leave any country, to seek and to enjoy asylum in other countries, and to change nationality. The situation of African refugees has some unique characteristics, caused to some extent by the historical relationship of states and nationalities. I propose that African states recognize their legal obligations and moral commitments to other Africans and to indigenous African institutions, and that if refugees desire to change their status, African host countries allow their long-deprived refugees to naturalize as citizens.

The Human Rights of Refugees

This chapter is intended to inform and persuade. It is thus part of the political process, as are all communications on this topic. I am concerned here with the human rights of refugees, particularly African refugees. The heart of my argument is simple: human rights must by definition apply to all humans. Unfortunately, refugees are not legally considered human. If they were, then they would be awarded rights already recognized as universal. The African Charter on Human and Peoples' Rights, the Universal Declaration of Human Rights, and the International Covenant on Civil and Political Rights agree on the universality of the rights that they contain (all citations in this chapter from these documents are taken from Hamalengwa, Flinterman, and Dankwa [1988]). As the Charter clearly states (Article 2): "Every individual shall be entitled to the enjoyment of the rights and freedoms recognized and guaranteed in the present Charter without distinction of any kind such as race, ethnic group, color, sex, language, religion, political or any other opinion, national and social origin, fortune, birth or other status."

Refugees may differ in "national and social origin . . . or other status" from the citizens of the host country, but that should not cause them to be less entitled than "every individual." Freedom of movement means that they should not be confined to camps and "schemes" (government-organized settlements). Freedom of economic opportunity means that they should be allowed to compete openly for employment and business opportunities. All other rights listed in covenants on human rights should apply to refugees as well. The African Charter states that "every individual" has many rights, among them the "right to leave any country including his own" (Article 12: 2) and the "right, when persecuted, to seek and obtain asylum in other countries" (Article 12: 3). Why should people be penalized when they exercise their rights to leave and seek asylum and thus become refugees? Naldi suggests: "It could be that the definition of the word 'individual' is not intended to include refugees but in the absence of any indication to that effect the word 'individual' must be taken to refer to any person" (Naldi 1989: 93-94).

I am most concerned about one specific right. The Universal Declaration of Human Rights states: "No one shall be arbitrarily deprived of his nationality nor *denied the right to change his nationality*" (Article 15: 2; emphasis added). Other immigrants are permitted to become naturalized citizens of their host country, and refugees should not arbitrarily be denied the right to change nationality and become citizens of their host country if they wish to do so. There may be regulations, delays, and requirements to be obeyed, as there are for "every individual," but there should not be an arbitrary denial of this right to people because of their refugee status. Whether the refugees are Angolan, Palestinian, Vietnamese, or Guatemalan, they are individuals with the same humanity as "every individual."

There are certain specific terms used by the Office of the United Nations High Commissioner for Refugees (UNHCR) in reference to refugees. The right to change nationality translates for refugees into the right to a durable solution in their host country, or country of first asylum, if the refugees so desire. As the precedent for this right has been established in the Universal Declaration, this right should be accepted universally.

Whether or not this happens everywhere, there are social and political precedents and realities in Africa (that may not exist or be as strong elsewhere) that support the implementation of this right for African refugees. Moral or cultural relativism is on the defensive in the universalistic environment of human rights, but Milne's reference to the particular morality of different societies points out that over and above a set of universal rights (the common morality), there may be some rights particular to only one society or culture area, Africa in this case. All rights do not have to be universal.

The Refugee Situation in Africa

The rest of this chapter is on African refugees, their defined status and rights, their numbers and characteristics, and the continual denial of their human rights. I begin by defining the concept of refugee and showing how the Organization of African Unity (OAU) countries broadened the United Nations (UN) concept to further their political agenda. The later extension to refugeelike situations and the historic growth of the refugee population in Africa during the past three decades reflect the continuing turmoil and abuses of human rights in the newly independent African countries. I then describe some of the key characteristics of African refugees, the violation of their human rights in their country of origin, and their settlement and continued denial of human rights in their host country. The popularity of self-settlement brings up important questions about the relationships of (1) the state (formerly colony), society, and nationality and (2) human rights and power.

Some Qualifications

The definition of refugees used here is that of the OAU, so the numbers of refugees reported in this chapter include some people who have fled mass distress situations, such as famines. Most census data in Africa are suspect, and statistics on populations in distress (or people who have died) are invariably only rough approximations. This is especially true for people who have migrated, because many have self-settled and are easily missed or undercounted.

I will not attempt in this chapter to review comprehensively the African scene or the situation of African refugees and their rights. My aims are more modest. Although I have studied Africa and its refugees for some twenty years, most of my insights and deeply held convictions are based on living for three years (spread over 1970–72, 1977, 1979, and 1989) with Luvale-speaking Angolan refugees and their Zambian hosts in northwestern Zambia. My descriptions and previous analyses of this case have been reported and published elsewhere (Hansen 1977, 1979a, 1979b, 1981, 1982, 1989, 1990; Hansen and Papstein 1979). As I have grown to understand these refugees and how they fit into their locality, learning to know them as people and as carriers of a culture, I have also learned to be critical of the way their rights are denied by Zambia and the way other refugees are treated in African countries.

Because of the weakness of census and sociological data on African refugees, I do not claim the situation of the Angolan refugees and their Zambian village hosts to be representative of all forcibly resettled people in Africa, nor do I know what proportion of refugees their situation resembles. However, there are indications from the reportedly high incidence of rural self-settlement and from other case studies that my analysis holds for a large number of other Africans (Harrell-Bond 1986; Rogge 1985; Betts 1980; Mageed and Ramaga 1986; Mazur 1988; Zartman 1970).

In more general terms, we know little about the approximately 4.5 million refugees in Africa (1989 statistics) or about the millions of other Africans who have been internally displaced over the past few decades. Very little has been written about these peoples. What is available is descriptive rather than analytical and is written primarily from the viewpoint of state-oriented outsiders. Almost nothing is known about the perspectives and assessments of the refugees themselves or of their local hosts. The African world from the perspective of the state and of state-oriented scientists and policymakers is a very different world from the one experienced and conceived by refugees and their local hosts. Given these limitations, this chapter must limit its focus to a few major issues.

Defining Refugees

The term "refugee" has been defined in various ways, each reflecting the orientation and intentions of its author. Some of the definitions are very broad, encompassing a wide variety of people who are forced to move. Even economically motivated migrants are sometimes included. An example of this is found in one of the first books on African refugees: "They are not refugees in the political sense, but that is their very real condition in terms of the cutting of old ties and the building of new" (Brooks and El-Ayouty 1970: xi–xv). Almost always, however, even broad definitions require that refugees be persons displaced by a forceful agent, such as war, natural disaster, famine, or government, while people who migrate for economic reasons (desire for a better life or better job) are not considered to qualify for refugee status.

The most explicit definitions are legal, political, and administrative. These definitions are restrictive rather than inclusive. They attempt to delimit refugee status precisely, in order to "establish dichotomous categories" (Zolberg, Suhrke, and Aguayo 1986: 153) of refugees and nonrefugees. For instance, the limits and restrictions are used to discriminate between refugees and

1. migrants who cross interstate borders and should be handled by the usual immigration legislation and procedures.
2. victims of hostilities, who may be fleeing the same sorts of forceful agents but remain within their country of origin (Wenk 1968).

There are even differences between refugees covered by international conventions and de facto refugees who may not be easily placed into these categories (Weis 1978).

Refugees have special problems and should therefore be given special consideration to ensure that their human rights are protected. In contrast to the ordinary migrant, the refugee no longer enjoys the protection of his or her own state (the state of origin) and requires some other state, or agency, to assume a protective role. The victim of hostilities remains within his or her own state and thus continues to be legally and politically the responsibility of (protected by) the state of origin. The reputed protection afforded by the state of origin to the victim of hostilities is fictive in many African cases, of course, because the state is unable, or sometimes unwilling, to perform its protective role. Or worse yet, the state itself is the source of hostilities. This leads to international concern to extend refugeelike assistance to victims of hostilities within states.

Separating people into a distinct refugee category defines who, or which government or agency, is responsible for that group's protection and welfare. This definition allocates responsibility for the provision of welfare to uprooted people, and thus for accountability by the appropriate state and possibly UN agencies. If refugee status is granted, then that individual enjoys certain rights in relation to the host state. According to Naldi (1989: 91), some of these rights are like those enjoyed by host-country citizens, while others are similar to those enjoyed by favored foreign nationals.

However, legal definitions may not address the actual criteria used in practice to grant refugee status and asylum. The right to asylum is not a customary right—that is, part of customary law—but is a conventional right, or based on international conventions. The individual's right to seek and enjoy asylum is not complemented by any state's corresponding obligation to grant asylum. The Universal Declaration and other UN conventions do not require states to grant asylum, so states retain absolute discretion in deciding whether or not to grant or refuse asylum in any given case. For instance, although a state may define the requirements for refugee status and an individual may fit these requirements, the state may conclude that the person is really an economic migrant, or it may decide not to grant asylum for other reasons. Exercising the right to become a refugee (the right to leave the country and seek asylum) does not mean the right will be recognized by a receiving country.

Besides recognizing this gap between legal definitions and practice, it is important to review the evolution of the legal status of refugee. Conventional definitions express the outcomes of the political process in which individuals, groups, and states have expressed and fought for their interests and goals. Laws define the criteria to become a refugee, the rights to be enjoyed by refugees, the responsibilities of states and other agencies, and the responsibilities of refugees towards their hosts. Laws are both the consequences and one of the weapons of political force and persuasion. Moral or legal gaps in protection, or in enforcing implementation, may spur political action, and states that fail their conventionally defined obligations toward people may find that used as a weapon against them in the international arena.

Refugees are defined by various international treaties and by the laws of many states. These legal definitions show their European origins and orientations. The first UN definition (in 1951), restricted to events before that date, allowed signatory states to restrict the definition further, to events occurring only in Europe (Convention Relating to the Status of Refugees). This was modified later by the UN (in 1966) to eliminate time (prior to 1951) and place restrictions (Protocol Relating to the Status of Refugees).

Both the Convention and the Protocol define a refugee as someone who flees from his or her country, or refuses to return if already outside it, because the person realistically fears persecution or death for religious, racial, or political reasons. Thus the UN definition applies to individuals (rather than to groups or populations) and specifies interstate movement, certain causes (war, civil unrest, or persecution), and a psychological and political judgment (there is fear, and it is well founded) (Brooks and El-Ayouty 1970: 225; Melander and Nobel 1978: 87; Melander and Nobel 1979: 24). The UN definition and criteria are the basis for most legal definitions around the world: "The concept of a refugee is known to customary international law although its precise definition is still unclear . . . [but] refugee law is now principally governed by conventional law and customary international law has been codified into the UN and OAU Conventions where it has been elaborated upon" (Naldi 1989: 90).

In 1969 the OAU adopted its own convention, the Convention Governing the Specific Aspects of Refugee Problems in Africa. This document incorporated the UN characteristics of a refugee within a broader definition that went beyond the individual and psychological (subjective) criteria used by the United Nations. According to the OAU, the objective existence of conditions such as "external aggression, occupation, foreign domination or events seriously disturbing public order" were sufficient grounds to give refugee status to individuals or populations that fled across state borders. Each person in the population did not have to prove an individual case for refugee status, given sufficient objective conditions affecting an entire population.

The OAU and UN agreed that refugee status requires interstate movement and specific causes forcing that movement, but the OAU's list extends acceptable causes to include occupation and foreign domination, i.e., colonialism. This allows the OAU to treat freedom fighters as a category of refugee (Brooks and El-Ayouty 1970: 272; Melander and Nobel 1978: 92; Melander and Nobel 1979: 118). Supporting anticolonial wars is stated as a political goal of OAU members in the Preamble to their Charter. It is "their duty to achieve the total liberation of Africa."

The phrase "events seriously disturbing public order" has been broadly interpreted. Accepted usage in Africa includes some people in mass distress situations who do not qualify as refugees under more restrictive definitions. Refugee status in Africa has been extended through the years to include people who flee areas of famine, and the UNHCR has become accustomed to responding to "refugeelike" situations. This broader usage was applied in a speech that President Nyerere of Tanzania made in 1979 to the First International Conference on Assistance to Refugees in Africa (ICARA). He defined refugees as "people who are now, or may in the future be, forced to flee from their homelands and seek refuge in another country in order to escape persecution, or death, or starvation" (quoted in CIMADE, INODEP, and MINK 1986: 142). He went on to note that the 1967 OAU conference on refugees had divided them into three categories:

1. political refugees, who were often more educated and more urban.
2. freedom fighters, whose flight was caused by external domination.
3. "the most numerous . . . men, women and children fleeing from war, from racial, religious, or cultural persecution or conflict, and from famines or other natural disasters" (quoted in CIMADE, INODEP, and MINK 1986: 144–45).

Eriksson, Melander, and Nobel (1981: 9) point out with more precision that eight different categories of people have qualified as refugees in Africa, with some categories predating the 1969 OAU Convention:

1. refugees fleeing from minority-rule regimes in southern Africa. These include members of national liberation movements.
2. refugees fleeing from independent African states as a result of the "consequences of colonialism . . . the arbitrary way in which the African continent was carved up among the colonial powers."
3. refugees fleeing from border disputes that are a consequence of colonialism.
4. refugees who are members of minority groups and are fleeing from ethnic and tribal disputes.
5. refugees fleeing from civil wars and other civil disorders that result from wars of secession.
6. refugees fleeing from the Moroccan occupation of their Sahrawi homeland.
7. refugees fleeing from gross human rights violations (for example, from Idi Amin's regime in Uganda).
8. refugees fleeing from natural disasters.

Note that in all cases (not just the seventh category) refugees are persons fleeing from gross violations of human rights. Some of the most basic rights are the ones to life, to liberty, to the security of the person, and to equal protection under the law. The above categories recognize as refugees people who have fled the violation, or threatened violation, of these basic rights in their country of origin.

Refugees (and victims of hostilities) are a clear indication of human rights abuse. The mere existence of refugees is an indictment of the conditions of life and lack of protection of human rights. The violator may or may not be the government of the country of origin, but in any event it has failed to protect basic human rights; otherwise, people would not flee. The initial violation of human rights is compounded when Africans, unfortunate enough to become refugees in the first place, continue to suffer the denial of their human rights for years, sometimes decades, in host countries. As we shall see below, long-term refugee status is an indictment of the lack of protection and a denial of human rights within host countries.

The Refugee Population in Africa

Almost two decades ago, Woronoff (1973) commented on Africa reaching an unfortunate demographic milestone in an article titled "Refugees: The Million-Person Problem." Shortly afterward, Gould (1974) reported on the slightly more than 1 million African refugees (1972 statistics); 50 percent of these originated in "wars of national liberation" against the Portuguese in Angola, Guinea-Bissau, and Mozambique. It was assumed that the creation of refugees was therefore an artifact of political transformation from colonies into states. Logically, liberation would mark the return of refugees to their homes, and no more refugees would be created. Africa freed of colonial rule would be a continent without refugees.

That proved to be a grand illusion. The end of colonial rule was accompanied by a rapid multiplication of refugees. By the beginning of 1980, more than 2.6 million Africans were refugees from newly independent states (Hansen 1981, 1982). Worse yet, these 2.6 million refugees did not include another 1.4 million Africans displaced and uprooted by wars or civil disturbances who remained within their state boundaries. The 4 million displaced Africans were victims of wars of Africans against Africans. Zimbabwe, Namibia, and the Republic of South Africa accounted for only 10 percent of the refugees, and during

Table 1. African Refugees by Host Country (December 1989)

Algeria	170,000	Malawi	628,150
Angola	91,150	Nigeria	5,200
Benin	1,200	Rwanda	22,200
Botswana	2,100	Senegal	5,000
Burundi	267,500	Somalia	834,000
Cameroon	51,200	Sudan	745,000
C.A.R.	3,100	Swaziland	28,800
Congo	2,100	Tanzania	265,150
Côte d'Ivoire	800	Togo	3,500
Djibouti	1,300	Uganda	102,000
Egypt	1,600	Zaire	340,700
Ethiopia	679,500	Zambia	143,600
Kenya	12,500	Zimbabwe	174,500
Lesotho	3,950		

Source: UNHCR World Map, *Refugees* (December 1989) 71: 21–23.

1980 many Zimbabweans were repatriating. Ethiopia itself produced more than half (58 percent) of the refugees. Hundreds of thousands of African refugees from earlier wars and disturbances (in Burundi, Equatorial Guinea, Rwanda, Uganda, and Zaire) continued to remain refugees outside their home state. Ethiopia, Uganda, Western Sahara, Chad, and Angola continued their civil wars and went on generating refugees.

By the end of 1986, it was estimated that at minimum there were more than 3 million refugees in Africa representing sixteen different countries. Twenty independent African states had smaller national populations than the total population of African refugees. The major generators of refugees were Mozambique, Ethiopia, Sudan, Angola, Burundi, Rwanda, and Western Sahara. With the exception of Western Sahara, all of the countries generating refugees also hosted refugees from neighboring countries.

By the end of 1989, only three years later, approximately 4.6 million Africans were refugees, with 4.4 million found in sub-Saharan Africa (UNHCR 1989; United States Committee for Refugees 1990). Table 1 lists the twenty-seven primary host countries and the number of refugees in each. In some cases, these totals include people who are not recognized as refugees but are in a "refugeelike" situation. Countries hosting fewer than 500 refugees are not listed.

Numerous as they are, the refugees in table 1 are but one subcategory of a larger number of forcibly displaced Africans similarly abused by forced or crisis-impelled migration. The larger category also includes internally displaced people who remain within their country of origin. Internally displaced Africans in 1989 included (1) victims of famine and war in Angola, Mozambique, Chad, Ethiopia, Sudan, and Uganda; (2) Ethiopians forcibly relocated by their government; and (3) South Africans of various "racial" categories who have been forcibly relocated as part of that country's apartheid policies. Statistics on internally dislocated Africans are even less reliable than are statistics on refugees. In 1989 there were approximately 7 to 9 million Africans internally displaced in seven countries: Angola, Mozambique, Chad, Ethiopia, South Africa, Sudan, and Uganda. These same states have also generated 78 percent of Africa's refugees.

Elsewhere I have argued that we need to examine as a whole this larger category of involuntary or crisis-impelled migrants in order to understand the dynamics of such situations (Hansen 1988a, 1988b; Oliver-Smith and Hansen 1982). In this chapter I am limiting discussion to interstate movement.

The Human Rights Dimension

African refugees are predominantly rural people who end up in another rural setting; this is essentially rural-rural migration. Some refugees come from urban areas, and some settle in urban areas in the host country, but urban refugees constitute a small minority.

Duration is another important characteristic. African refugees have been refugees for a long time. This is a major reason why the numbers keep growing every year. Most of the 4.6 million refugees in Africa in 1989 were not new arrivals. Each time there is an outbreak of fighting or another famine situation, refugees swell a preexisting population who migrated earlier. The earlier population is relatively stable; that is, most of its constituent members continue to (1) stay in the host country and (2) be counted as refugees.

"Refugee" connotes a temporary or transient condition. But one of the key issues about refugee status is how it ends. When does a person stop being a refugee, and why? This is a complex issue with political, legal, sociological, and philosophical dimensions that cannot be discussed here. What I want to point out in this chapter is the human rights dimension of the African refugee situation.

The "achieved" status of refugee is that of a rights-deprived person, like that of a slave. Refugees are not treated as if they were recognized as human, with the rights that "every individual" has. Exchanging refugee status for another requires a decision or action by the society or government of the state in which the refugee resides. To a great extent, the stability of the African refugee population is a result of the failure or refusal of African host governments to allow refugees to stop being refugees, to exchange or shed their refugee status for another status.

The UNHCR talks about "durable solutions," which are ways for refugees to stop being refugees. One durable solution is for refugees to repatriate. A second solution is for refugees to settle permanently within, and become citizens of, the host country where they first received asylum. The third solution is for refugees to resettle in another host country that allows them to settle permanently. In essence, the second and third solutions are for the refugee to integrate into a host country, while the first is for repatriation.

The UNHCR notes repeatedly that repatriation is the preferred solution. I disagree. In a world where all wars last only days, repatriation would quickly place people home. However, wars in Africa are not brief. When, for example, will the wars in Angola, Ethiopia, Mozambique, and Sudan finally end? As I note below, integration is a solution now, whereas repatriation is a solution for sometime in the future.

Refusal by host governments to allow refugees to settle permanently maintains millions of Africans in the rights-deprived status of refugee. These people suffered violations of their human rights for weeks, months, sometimes years in their own countries before becoming refugees. They then continue to suffer denial of their human rights in their host countries for years, sometimes decades.

How can the long-term denial of human rights to millions of Africans be considered moral conduct in any country, but particularly in countries that publicly pride themselves on being humanistic and supporters of human rights? Economic costs may be raised as an issue because the 1966 International Covenant on Economic, Social and Cultural Rights states: "Developing countries, with due regard to human rights and their national economy, may determine to what extent they would guarantee the economic rights recognized in the present Covenant to non-nationals" (Article 2: 3). But this same qualification was not extended in the International Covenant on Civil and Political Rights. Developing countries were not excused from extending civil and political rights for economic reasons. In any event, probably the great majority of long-term African refugees have been self-supporting for years. For the most part, they have become as productive as other rural people. In only rare instances are refugees security risks, although the threat to national security is often a useful shield for dubious conduct. The question of state and interstate security will be treated in more detail below.

The refusal by African governments to recognize the human rights of refugees who entered that status decades earlier is even less defensible when we examine the historical background of many refugee situations. African claims to freedom of movement rest both on internationally agreed-on covenants and on the fact that modern borders quite often cut through older ethnic territories and societies. Colonial and postcolonial borders placed kinfolk and coethnics in differing states with differing citizenship and even differing external languages.

Self-Settlement and Hospitality

Two common characteristics of rural African refugee situations are self-settlement and hospitality, features that are generally surprising to observers already familiar with refugees in other regions of the world. Many of Africa's refugees practice self-settlement, which is sometimes misleadingly called "spontaneous" settlement, as if it occurred without any conscious direction. Self-settlement usually refers to refugees settling themselves in existing villages, or starting their own villages, near the international border. On their own, the refugees work to reestablish an independent rural livelihood and life-style similar to the one abandoned in their country of origin. Self-settlement may be aided by governmental or foreign assistance, but most of Africa's self-settled refugees have not received any direct assistance from the state. Urban self-settlement occurs as well, but for a much smaller number of refugees. Here I refer only to rural self-settlement.

Local residents (hosts) are usually hospitable to refugees and share many local resources. African hospitality has been lauded by politicians as an inspiring moral tradition and has been ideologically embedded into theories of African socialism or humanism. Hospitality varies with circumstances, including the extent to which land and employment are available locally, and may be diminishing, disappearing, or even being replaced by antipathy as refugee numbers grow and African national economies continue to stagnate.

The importance, meaning, and value of these two features have been debated by politicians and social scientists. Both hospitality and self-settlement express an African social reality largely neglected in human rights arguments. This is due in part to the social reality of refugees and their local hosts being largely ignored in international and legal debates. It is also due to the social reality of Africa being ideologically transformed beyond recognition by the political demands of anticolonialism and African state formation.

Refugee settlement decisions have always been linked with national and international security policies. Self-directed versus government-managed settlement was debated publicly for the first time in Africa in an international meeting at Addis Ababa in 1967. The conference recommended that self-settlement in the border areas be promoted if local resources could be generated for the refugees and if the security of refugee settlement areas in the host country was not threatened by violence from the country of origin. If this proved impossible, the host country should develop government-organized settlements in areas farther away from the border. The ICARA conference in 1979 recommended that those opting for self-settlement be granted greater national and international assistance and that research be conducted to clarify the conditions of self-settled refugees (Eriksson, Melander, and Nobel 1981).

National and international policies have not changed in spite of these recommendations. Governments and humanitarian agencies prefer that rural refugees live in camps, or schemes, Anglophone Africa). Despite the obvious popularity of self-settlement to refugees, most national and international assistance since 1967 has been allocated to government-organized schemes. Governments favor such schemes for several reasons: concerns about national security (the most often publicized reason), fears that the absorption capacity of self-settlement areas is too limited because the development of schemes is congruent with normal development programs (what Chambers [1979] calls "project bias"), and because officials know very little about the short- or long-term consequences of self-settlement versus scheme settlement.

National security and the reluctance of states to insult or threaten their neighbors are often cited as reasons to oppose self-settlement and to remove refugees from border areas into government-directed schemes. These concerns are expressed in the African Charter on Human and Peoples' Rights (1981) as follows: "States parties to the present Charter shall ensure that . . . their territories shall not be used as bases for subversive or terrorist activities against the people of any other State party to the present Charter" (Article 23: 1–2).

The OAU Convention Governing the Specific Aspects of Refugee Problems in Africa (1969) expresses the same concern (Article 3: 2) and notes in its Preamble that leaders of African governments are aware that "refugee problems are a source of friction among many Member States," desire to eliminate the "source of such discord," and are anxious to distinguish between a refugee and "a person fleeing his country for the sole purpose of fomenting subversion from outside" (Preamble 3–4). In order to achieve national security and eliminate interstate discord, the Convention further states: "For reasons of security, countries of asylum shall, as far as possible, settle refugees at a reasonable distance from the frontier of their country of origin" (Article 2: 6).

The statement about removing refugees from border areas for security reasons is directly counter to the human right of freedom of movement within a country. Naldi notes:

> States granting the right of asylum are, for reasons of security, under an obligation to settle refugees a reasonable distance from the frontier of their country of origin. This requirement would appear, *prima facie*, to be incompatible with Article 26 of the UN Convention and Article 12, paragraph 1 of the Banjul Charter which states that every individual shall have the right of freedom of movement and residence within the borders of a state. It could be that the definition of the word "individual" is not intended to include refugees but in the absence of any indication to that effect the word "individual" must be taken to refer to any person. (Naldi 1989: 93–94)

The question of national security is raised far too often to disguise the denial of human rights. The vast majority of African refugees are neither politically active nor militant in their country of origin. In fact, the majority are women and children, and many are old. Almost all of them, including most of the men, are "innocent bystanders" fleeing warriors (or famine), as was noted by President Nyerere in the speech quoted earlier. Only a small segment of all refugees are politically or militarily active. Usually these are active members of recognized political movements and can be separated from the other refugees if desired. During the wars of liberation in the 1960s and 1970s, politically active refugees (or freedom fighters) were often housed in separate camps or training facilities. During those years, the numbers of putatively active freedom fighters were increased by the fact that some African host countries would accept as refugees only those who were, or would attest to being, active members of a liberation movement. Contrary to the spirit of human rights, host countries allowed liberation movements the power to deny refugee status to people coming from strife-torn colonies if the incoming refugees were not active members of that particular movement.

Self-Settlement, Power, and Human Rights

The viewpoints of African states have been presented above. The arguments among social scientists about self-settlement and hospitality may be reduced to two opposing positions. The common view held by most observers focuses on the material poverty of local hosts and the vulnerability of refugees (Chambers 1979, 1986; Kibreab 1985). Refugees are unprotected from being abused when they self-settle. Local hosts also suffer, the poorest suffering most, because the arrival of more mouths to feed increases costs and scarcity of food (as well as land and employment) and decreases wages. Self-settlement allows governments to escape legal obligations by pretending instead that traditional African hospitality is at work, when what is really happening is impoverishment and abuse. A subtitle in Kibreab (1985: 69) notes that "Hospitality in a State of Poverty Is Inconceivable."

A minority opinion focuses on (1) the existence of coethnics on both sides of many national borders, which diminishes the dislocation; (2) the social and psychological benefits to refugees who can reestablish a normal existence more quickly; and (3) the need and right to enjoy some measure of self-control (Hansen 1977, 1979b, 1982, 1990). The historical backgrounds of many African refugee situations reveal that the precolonial territories of many ethnic groups (previously tribal peoples) have been divided by colonial borders. Refugees remaining near the border may therefore remain in familiar territory, often among relatives. Refugees remaining in such host villages lose less of their identity and fewer personal resources.

I have analyzed elsewhere refugees and self-settlement in terms of power and control (Hansen 1982). If power is the ability to influence actors and their actions, then one dimension of this is self-control, or power over oneself and one's own actions. There are grounds for assuming that a certain amount of self-control and power over others seems to be a basic human need (May 1972). If this is so, then there is, or should be, a human right to exercise some measure of self-control. The international conventions and the African Charter may recognize this right in their references to liberty and dignity.

One of the defining features of refugees is some degree of powerlessness. Flight represents an attempt to utilize whatever power a person still possesses to escape from a threatening situation. Changes in the sociopolitical environment of their original residence diminish people's power and self-control and therefore strip them of their rights even before they leave. Flight further reduces the individual's power and self-control. The extent to which refugees actually suffer as a result of their uprooting and flight varies from one situation and individual to another. For almost everyone, however, the process of becoming a refugee is a transition from more rights, more security, and relative prosperity to fewer or none and to poverty.

Settlement after flight occurs in a context of deprivation and anxiety. The refugees suffer a series of losses: physical, social, political, and economic. They become aware of the fact that they are living in danger. They try to maintain whatever power they can because of its fundamental importance to their personal well-being and its usefulness. Unfortunately, this understandable desire by refugees to conserve and nourish their diminished self-control and power over others is not often understood or appreciated by private and governmental institutions (Leighton 1945; Oliver-Smith 1986). As a consequence, assistance programs often undercut even more the already weakened power of refugees and deny them their right to self-control. Having survived to varying degrees the loss of power and the violation of their human rights in their place of origin and subsequent flight, refugees face a continued denial or violation of their human rights in their host country.

From the perspective of the refugee, self-settlement in the border villages is a sensible decision in terms of power. The village world is a familiar one, where the refugee may be able to transfer and maintain some status, rank, and prestige from his or her previous existence. Though material wealth is usually greatly reduced in flight, the refugee can continue to live in a world where his or her previous experience, skills, and acquired knowledge may be put to use to rebuild a new life. Self-settlement is even more attractive to refugees with host relatives. Being received by kin and staying among them means that the refugee maintains more of his or her previous social identity. Kinship relationships with the accompanying reciprocity-based rights and obligations mean that the refugee maintains more power over other people and more stability and power over his or her own life. These reasons provide powerful support for the popularity of self-settlement.

Whatever the merits of the various arguments, the great majority of African refugees in the past have self-settled, despite government preferences (and sometimes demands), major amounts of material assistance given in the schemes, and the concerns of social scientists. In 1975, 75 percent of African refugees were self-settled, while only 24 percent were in schemes and only 1 percent were in cities (Chambers 1979). In the ICARA conference, African governments estimated that more than 60 percent of African refugees were self-settled (UNHCR 1979). Refugee statistics are unreliable, but large numbers, perhaps the majority, have continued to self-settle during the 1980s (Mazur 1988).

A Case of Successful Integration of Self-Settled Refugees

In 1989 I returned to Zambia to continue my longitudinal study of self-settled Angolan refugees in border areas of Zambia and to contrast the well-being of those refugees with others of the same cohort who had lived all of those years (late 1960s to 1989) in a government-directed settlement project. The scheme-settled Angolans had been moved from the Luvale-speaking border to a district inhabited by another ethnic group. All of the refugees in my study arrived in Zambia as adults (fifteen years or older) during the late 1960s and were still living in Zambia in 1989. The following paragraphs are from my conclusions to that study (Hansen 1990: 34–35).

Differences in Integration. Self-settled refugees of both genders were much more integrated into Zambian society than were scheme-settled refugees. Approximately half of the men and women in the scheme in 1989 wanted to repatriate, whereas none of the self-settled wished to do so. One-fifth of scheme-settled refugee men and women still felt themselves to be strangers in Zambia, whereas none of the self-settled felt that way. None of the scheme-settled refugees (to the best of my knowledge) had Zambian registration cards, although some of them had cards when they were self-settled. All of the currently self-settled refugees had Zambian registration cards and therefore de facto citizenship. The integration of the self-settled refugees was supported by the local villagers, who viewed the refugee-host relationship in kinship terms. The relatively weak integration of the scheme-settled refugees was partially caused by the attitudes and behaviors of the Zambian villagers and townspeople living around the scheme.

Differences in Psychological Security and Independence. The Zambian government affected the psychological security and independence of both sets of refugees, although in distinct ways. There was a pervasive fear among self-settled refugees that the government might still take them away from the village to the scheme and perhaps deport them to Angola—i.e., the threat to the psychological security of the self-settled refugees came from the Zambian government. The scheme-settled refugees did not seem to be afraid. On the other hand, scheme-settled refugees were insecure in another way. They did not believe that they had the power to determine their future. They believed that the government would decide whether they were repatriated or not—i.e., repatriation would be not a voluntary but a government-determined act.

Poorer Zambians versus Richer Angolan Refugees. Scheme-settled refugees were materially better off than self-settled refugees, who were more integrated and felt at home. Many scheme-settled refugees remained "refugees" after twenty-three years in Zambia, whereas self-settled refugees were no longer "refugees" in their eyes or in the eyes of their local hosts. Instead, self-settled refugees were now perceived by themselves and their neighbors as (generally poor) rural Zambians. Therefore, in the simplest terms the long-term consequences of the two settlement strategies were that the self-settled refugees were now poor de facto (though not de jure) Zambians, while the scheme-settled were richer but still Angolan refugees.

Defining and Recognizing a Durable Solution. The UNHCR tries to promote "durable solutions" for refugees. Attaining economic self-sufficiency is not seen as sufficient for achieving a durable solution. Agricultural settlement schemes, which are designed to allow the refugees to achieve economic self-sufficiency, are seen only as long-term holding actions, cost-effective ways to maintain refugee populations for a long time. What constitutes a durable solution? Durable solutions occur when refugees stop being refugees.

The self-settled refugees I interviewed and observed were no longer "refugees"—the term no longer applied. They thought and said that they were villagers, and their local hosts agreed. The "Angolan refugees" did not think that they were still Angolans, strangers, newcomers, or refugees. I could identify people as having been refugees in 1970–72, when I took a village census. Some of them were willing to admit in 1989 that they had come from Angola during the war (while others were too apprehensive to admit to having been refugees), but each one said that he or she now was a *mwenyembo* (villager). They had stopped being refugees. They had exchanged that status for the status of villager. I felt that they were correct; it was wrong to still categorize these self-settled people as refugees. The situation of the self-settled Angolan refugees in Zambia constituted a durable solution. If this was not a durable solution, why not? If these people had not achieved complete integration, a durable solution, then how are durability and integration defined and achieved?

This case shows self-settled refugees, with the help of their local hosts, achieving de facto integration. All of them had also acquired Zambian national identification cards and had become de jure Zambians. However, the Zambian legal code does not provide for the possibility of refugees becoming citizens. There is a provision for naturalization of immigrants, but there is no agreement that refugees can be naturalized. Having entered the country with the status of refugee, the refugee is not permitted to drop or exchange the status. When I reported to the Zambian commissioner for refugees and his staff the differences between self-settled and scheme-settled in terms of the latter still considering themselves to be "strangers" in Zambia, the commissioner was careful to point out that given Zambia's current legal code, all of the refugees must remain strangers (refugees) forever.

The Human Rights of African Refugees, Nationality, and the State

> In 1884–1885, the European imperial powers met in Berlin and without the consent or participation of the African people, demarcated the Continent of Africa into colonies or spheres of influence. In many cases, kingdoms or tribes were split with such reckless abandon that they came under two or three European imperial powers. This event was the genesis of many present-day conflicts and virtually insoluble problems in the African Continent. (Elias 1988: viii)

The movement of many African people across state borders, yet within ethnic (or precolonial) territories, raises a number of important questions about the relationship of the state (formerly colony), society, and nationality in Africa. Which borders are national ones: those that separate new states or those that separate long-established and still dynamic ethnic groups? Which social and political groupings are the appropriate ones to be called nations: only the states, only ethnicities, or both? Are African states really nation-states, or are they states that hope to become nation-states? When do people become refugees? Is it when they cross state borders, or when, within the host state, the involuntary migrants are forced to move again, this time outside of their ethnic territory? How do Africans indigenously conceptualize refugees?

African leaders have adopted and continued to use political forms and precedents that grew from, and were organically related to, the European experience. Formal declarations of independence from direct European rule do not mean actual independence from European conceptual dominance. African leaders and peoples have gone through tremendous political changes in the past hundred years. These profound changes have included the transformation of African societies and polities. They are still composed of indigenous African units, such as the lineage, village, tribe, and chieftainship, but they have been transformed around European units, such as the colony, district, political party, and state.

The most obvious and powerful expressions of the continued African conceptual reliance on European political forms are the African states themselves. The states are direct and uncritical successors of the colonies. Both colony and state are forms introduced by the Europeans. The colonies and the shapes of colonial territories that were created by European powers reflect variable penetration by outsiders into the interior, thwarted and achieved ambitions, and (often intentional) ignorance of preexisting tribal territories. When African states gained their "independence," leaders of these new states assumed the boundaries and internal structures of the colonies, sometimes with minor cosmetic changes in names (Northern Rhodesia became Zambia; the Gold Coast became Ghana, etc.). Though they were African themselves, the leaders ignored African identities, territories, and boundaries in favor of European-defined ones.

The term "nation" refers to a group that shares a common history and identity and is aware of that; they are a people, not just a population. Using that definition, ethnic groups (once called tribes) in Africa are also nations. None of the new African states were originally nation-states because none of them were nations as well as states. Each of the new states contains more than one nation. In their border areas, many new states contain parts of nations because the European-inspired borders cut across existing national territories. Thus one of the major tasks confronting the leaders of new African states was creating nations.

This task was often referred to as creating a national consciousness, but that was misleading. There was no nation to become conscious of; the nation had to be created concurrently with a consciousness.

The social and political transformation from African indigenous forms to ones introduced from Europe has not been easy nor entirely successful. Many current problems can be traced to the structures accepted from the Europeans (Zolberg, Suhrke, and Aguayo 1989). Many African people are caught in the conflict between African and European precedents and forms. The difficulties of fitting Africans into European-based forms during the last three decades are evident in examining the prevalence and situation of African refugees, whose creation and continuing presence also demonstrate the widespread failures of African states to satisfy basic human rights and needs.

Whether or not most of them would be able to phrase it in our legal terminology, African refugees want their human rights restored in their host countries. Their claim to have their rights restored—i.e., their insistence that African host countries stop denying refugees their human rights—rests on both universal and particular grounds. The universal basis for their possession of human rights is the set of internationally agreed-on covenants. The particularly African bases for their claims to freedom of movement and sociopolitical membership are the moral commitment of African states to human and peoples' rights and the continuation in all African states of strong, indigenous sociocultural units that predate the European-derived state. Ultimately, we must question the sovereignty of African states to exclude these people and to deny them their human rights.

Conclusion

The creation of refugees expresses the violation and abuse of human rights in the society and country of origin. People become refugees to escape this violation and abuse. The continuation of the rights-deprived refugee status in the receiving country continues the denial of human rights. The continued existence of millions of refugees in our world expresses the denial of human rights in both the originating and receiving countries. Refugees typically find themselves in a no-win situation wherever they are.

African states have adopted European-derived colonial boundaries that cut across and divide many indigenous ethnic (once called tribal) territories. These newer colony-become-state territories often separate family members and coethnics in adjacent states. Lineage, clan, and ethnic relationships and reciprocal obligations continue to have meaning for Africans today, even if their states have usurped the term "nation" for themselves.

Self-settlement by African refugees and the hospitality of local African hosts reveal several things. First, many African refugees are remaining within their ethnic territories, although they cross state borders. Second, Africans continue to recognize family and ethnic claims to hospitality, shelter, and residency, even if these claims are not recognized by African states and their legal codes. Third, as demonstrated by my Zambian case data, self-settled refugees, with their own resources and local hospitality, may be more able to integrate and achieve a more durable solution than may scheme-settled refugees, who have received a good deal of national and international assistance.

For whatever reasons, a large number of African refugees, perhaps the majority, have preferred to self-settle. In spite of this demonstrated preference, African governments have made a policy of resettling refugees away from international borders into government-managed camps and projects. National and international assistance has been largely restricted to refugees in these official locations, so self-settled refugees generally receive no assistance from the national government or international agencies. Host governments may define this policy as one dictated by concerns about national security. I believe this to be a convenient but ill-founded excuse. The great majority of refugees are not security risks, and the fighters and provocative agents can usually be identified.

Some refugees voluntarily go to the government-managed locations because they want or need assistance, but other refugees are forcibly resettled. This is a violation of their human right to free movement within a territory. This involuntary resettlement is an illustration of policies and programs that define themselves as beneficial but are actually detrimental to the welfare of the people affected. Forced resettlement deprives refugees of self-control and further reduces their power.

My research suggests that African refugees and their local hosts have a very different definition of "refugee" from that held by African states and the OAU. In local African eyes, fleeing outside one's own ethnic territory often makes that person a refugee. By forcibly relocating refugees away from international borders (where they may have their own kith and kin) and into areas controlled by different ethnicities, host governments create refugees. To be sure, what to do with large numbers of involuntary migrants in Africa remains a thorny and sensitive issue.

Future research that highlights the no-win characteristics of the predicament of such people is important for the purpose of ensuring that their problems do not get overshadowed by the concerns of others on the growing human rights agenda. Repatriation must not be considered the sole goal for solving refugee problems. Naturalization and integration should be increasingly available as a choice. In a better and more democratic world, human rights should apply to all people, refugees included.

Author's Note

A number of my colleagues and students have worked with me on this chapter and contributed to my ideas. Special thanks to Winston Nagan, Tony Oliver-Smith, and Buzzy Guillette. Two students, Mark Walkup and John McDonnell, spent many hours discussing human rights and refugees at my house and brought me many references. Goran Hyden and Ronald Cohen have been very patient editors, for which I thank them. My wife, Holly Williams, knows how much I owe to her. I am responsible for any errors and controversies.

References

Betts, Tristam. 1980. *Spontaneous Settlement of Rural Refugees in Africa*. London: Euro Action—ACORD.
Brooks, Hug C., and Yassin El-Ayouty, eds. 1970. *Refugees South of the Sahara: An African Dilemma*. Westport, Conn.: Negro Universities Press.
Chambers, Robert. 1979. "Rural Refugees in Africa: What the Eye Does Not See." *Disasters* 3 (4): 381–92.
———. 1986. "Hidden Losers? The Impact of Rural Refugees and Refugee Programmes on Poorer Hosts." *International Migration Review* 20 (2): 245–63.
CIMADE, INODEP, and MINK. 1986. *Africa's Refugee Crisis: What's to Be Done Now?* London: Zed Books.
Elias, T. O. 1988. *Africa and the Development of International Law*. 2d ed. Edited by Richard Akinjide. Dordrecht: Martinus Nijhoff.
Eriksson, L. G., G. Melander, and P. Nobel, eds. 1981. *An Analysing Account of the Conference on the African Refugee Problem, Arusha, May 1979*. Uppsala: Scandinavian Institute of African Studies.
Goodwill-Gill, Guy S. 1983. *The Refugee in International Law*. Oxford: Clarendon Press.

Gould, W. T. S. 1974. "Refugees in Tropical Africa." *International Migration Review* 8 (3): 413–30.

Hamalengwa, M., C. Flinterman, and E. V. O. Dankwa, comps. 1988. *The International Law of Human Rights in Africa: Basic Documents and Annotated Bibliography*. United Nations Institute for Training and Research. Dordrecht: Martinus Nijhoff.

Hansen, Art. 1977. "Once the Running Stops: The Social and Economic Incorporation of Angolan Refugees into Zambian Border Villages." Ph.D. diss., Department of Anthropology, Cornell University.

———. 1979a. "Managing Refugees: Zambia's Response to Angolan Refugees 1967 to 1977." *Disasters* 3 (4): 375–80.

———. 1979b. "Once the Running Stops: Assimilation of Angolan Refugees into Zambian Border Villages." *Disasters* 3 (4): 369–74.

———. 1981. "Refugee Dynamics: Angolans in Zambia 1966 to 1972." *International Migration Review* 15 (53–54): 175–94.

———. 1982. "Self-Settled Rural Refugees in Africa: The Case of Angolans in Zambian Villages." In *Involuntary Migration and Resettlement: The Problems and Responses of Dislocated People*, ed. Art Hansen and Anthony Oliver-Smith, pp. 13–35. Boulder, Colo.: Westview Press.

———. 1988a. "Coping with Famine, Drought, and War in Sub-Saharan Africa." *Studies in Third World Societies* 36: 227–54.

———. 1988b. "Variability within the Processes of Involuntary Migration and Resettlement." Paper presented at the International Symposium on Involuntary Resettlement at the Twelfth International Congress of Anthropological and Ethnological Sciences, Zagreb, Yugoslavia.

———. 1989. "Preliminary Report on Policy-Oriented Refugee Research about the Long-Term Consequences of Two Settlement Options for the Security, Rehabilitation, and Sustainable Development of Refugees and Their Local Hosts: Based on a Case Study of Angolan Refugees (1966–1989) in Zambia." Paper presented at a seminar at Queen Elizabeth House for the Refugee Studies Programme, Oxford.

———. 1990. *Refugee Self-Settlement versus Settlement on Government Schemes: The Long-Term Consequences for Security, Integration and Economic Development of Angolan Refugees (1966–1989) in Zambia*. Discussion Paper Number 17. Geneva: United Nations Research Institute for Social Development.

Hansen, Art, and Robert J. Papstein, eds. 1979. *The History of the Luvale People and Their Chieftainship*. Los Angeles: Africa Institute for Applied Research.

Harrell-Bond, Barbara. 1982. *Ugandan Refugees in the Sudan. Part III: Administration in Planned Rural Settlements*. Universities Field Staff International (UFSI) Reports 1982/No. 50.

———. 1986. *Imposing Aid: Emergency Assistance to Refugees*. London: Oxford University Press.

Kibreab, Gaim. 1985. *African Refugees: Reflections on the African Refugee Problem.* Trenton, N.J.: Africa World Press.

Leighton, Alexander H. 1945. *The Governing of Men: General Principles and Recommendations Based on Experience at a Japanese Relocation Camp.* Princeton, N.J.: Princeton University Press.

Mageed, Fawzi A., and Philip Ramaga. 1986. *Spontaneously Settled Refugees in Juba: A Socio-Economic Study.* Khartoum: Office of the Commissioner for Refugees.

May, Rollo. 1972. *Power and Innocence: A Search for the Sources of Violence.* New York: W. W. Norton.

Mazur, R. E. 1988. "Refugees in Africa: The Role of Sociological Analysis and Praxis." *Current Sociology* 36 (2): 43–60.

Melander, Goran, and Peter Nobel, eds. 1978. *African Refugees and the Law.* New York: Africana.

———. 1979. *International Legal Instruments on Refugees in Africa.* Uppsala: Scandinavian Institute of African Studies.

Milne, A. J. M. 1986. *Human Rights and Human Diversity.* London: Macmillan.

Naldi, Gino J. 1989. *The Organization of African Unity: An Analysis of Its Role.* London: Mansell.

Nedjati, Zaim M. 1978. *Human Rights under the European Convention.* European Studies in Law, vol. 8. Amsterdam: North-Holland.

Oliver-Smith, Anthony. 1986. *The Martyred City: Death and Rebirth in the Andes.* Albuquerque: University of New Mexico Press.

Oliver-Smith, Anthony, and Art Hansen. 1982. "Involuntary Migration and Resettlement: Causes and Contexts." In *Involuntary Migration and Resettlement: The Problems and Responses of Dislocated People,* ed. Art Hansen and Anthony Oliver-Smith, pp. 1–9. Boulder, Colo.: Westview Press.

Rogge, John R. 1985. *Too Many, Too Long: Sudan's Twenty-Year Refugee Dilemma.* Totowa, N.J.: Rowman and Allenheld.

———. 1987. "When Is Self-Sufficiency Achieved? The Case of Rural Settlements in the Sudan." In *Refugees: A Third World Dilemma,* ed. John Rogge, pp. 96–98. Totowa, N.J.: Rowman and Littlefield.

Scudder, Thayer. 1981. *From Relief to Development: Some Comments on Refugee and Other Settlement in Somalia.* Working Paper No. 4. Binghamton, N.Y.: Institute for Development Anthropology.

United Nations. 1981. *The Refugee Situation in Africa: Assistance Measures Proposed.* International Conference on Assistance to Refugees in Africa (ICARA), Geneva, 9–10 April.

United Nations High Commissioner for Refugees (UNHCR). 1979. *Report of Committee B on Social, Economic, Institutional, Administrative and Financial Problems.* Conference on the Situation of Refugees in Africa, Arusha, May.

———. 1989. *Refugees.* No. 71 (December). Geneva: Public Information Service.

United States Committee for Refugees. 1990. *World Refugee Survey: 1989 in Review*. Washington, D.C.: American Council for Nationalities Service.

Weis, Paul. 1978. "Convention Refugees and De Facto Refugees." In *African Refugees and the Law*, ed. Goran Melander and Peter Nobel, pp. 15–22. New York: Africana.

Wenk, Michael G. 1968. "The Refugee: A Search for Clarification." *International Migration Review* 2 (3): 62–69.

Winter, Roger. 1984. "Refugee Protection in Africa: Current Trends." Paper presented at the Washington Institute for Values in Public Policy Conference on U.S. Policy toward Africa, Washington, D.C., 19 September.

Woronoff, Jon. 1973. "Refugees: The Million-Person Problem." *Africa Report* 18, no. 1 (January–February): 29–33.

Zartman, William. 1970. "Portuguese Guinean Refugees in Senegal." In *Refugees South of the Sahara*, ed. H. C. Brooks and Y. El-Ayouty, pp. 143–61. Westport, Conn.: Negro Universities Press.

Zolberg, Aristide R., Astri Suhrke, and Sergio Aguayo. 1986. "International Factors in the Formation of Refugee Movements." *International Migration Review* 20 (2): 151–69.

———. 1989. *Escape from Violence: Conflict and the Refugee Crisis in the Developing World*. Oxford: Oxford University Press.

7

"Life Is War": Human Rights, Political Violence, and Struggles for Power in Lesotho

ROBERT SHANAFELT

She was kidnapped on the outskirts of the city of Maputo, with her baby still suckling. Her child was crying, either hungry or upset by the long march which she and her mother were forced to endure.

The bandits felt threatened by the child's crying. They were afraid of being heard and reported to the armed forces. They were worried. They scolded the mother. They indicated that she should make the child shut up.

Among them, a bandit already, was a child who looked about ten (though perhaps a little older, as his growth was stunted by malnutrition). He proposed to his chiefs, "This child is making a lot of noise. Can I kill her?"

And the mother said that when she heard this she sweated with horror. She looked to see who was speaking and saw that it was a mere child. She thrust her breast into her baby's mouth. He [sic] sucked at the milk and fell asleep.

She ended, "I was lucky. What would have happened to the baby if she had not gone to sleep. How can a child be a killer? He spoke so coldly that I'd no doubt he'd have done it. . . . " (Magaia 1988: 107–8)

In chapter 1 Cohen argues that personal security and safety are bedrock features that define human rights claims. I agree. Other rights described in this book are certainly important. But claims to just demands are difficult to express or protect when people have the feeling that by simply going about their everyday lives they are in random danger of being hurt, arrested, or robbed by the lawless who live outside, or just as often inside, the authority of the state. In many parts of Africa this sort of insecurity is only intermittent or even rare. At other times or places it is woven into the fabric of ordinary expectations. The point is, however, that without legitimated and legalized human rights protection, reinforced through constant practice, the *potential* for such insecurity is constant.

The ubiquitous venality of African life and the violence that can suddenly visit innocent and defenseless people are widespread throughout the continent, especially in southern Africa (see chapter 4 and the publications of Africa Watch and Amnesty International). Unfortunately, the searing horror of it all too often gets sanitized in academic discussions. This masks the fear, often the terror, when human rights abuses are embedded into the civil and political life of the state. More positivistic theory such as that recently published by Gurr (1989) and his colleagues covers a large range of antecedent variables, but as with most accounts these look for systematic and mechanistic models of proximate causation. I will analyze the Lesotho materials in a similar fashion toward the end of this chapter.

First, however, I want to portray the African human rights predicament from the perspective of those who experience its perfidy. Hannah Arendt (1970) comes closest to discussing this more direct kind of understanding when she examines violence and authoritarianism not for their causes but for their effects. In African studies Schatzberg's (1988) recent work on Zaire makes the point as well but not quite as directly since his ultimate goal is to link state insecurity to human rights concerns. In contrast and following Parkin (1986) I wish to add a more hermeneutical approach, that of making directly available to the reader what it is like to experience human rights abuses in Africa. This does not rule out a more positivistic orientation, and as noted I will look at causal features of this particular case at the end of the chapter. But in my view the primary purpose of this book is to argue for the inextricable coupling of development to human rights. Although much ink has been spilled to support the notion that they are not necessarily linked in Africa, this chapter and others in this volume make the opposite point of view particularly compelling, namely, that African development of any sort is necessarily coupled to human rights protection and practice. In what is to follow, then, I take the portrayal of the experience itself to be my part of the task. Theory in the positivist sense is added to the end as interpretive commentary rather than primary focus, to complete the picture.

Although the passage cited above is not from Lesotho, the cry of this anguished mother clearly cuts across national boundaries. A mother's pained cry from Mozambique is linked to Lesotho as the men of Lesotho and Mozambique are linked in a common life in South Africa's mines; it is linked as citizens of both nations are vulnerable to the disruption and violence brought about by high rates of labor migration, South African apartheid policies, and chaotic processes of culture change. The horror experienced by one mother and her child is meant to set the tone for my discussion; for no dispassionate reportage can adequately bring home the experiences of individuals such as she, a woman concerned for the safety of her child and unable to understand the world of violence in which she suddenly finds herself. She is shocked and dazed by the overturning of the moral universe that the Mozambique National Resistance (MNR) bandits have brought about. And her shock is at least as great as that of those of us who are able to think abstractly about human rights free from the fear she is facing.

Given the frequency of mass killings and other forms of political violence the world over, anyone with access to a newspaper and a history book has reason enough to be less shocked. Such things have become all too commonplace. Sometimes such killings appear to take place in dispassionate obedience to a chain of command, but those who pull the triggers may also do so with a great deal of enthusiasm. Perhaps we need to take more seriously the view that control over the instruments of violence is capable of bringing tremendous pleasure—what Nietzsche (1967: 65) described as "the pleasure of being allowed to vent . . . power freely upon one who is powerless." At least the link between psychology and power needs to be taken into account.

The link between personal gratification seeking and power is certainly present in Africa. Schatzberg (1988), for instance, gives numerous examples from Zaire. One of these is from the official correspondence of a Zairian administrator who found it fit to describe local soldiers as bandits who "invade villages, rape married women and girls, [and] *permit themselves everything*" (quoted in Schatzberg 1988: 52; emphasis added). Something of a sociological principle (although admittedly somewhat circular) could be formed around this single sentence: armed men will tend to "permit themselves everything" to the extent that there are weaknesses in contravening ideological and coercive systems of power and authority. In other words, armies rampage where there exists a power vacuum. This insight goes back at least as far as Machiavelli, but it is also not lost on the ordinary people of contemporary Africa who are the victims of such brutal treatment.

The violence and political repression experienced in Africa and other parts of the world more than indicates that some find for themselves pleasure amidst chaos and terror. But to understand this violence more is required than an appreciation that individuals can enjoy violent situations that allow them to give free rein to their desires. Only occasionally does human psychology manifest itself in what has been described as a "culture of terror" (Taussig 1984). It is obvious that violence of the sort practiced by the MNR bandits is foreign to the experience of the mother from Mozambique. Values affirming human dignity and worth may even be part of the background of individuals who have in fact become murderous. Normal men in Mozambique have become deviant in a deviant situation. For explanation of the conduct of such individuals we need also to examine the milieu that generates conformity to "inhuman" values and to ask more searching questions about the relationship between power and violence. A milieu of violence in a society may be either a temporary aberration or it may reflect a condition endemic to the society as a whole. But even as one moves from the former to the latter situation, the resistant voices of victims are still to be heard. In Lesotho "rights talk" is one manifestation of the exchanges that are occurring between those who control the means of violence and those who have felt them. In such cases either of two extreme conditions may result: successful organization and resistance to violent oppression or a general breakdown of formerly held humanistic values in favor of a "culture of violence." In Lesotho organized resistance to the state is taking place, but it is by no means clear that its people will be able to overcome the patterns of violence that have beset them.

In this essay I shall use "political violence" to mean violence carried out by individuals who represent governments, who are reacting against governments and/or their representatives, or who engage in acts of violence against the community for the immediate benefit of a small group. This definition is admittedly somewhat arbitrary in that all acts of violence involve power and are thus "political." I mean only to call attention to the sort of violence that is used to preserve or overthrow established systems of status and authority.[1] And, while violence and power are linked, I concur with Arendt (1970) that they are not the same. "Power and violence," she tells us, "are opposites; where one [violence] rules absolutely, the other is absent. Violence appears where power is in jeopardy, but left to its own course it ends in power's disappearance" (Arendt 1970: 56). This latter point is quite important for understanding violence in southern Africa, and I shall return to it.

Specific cases of political violence in Lesotho will be discussed in terms of several factors that are crucial for understanding violence in general. In particular, four causal factors will be discussed: the possible psychological motives of the perpetrators, the place of violence in the South African cultural context, the material conditions of the society, and the nature of the system of governance and rule experienced at the local level. Of course, psychology, culture, and material interests are interlinked; they are separated here chiefly because the examples to be discussed seem to be more clearly motivated by one factor over another. Prior to discussing these specific causes, however, I provide a brief account of the human rights situation in Lesotho since formal independence was declared in 1966.

The Context of Violence in Lesotho

Although politics in Lesotho cannot be understood without reference to the machinations of South African policymakers, it is nonetheless evident that it has an important internal dimension. Indeed, as Edgar (1987) notes, South Africa can, if it chooses, safeguard its interests without having to obtain complete control of Lesotho's state bureaucracy. There is intense competition in Lesotho for political office because of the material benefits such offices provide. Because these offices are quite limited in number, a degree of tension and division is ensured irrespective of South Africa's actions. Lesotho is, after all, a landlocked and very dependent microstate, and its people aspire to levels of prosperity evident in South Africa.

Still, as will be made clear below, South Africa has not been content to exert its influence merely by handing out a bit of its largess to a few well-chosen politicians. Although it has almost certainly done that, it also has not stopped short of economic pressure and violence against the general population. Nonetheless, South Africa, like the United States in relation to Central America, would like at least the illusion of independent, legitimate governments in its hinterland. To this end it has often given Lesotho's bureaucrats a long tether, later attempting to rein in that tether if the bureaucrats begin to act as if it were not there at all.

To understand some of the internal dynamics of Lesotho's politics, one needs to be aware that elections are in the interests neither of the chieftaincy nor of those bureaucrats who have become entrenched in power. For one thing, populist, antichief candidates associated with the Basotho Congress party (BCP) have done well in those few elections that have been freely contested, particularly in the lowlands (Breytenbach 1975: 68–70, 85). And when chiefs find themselves competing for office, things can become quite unpleasant. Such competition existed between King Moshoeshoe II and his cousin Leabua Jonathan[2] as they sought to define the nature of the king's position in the newly independent Lesotho. In fact, repression of political opposition in independent Lesotho can be traced to the day in 1965 when a preindependence rally held by supporters of King Moshoeshoe II was attacked by members of the police and security forces, purportedly on the orders of supporters of Jonathan's Basotho National party (BNP; Khaketla 1972: 142–49). Jonathan sought to restrict the king's authority and vest it in himself, the prime minister. The king's supporters wanted a monarchy with real power. At this time, Jonathan was on friendly terms with the South Africans and openly received their contributions for his campaign, but it is not likely that the South Africans were involved in this incident.

Jonathan's rule turned increasingly harsh after he aborted the elections of 1970. He declared them void and refused to relinquish power when it became apparent that his BNP was going to be defeated by candidates from the populist BCP (Breytenbach 1975: 108). There was probably a coup attempt in 1972 and another more serious military challenge in 1974. The coup attempt in 1974 was followed by ruthless reprisals in which hundreds associated with the opposition BCP were allegedly killed (*New African* 1989: 175).

Richard Weisfelder, a longtime observer of Lesotho's political scene, described the human rights situation as of 1975 in the following terms:

> Since 1970 Lesotho has been treading the all too familiar path of arbitrary government, suppression of dissent, and sporadic violence. Unexpectedly, the adoption of this authoritarian format was accompanied by a distinct worsening of relations between Chief Jonathan's government and the South African regime. Basotho spokesmen stepped up their attack upon racial injustice under apartheid, denounced the forthcoming independence of Transkei as fraudulent, and warned that Pretoria's failure

to promote equality and majority rule could only lead to bloodshed. Meanwhile, carbon copies of notorious South African laws have been added to the Lesotho statute book, including provisions for detention without access to counsel or courts and for indemnification of public figures from prosecution for abuses of power. (Weisfelder 1976: 22)

After the first attempts to remove Jonathan failed, some members of the BCP fled to South Africa, Botswana, and Zambia. The Lesotho Liberation Army (LLA) was formed shortly thereafter to wage an armed struggle against the BNP regime. The LLA was particularly successful in infiltrating Lesotho's northern districts of Leribe, Butha-Buthe, and Mokhotlong but was also quite active in areas bordering South Africa's Transkei. In 1980 ten LLA suspects were shot dead in Butha-Buthe in an ambush set up by Lesotho's Paramilitary Unit (PMU). Hundreds of villagers fled to South Africa to escape the security forces as they proceeded to raid villages in search of escaped rebels.

Because of the ease with which LLA attacks were launched from South African (or Bantustan) territory, it soon became clear that the organization was operating with at least the tacit approval of the South African government. Journalists interviewed witnesses who claimed to have seen mortar attacks launched against Lesotho from South African territory. They also verified that LLA supporters were operating from bases in the Transkei (Cason and Fleshman 1985: 3). In a recent inquiry on violence at South African gold mines it was further revealed that South African security police employed agents provocateurs in the mining compounds to promote anti-Jonathan sentiment among mine workers from Lesotho (Pallister, Stewart, and Lepper 1988: 143).

In the early 1980s a number of prominent politicians on both sides of the conflict were assassinated. In June 1981 a member of parliament, Matjato Chakela, was killed at her home in Peka. This was followed by an attack on the life of another MP, Leloko Jonothane. In September 1981 the bullet-ridden bodies of Edgar Motuba, editor of the opposition Protestant weekly *Leselinyana la Lesotho,* and two of his friends were found dumped in a ravine. Also in that year Michael Ramorothole, a leading BCP member, was abducted and murdered. There was also an attempt on the life of B. M. Masilo of the Lesotho Council of Churches. It is difficult to ascertain who is responsible for which killings and whether claims of responsibility can be trusted. On the one hand, government opponents claim that Lesotho's two-thousand-man PMU forces operated a death squad known locally as

Koeeoko, "the Beast" (Legum 1981: B623; Legum 1984: B632–B634). On the other hand, the LLA reportedly claimed responsibility for attacks on the lives of a number of government officials. Among those killed were Minister of Works Jobo K. Rampeta, Chief Seeiso Majara (son of the minister of mines), and two members of the family of the minister of agriculture. The LLA reportedly also claimed responsibility for the shooting death of Koenyama Chakela, a BCP leader who had returned to Lesotho after accepting an offer of amnesty.

South Africa's most notorious public act of violence against Lesotho also occurred in the early 1980s. In December 1982 South African commandos launched a nighttime raid against an apartment complex and several houses in Maseru. The South Africans were worried about ANC infiltrations into their territory and about possible planned "deeds of terror" to be launched from Lesotho over the Christmas holidays. South African spokespersons claimed they raided a "military base," but no evidence of one was ever produced. Foreign journalists supported Lesotho's contention that those killed were innocent of harboring anything other than a few guns for their own protection. Many of the forty-two people killed were shot in their sleep. Among the victims was a fourteen-year-old boy and a twenty-five-year-old mother of two who was shot as she peered through her window to see what was happening next door (United Nations 1983: 16; Hanlon 1986: 5–7; IDAF 1985).

Despite this attack on Lesotho's sovereignty, the raid seemed to have had little impact on governance in Lesotho and may even have helped turn Jonathan more actively anti–South African. After 1982 he became increasingly vocal in his opposition to apartheid policies. In 1983 he closed the Taiwanese embassy and established diplomatic relations with China, the Soviet Union, and North Korea. Some Basotho were sent abroad for military training and Jonathan welcomed North Korean military advisers into Lesotho. The South African government closed or slowed down traffic at the borders numerous times from 1983 to 1985 to show its displeasure with these actions. Nonetheless, there was a marked decline in LLA activity in 1984 and 1985. Then in December 1985 there was another South African raid on Maseru. This time the operation took the form of a hit squad. Nine people were murdered.

The climate of fear generated by the South African actions was exacerbated by Jonathan's response. Earlier in the year Jonathan had handed out weapons to members of his BNP youth league. They used them allegedly to threaten South African exiles and other dissident students on the campus of the national university (Edgar 1987). They also terrorized the general population (Eldredge 1989: 20). For example, on 1 January 1986 security forces and young men with weapons reportedly supplied by the youth league opened fire on a crowd of people who had gathered to attend a New Year's Day pop concert. At least one was killed and a number were wounded.

Fortunately for the people of Lesotho the coup of 16 January 1986 took place with a minimum of bloodshed.[3] People welcomed the end of Jonathan's terror, but looked forward with no great optimism to the system of military rule that was set up to take its place. Initially many were happy the king was to be given more freedom to speak his mind, but it soon became clear that freedom would not increase under the new military ruler, Justin Khetsing Lekhanya. Displeasure with his rule did not take long to materialize. Rumor had it that already by March 1988 three attempts to remove him by military subordinates had been tried (*Africa Confidential* 1988: 6). It is widely believed in Maseru that the only thing that has saved him is the support he receives from South Africa. Further, in 1989 charges of murder were laid against him and because of them the king asked him to step down. Yet, despite Lekhanya's personal admission of shooting a young student, George Ramone, in the back (*Moeletsi oa Basotho* 11 November 1989: 1), he did not resign and was eventually exonerated by a government-convened commission of inquiry.[4] Since then he has been successful in turning the cards on his opponents and some of *them* have now been charged with murder. The rift between the king and Lekhanya widened until the king was forced into exile in 1990.

In February 1990 Lekhanya arrested four members of the military council and replaced a number of senior government officials. Soon afterwards he charged that the king's cousin, former Minister of Defense Sekhobe Letsie, was involved in ordering the 1986 murders of Vincent Makhele and Desmond Sixishe and their wives; both men were cabinet ministers with considerable power in the Jonathan government (*Leselinyana* 23 February 1990: 1). The government also charged that the minister of planning, Michael Sefali, had knowledge of the murder of the four (*Lesotho Today* 29 March 1990: 1). In an incident that followed quickly on the heels of these events, the king was sent out of the country. The king and his supporters maintain that the king was forced into exile by Lekhanya (*Mirror* 23 March 1990: 1). To many observers the fact that all of those arrested in connection with the murders are supporters of the king and/or his pro-ANC views makes charges of murder suspect.

Indeed, since the coup the military government has been openly friendly to South Africa. It has allowed a South African trade mission to be opened in Maseru, agreed to go ahead with a major dam project designed to supply water and electricity to South Africa's industrial heartland, and welcomed construction of a new military hospital by the South African Defense Forces. In addition, a number of political refugees and activists have been forced to leave the country. An expatriate clergyman charged that in the year following the coup South African police and security forces were given a free hand to enter the country in pursuit of political activists (Legum 1988: B660). In the same period, official representatives of the ANC were forced to quit Lesotho and some of its members living in exile there were attacked. This continued in 1988 and 1989. For example, in March 1988 Mazizi Maqekeza, a South African exile and member of the ANC, was shot dead by an unknown assailant while under police custody in the hospital. He and another ANC member had been arrested the previous month following a shooting incident in which a third ANC man was killed by the police. The second man arrested is reported to have "disappeared" while in custody (Amnesty International 1989: 61).

And the military regime has not been reluctant to use violence to remove its internal opponents. Three military officers died in detention in March 1987. Further, a former member of the military council and several enlisted men have recently been put on trial for the abduction and slaying of Sixishe and Makhele and their wives (Legum 1988: B661).

On the more positive side, however, the military government has shown a certain tolerance of vocal opposition. Local papers regularly publish articles critical of the regime and report on its abuses. Nonetheless, there are limits. An editor of a newly established weekly was arrested, then deported, for reporting on the financial dealings of a prominent government minister (Eldredge 1989: 21). In June 1990 the government began a new phase in its dealing with opposition by convening a constituent assembly with the stated goals of discussing the formation of a new constitution and a return to civilian rule. The impact of this will be discussed in a later section.

Besides the political violence of the state and its opponents, Lesotho's people suffer from increasing rates of crime. In February 1988 Lesotho's chief justice reported serious crime had increased three to four times since 1983 (*Lesotho Today* 11 February 1988: 1). Like South Africa as a whole, Lesotho has particularly high rates of murder and assault. In 1987 there were reportedly about 33 murders per 100,000 people in Lesotho (Shanafelt 1989: 54). This is a rate comparable to that found in South African townships such as Soweto but quite high on the world scale—being, for example, some three times higher than that reported for the same year in the state of Texas (*World Almanac* 1989: 818).[5] Lesotho's political and economic situation as an extremely vulnerable quasi state and a labor reserve dependent on migrant labor have joined to produce sizable subcultures of violence and brigandage in what from the outside may appear to be sleepy villages and towns. Far from representing the inchoate political aspirations of the people, such subcultures of violence are vilified by those with the most respect for "traditional" moral values and justice. Women who have spent their entire lives tilling the soil and men who have become accustomed to earning their daily wages from mine labor are horrified by the attacks made on them by the young bandits whom they refer to as *lintja* (dogs). While not on the scale of the terror in Mozambique, the terror in Lesotho is evident nonetheless.

Understanding Political Violence in Lesotho

The Psychology of Violence[6]

As the old adage goes, power corrupts, but a footnote should be added that it also inflates egos. Even in weak states like Lesotho individuals expect that political and military office will lead to benefice and that subordinates should unquestioningly obey an authority's commands. When these expectations are frustrated violence frequently results. The accounts related below give examples from everyday life in Lesotho in which violence is linked to frustrated power or to attempts to wield authority in ways the general populace does not consider legitimate. For the unarmed citizen facing the police or the military it is dangerous to (1) resist the whims of individual soldiers or police officers, (2) show any sort of disrespect toward police/military authority and esteem, and (3) expect the military or police to carry out its role with Weberian rational efficiency. However, soldiers and police cannot always rely on their superior weaponry for security. Often civilians fight back when confronted with military excesses.

Armed forces, including those off duty, become violent when others refuse to bend to their wills; civilians resist abuses. Example one: At a high school located in a mountain village, two off-duty policemen and a female companion demanded to see a female student. When their request was refused they began to physically assault two teachers. On seeing what was happening, a large group of students tried to come to their teachers' aid. The soldiers fired warning shots into the air to keep the students at bay before vacating the premises (*Leselinyana,* 9 October 1987). Example two: An inebriated off-duty policeman attending a dance party suddenly stood up and demanded the music be turned off and the party stopped because, he claimed, it was an illegal gathering. He was unable to give any explanation for his behavior, as proper papers had been obtained. Nonetheless he continued to demand that his will be obeyed. He made threats and brandished his gun, but brave partygoers managed to push him outside. Finally he left and the party continued (author's diary, 1983). Example three: An internal security policeman (*Lepolesa la mautloela*) named Teboho threatened numerous people with a gun for two days as he walked around his village. This occurred after Teboho quarreled with and threatened to shoot a man. This man later claimed the security agent was angry because he was refusing to make his sisters available to him. Teboho was angered further when his opponent successfully wrestled his handgun from him and had it put away for safekeeping in someone else's house. In response he sought the assistance of several other policemen and armed himself with his government-issued rifle. He informed the other policemen that his handgun had been stolen from him. Teboho was still seeking his opponent several days later (*Moeletsi,* 2 October 1988: 5).

Police and military will not tolerate disrespect or questioning of their authority. Example one: A man was beaten and handcuffed at a football match simply for asking why a boy attending the match had been taken into custody (*Moeletsi* 29 May 1988: 1). Example two: A drunken customer at a rural shop began to shout abuses at the other customers. Among those insulted were two off-duty policemen. One of the policemen punched and kicked the drunk. After this both policemen left, but they soon came back to kick him some more. Again they left, this time to return armed. They proceeded to open fire on the shop, spraying it with bullets. When the shopowner attempted to stop the men, one of them assaulted her. At this point witnesses from the village quickly came to her rescue. One of the policeman attempted to shoot at the shopowner's defenders, but when his gun misfired they chased him down and beat him severely (*Moeletsi* 28 September 1988: 6).

Policy and caprice at roadblocks. Roadblocks are always potentially dangerous; at these sites state forces and individual will confront one another on a daily basis. Moreover, at roadblocks goods can be easily extracted from the general populace. And to this ever-present possibility of corruption must be added the reality of caprice. Despite its tiny army, Lesotho is little different from other places in Africa in this regard. Soldiers may be drunk or eager to assert their authority as soldiers or as men. Anyone who mistakenly misses a roadblock is in danger of being shot. Particularly during Jonathan's rule, the military was noted most for its indiscipline. But the situation is not all that different under the new government. For example, it may never be known whether it was policy or caprice that led to the death of one unfortunate man, Sootho Matala, at a roadblock in June 1988. Traffic police shot and killed Sootho, son of a prominent local chief, after he was slow to stop at a roadblock. The family reported that he was returning with a group of women who had asked to be taken to church. When he overran the roadblock the police shot out one of his tires. After stopping the vehicle, Sootho panicked and tried to run away. According to eyewitness accounts reported in the newspapers, when Sootho was caught he raised his hands without saying a word. Although it was obvious that he was unarmed, police opened fire, putting three bullets into him (*Moeletsi* 24 July 1988: 1). This is not merely an isolated incident. More recently the wife of a Protestant minister was wounded by police bullets when her husband refused to stop in the dark at a poorly marked roadblock (*Moeletsi* 26 November 1989: 1).

Violence and Its Social and Cultural Context

Violence cannot be explained simply as a response triggered by the frustration of a desire (although it may include that), nor is it always reducible to rational self-interest. Violence always occurs within a sociocultural context and in terms of systems of moral valuation. Spiegel and Boonzaier (1988) and others have pointed out that it is difficult if not impossible to speak of "traditional" African culture given the effects of labor migration, changes in material conditions, and the lengthy history of cross-cultural interaction in South Africa; nonetheless, when it comes to violence it may not be inappropriate to ask about the articulation between historical processes of change, contemporary circumstances, and older "African" frameworks of understanding. In this regard, something can be said about the experience and understanding of violence in the Lesotho context.

In Sotho language and practice there has existed a certain ambiguity about the nature of violence and its appropriateness. This ambiguity is reflected in, for example, the common Sotho greetings *Lumela* (Agree) and *Khotso* (Peace), which are overtly about peace and harmony but at another level refer to war and conflict (*Leselinyana la Lesotho* 11 September 1988: 2). Ambiguity is also found in attitudes about what constitutes humanity and justice. On the one hand, to be human requires one to be part of a general community of others and to show proper respect for the social order (*ho hlompha molao*). On the other hand, those who violate this order—thieves and witches (*baloi*), for example—in some sense forfeit their humanity (*botho*)[7] and their rights.

While political discourse since the nineteenth century has often focused on values of peace and diplomacy, these exist in uneasy conjunction with the militaristic attitudes that evolved during the periods of warfare and cattle raiding of the previous century. In contemporary times youths tend livestock in situations of tremendous physical hardship for themselves and extreme competition with their neighbors for available pasturage. In order to survive they are taught to be aggressive and to fight when called on to do so (Shanafelt 1989: 66–69). Most assuredly the modern context is South African, not simply Sotho. But if anything, the violence of life in the South African setting has reinforced those aspects of Sotho culture that already stressed violence. Violence can be the only road to survival in mine compounds and urban locations. Perhaps because of the awareness of this situation, Lesotho's courts are peculiarly lenient when dealing with those cases of assault and attempted murder that occur within the country's borders. Dockets examined by me for the ten-year period between 1975 and 1985 in the border town of Maputsoe revealed that a typical punishment for assault with a deadly weapon was only three months in jail or an R 30 (U.S. $15) fine.

Another factor contributing to the erosion of formerly cherished Sotho and Christian values of humanity, peace, and justice is alcohol abuse. Wallman's (1972) description of alcoholism and anomie in Lesotho as part of a "non-development syndrome" may have been misconceived, but she was correct to point out the relationship between these factors and Lesotho's situation as a labor reserve economy. The brewing of alcohol is one of the principal ways rural women have of capturing some of the capital of miners and bringing it back into the countryside. Unfortunately, an unintended consequence is increasing anomie and alcohol abuse. This has been publicly acknowledged as a serious problem. Prince Mohato Seeiso has recently joined in a campaign against the rampant alcohol abuse in the country, but such campaigns can hardly be taken seriously when at the same time the government has spared no effort in the construction of liquor distribution points in every district of Lesotho.

Respected adults in Lesotho often see the new problems of theft and banditry as resulting from a decay of values. They point out that youth no longer show respect (*ho hlompha*) and are running about without proper guidance (*molao*). Violence for the sake of violence and for the purpose of striking terror into the hearts of its victims is becoming a feature of everyday life. The best—and most terrifying—example of this is the attack on a bus that occurred in Quthing district in June 1989. The bus, on its route along the steep and winding dirt road between the rural village of Sinxondo and the district center of Moyeni, was waylaid by five men, each of whom carried an AK-47 rifle. The armed men jumped out on the road in front of the bus, then proceeded to open fire. On entering the bus, the bandits emptied several rounds into the body of the already wounded bus driver, then took the ticket money. With the passengers still inside, they set the bus alight before fleeing. One of those inside said she heard one of the bandits laughing as he fled. Fortunately, most of the passengers were able to escape the bus before it was engulfed in flames. Besides the driver, two passengers died in the incident and several were seriously injured (*Moeletsi* 2 July 1989: 1).

Material Interests and Violence

When elders blame increasing violence on lack of respect for morality, or on the normlessness of youth, they may reject the notion that this has been brought about by labor migration. Labor migration has been going on a long time, they argue, but violence at this level has not. Nonetheless, a factor that has changed which no one denies is the increasing landlessness of the population and the consequent inability and/or lack of interest among youth in maintaining a rural life-style. This must be linked to labor migration, for without a rural base it is difficult for migrants to maintain any sense of stability or security for their futures. And such land shortage can lead directly to political violence.

For example, a rash of killings was reported in the area of Mphosang after the death of the chief responsible for allocating rights to land. His former subordinates tried to take advantage of this situation by reallocating land among their friends, relatives, and supporters. Violence broke out when these reallocations were contested by the previous "owners" (*Moeletsi* 10 July 1988: 2). Similarly, a dispute over grazing rights led to death in the winter dry season of 1988. According to *Moeletsi* (18 June 1989: 6) a local chief got into a dispute with members of the Qacha's Nek district development committee when they impounded his livestock. The committee alleged that the cattle were being grazed illegally in reserved pastures. The chief was enraged by their actions and he or a member of his party killed one of the committee members in the fight that ensued. In retaliation, relatives of the victim returned and stabbed the suspected murderer, killing him.

As the incident of the bus burning indicates, the bandits who are attacking their fellows frequently show little concern for anything but personal profit and their chances of escaping the law. Assault and armed robbery of this sort is not merely confined to the towns but has become endemic throughout the countryside. One group of rural bandits has the nickname *Batho ba nako 'ngoe* (One-time people). They prey particularly on migrants from rural villages who make weekend visits to their families from South Africa. Victims may be stripped of their clothing and possessions. Sometimes they are then killed (*Moeletsi* 12 June 1988: 2; Shanafelt 1989: 53). Gangs of thugs may also terrorize individuals as they go about their ordinary shopping routines in the larger towns of a district (*Moeletsi* 21 January 1990: 1).

Some commentators from Lesotho have related these new sorts of crimes to high rates of unemployment, to class differentiation within Lesotho, and to political strife in general. Political motives especially have been suspected in some of the latest thefts that have been well organized and also quite lucrative. The years 1987 and 1988 saw several armed robberies that netted sums ranging from R 40,000 (U.S. $20,000) to more than R 90,000 (U.S. $45,000). In a letter to the editor of *Moeletsi*, one commentator argued that some people were stealing in order to feed their families, while others were members of factions that supported the ANC or sought to overthrow the Lesotho government (*Moeletsi* 9 October 1988: 2). Another letter complained that there was a lack of respect for human rights in Lesotho because of the extreme differences in wealth between the elite and the many who lack basic necessities (*Moeletsi* 31 July 1988: 2).

Governance and Violence

In his work on Zaire, Schatzberg (1988) suggests that there is a direct relationship between the degree to which leaders feel secure in their power and the degree to which they rule through repressive means. The type of insecurity to which Schatzberg refers is almost certainly present in Lesotho, but to it is coupled the insecurity of the South African state. In Arendt's terms, both political domains have relied on violence because they lack power and legitimacy. Ironically, however, by ruling through violence they assure that legitimacy will always be low. As Arendt argues: "To substitute violence for power can bring victory, but the price is very high; for it is not only paid by the vanquished, it is also paid by the victor in terms of his own power" (Arendt 1970: 53).

Since the 1986 coup the violence of the Lesotho and South African governments has been more clearly combined. Attacks on the ANC within Lesotho have already been noted, but other groups have not been immune. Many incidents of police brutality have been reported (*Moeletsi* 24 July 1988: 1). Individuals suspected of criminal or "subversive" activity have reportedly been picked up and taken across the border, where they are tortured by the South African police. In December 1987 one of the leaders of a group called the Lesotho Patriotic Youth Organization alleges he was abducted at gunpoint by three Afrikaans-speaking men who seemed to be of mixed race. They handcuffed and assaulted him, then drove him to a wooded area and carried out a mock execution before letting him go (*Moeletsi* 21 February 1988: 1). Similarly, when an LLA splinter group hijacked a bus of pilgrims on their way to see the pope in September 1988, it was South African commandos who stormed the bus and freed the passengers. A postmortem examination of one of the hijackers—who was reportedly only superficially wounded when taken into custody—revealed that he had had his throat slit and his skull smashed (Amnesty International 1989: 61).

The nature of the cooperation between Lesothoan and South African security forces is exemplified further by the so-called state of emergency against crime, which was announced in Lesotho in February 1988 (and which remains in force). After this the South African police became increasingly involved in Lesotho's internal affairs and were regularly seen within the country. With the assistance of the Lesotho police they conducted a draconian crackdown against suspected automobile thieves. Suspected thieves were among those who were reportedly abducted in Lesotho and tortured in South Africa (*Moeletsi* 16 October 1988: 1). The crackdown had considerable impact on public transport. In some districts a large number of vans used as taxis were confiscated. Many taxi drivers were beaten and taken into custody. While the campaign against crime is real, it also serves as a justification for continuing military rule. It has resulted in increased coercion in general and is a further indication of Lesotho's new desire to please South Africa.

The military government has made some attempts to increase its legitimacy. For example, it has held municipal elections in the capital city, Maseru. But the elections were not particularly well managed and few people voted. They were rejected by a number of prominent political leaders, who issued press statements calling for parliamentary elections and the restoration of the constitution adopted at independence in 1966 (Eldredge 1989: 22). More importantly, a new national assembly has also been called by Lekhanya's government to discuss the creation of a new constitution and the return to civilian rule in 1992. While many prominent political figures threatened initially to boycott this assembly, most eventually agreed to take part. Among them was former BCP head and exile Ntsu Mokhehle. Nonetheless, despite such participation it is not clear that the assembly is considered legitimate in the eyes of most of the people. A conference held in Maseru to discuss the future of Lesotho, for example, resolved that the national assembly was unrepresentative and had no mandate from the people (*Lesotho Today*, 19 July 1990: 3).

The political turmoil is leading to more active opposition. People have begun to compare their government to that of a Bantustan and are asking when the soldiers will "return to their tents." From 30 May until 29 August 1990 teachers waged a strike for higher pay, which forced the partial closure of many schools; despite government threats and declarations of the strike's illegality, teachers refused to call it off. In the second week of August, five members of the Lesotho National Teacher's Coordinating Committee were detained for several days under the provisions of the 1984 Internal Security Act. On 27 August, students reportedly marched through Maseru to present a petition to Lekhanya, their chief concern being a resolution of the strike. They were met by police and military forces, who declared their march an illegal gathering. Observers reported seeing students teargassed and beaten by soldiers. Several young men were also shot in other parts of town, again allegedly by government forces. Lesotho's acting minister of information, Kelebone Maope, told a BBC reporter that there were several incidents of violence on the part of youths, including the stoning of cars. One seventeen-year-old was shot by police, allegedly as they gave chase to stone throwers. This killing occurred in a week in which police reportedly also shot to death another youth in Maseru and assaulted and shot two shoe repairmen in a nearby village (*Work for Justice* 1990). It is clear that the Lesotho government is ruling by violence; what authority it has is increasingly tenuous.

Conclusion

Many of the human rights abuses that have been reported here can be linked to South African apartheid policies and the disruption caused by labor migration, but South Africa should not be used as a scapegoat to absolve from blame individuals within Lesotho. It is very unlikely that an end to apartheid will bring an automatic end to human rights abuses in the South African periphery.

Much of the conflict within Lesotho can be traced to struggles for positions of power and authority within the state and to general competition for valued and scarce resources. But these factors are not written against a cultural and psychological blank slate. Culture and psychology in Lesotho have been shaped by the collective experience of migrant labor and diminishing agricultural resources. This shared experience serves to reinforce militaristic values at the expense of norms that stress social harmony and peaceful cooperation. And positions of authority within the Lesotho state have given individuals ample opportunity to seek personal gratification, wealth, and prestige at the expense of others.

Violence is a concept with a multiplicity of references and metaphorical extensions (Parkin 1986: 204). But our attempts to describe and explain it have been made in terms of the experiences of individuals who suffer from it. There is little doubt that the cases of murder and assault described here violate "Sotho" standards of justice. And while the words used to describe these actions may be difficult to translate, the acts of violence themselves can be compared to actions elsewhere.

There are regular, perhaps universal, aspects of human psychology, social life, and governance that are conducive to the perpetuation of violence. For example, individuals who control the instruments of power (e.g., capital or arms) are likely to have high estimations of self-worth, if only for the moments when their access to these instruments is least regulated. When the control of arms is given to young soldiers with little ideological commitment to a higher authority, then these feelings may become intoxicating and violence may occur as a result. Such "intoxication" is best checked where norms and standards that reject the use of violence as a means to an end have been internalized. This is where anomie may have a role in the perpetuation of violence.

To understand violence, the nature of material conditions and group interests must always be taken into consideration. Scarcity may force otherwise peaceable people to engage in acts of violence merely to stay alive. In such cases, governments frequently resort to violence—and violence may become a matter of policy—because they are weak and there exists an intense struggle for the material benefits that accrue to their systems of patronage.

Lesotho's geographic situation and dependency on South Africa are unique, but its human rights situation is not. Governments here, as in many other parts of the world, have ruled more through violence than through consensus. For many in Lesotho violence and corruption have become a way of life and a highly developed subculture of violence and graft has emerged. Yet the *tsotsis* and political hooligans have not completely conquered those who believe in accountability and the rule of law. Brave lawyers have challenged the legitimacy of Lesotho's "state of emergency," academics have voiced their disapproval of the establishment of an appointed national assembly, and teachers and other workers have made the strike a common fact of life in Lesotho. Many have also risked their lives in other ways to voice opposition to the senseless killing of friends and relatives. One may say, in simplified Hegelian terms, that state violence and general political disorder have given rise to their antithesis in demonstrations for just wages, representative democracy, and respect for human rights. How far this is an accurate proposition for Lesotho, and indeed for South Africa, the next few years will tell.

Notes

"Life is war" is a rough translation of *Bophelo ke ntoa*, a phrase increasingly used in Lesotho by people describing contemporary circumstances.

1. This definition is similar to the objective definition suggested by Mers (1975).
2. Both the king and Jonathan are descendants of Lesotho's founder, Moshoeshoe I.
3. For details of the coup and the factions behind it, see Edgar (1987) and Legum (1988).
4. Lekhanya defended his actions by claiming Ramone was fleeing the scene after an attempted rape. Circumstances of the shooting give rise to suspicion that the young man may have crossed Lekhanya because he was angry about the latter's visits to women on the agricultural college campus. The commission of inquiry, however, accepted Lekhanya's version.
5. It needs to be noted, however, that murder rates in the United States have risen dramatically in the past several years. Washington, D.C., for example, reported a rise from 197 killings in 1986 to more than 430 in 1989. Washington now has the highest murder rate in the country, at 69 per 100,000 (*New York Times* 31 December 1989: 14).
6. Most of the following accounts are taken from the Sotho-language paper *Moeletsi oa Basotho*. In some cases the paper was only able to get one side of the story, so readers should keep in mind that these are allegations that the author has not always been able to substantiate independently. Nonetheless, familiarity with many such incidents makes the author feel confident of their general accuracy.
7. The Sotho proverb *Lesholu ke ntja, le lefa ka hloho ea lona* (A thief is a dog who pays with his head) is commonly heard in Lesotho these days. About the proverb, Sekese (1981: 188) wrote: *"Kahlolo ea masholu e bapisitsoe le ea lintja tse utsoang. Motho ea utsoang, eba o s'a tlotlolotse lebitso la botho ba hae, bo neng bo tshoana le joa batho ba bang; o se a sebelisana le lintja."* (The judgment concerning thieves can be compared to that made concerning thieving dogs. A person who steals has effectively erased his right to full humanity like other people; he is already one with the dogs.)

References

Africa Confidential. 1988. "Lesotho's King versus General." 4 March.
Amnesty International. 1989. *Amnesty International Report*. New York: Amnesty International.
Arendt, Hannah. 1970. *On Violence*. New York: Harcourt, Brace and World.

Breytenbach, W. J. 1975. *Commoners and Crocodiles in Lesotho*. Pretoria: Africa Institute of South Africa.
Cason, J., and M. Fleshman. 1985. "Lesotho May Vote after Fifteen Years." *Africa News* 24 (2): 1–3.
Edgar, Robert. 1987. "The Lesotho Coup of 1986." In *South Africa Review Four*, ed. Glenn Moss and Ingrid Obery, pp. 373–82. Johannesburg: Ravan.
Eldredge, Elizabeth. 1989. "Lesotho: Of Coups and Commoners." *Southern Africa Report* (Toronto) 5 (2): 20–22.
Gurr, T. R., ed. 1989. *Violence in America*. Newbury Park, Calif.: Sage.
Hanlon, Joseph. 1986. *Apartheid's Second Front: South Africa's War against Its Neighbours*. Harmondsworth: Penguin.
International Defense and Aid Fund (IDAF). 1985. *Massacre at Maseru: South African Aggression against Lesotho*. London: International Defense and Aid Fund.
Khaketla, B. M. 1972. *Lesotho, 1970: An African Coup under the Microscope*. Berkeley: University of California Press.
Legum, Colin, ed. 1981, 1984, 1988. *Africa Contemporary Records: Annual Survey and Documents*. New York: Africana.
Leselinyana la Lesotho. 1987. 9 October.
———. 1988. "Moetlo le Bolumeli" (Letter to the editor, "Custom and Faith"). 11 September, 2.
———. 1990. "Liphetoho 'Musong" (Change in the Government). 23 February, 1.
Lesotho Today. 1988. "Grave Crime Up." 11 February, 1.
———. 1990. "False Name Was a Joke." 29 March, 1.
———. 1990. 19 July, 3.
Magaia, Lina. 1988. *Dumba Nengue. Run for Your Life: Peasant Tales of Tragedy in Mozambique*. Trenton, N.J.: Africa World Press.
Mers, Perry. 1975. "The Nature of Political Violence. *Social and Economic Studies* 24 (2): 221–38.
Mirror (Lesotho). 1990. 23 March, 1.
Moeletsi oa Basotho. 1988. 21 February, 1.
———. 1988. 29 May, 1.
———. 1988. 12 June, 2.
———. 1988. 10 July, 2.
———. 1988. 24 July, 1.
———. 1988. 31 July, 2.
———. 1988. 28 September, 6.
———. 1988. 2 October, 5.
———. 1988. 9 October, 2.
———. 1988. 16 October, 1.
———. 1989. 18 June, 6.
———. 1989. 2 July, 1.

———. 1989. 11 November, 1.
———. 1989. 26 November, 1.
———. 1990. 21 January, 1.
New African. 1989. New African Yearbook 1987/1988.
New York Times. 1989. 31 December, 14.
Nietzsche, Friedrich. 1967. *On the Genealogy of Morals and Ecce Homo.* Reprint. New York: Vintage.
Pallister, D., S. Stewart, and I. Lepper. 1988. *South Africa Inc.: The Oppenheimer Empire.* London: Simon and Schuster.
Parkin, David. 1986. "Violence and Will." In *The Anthropology of Violence,* ed. David Riches, pp. 204–23. Oxford and New York: Basil Blackwell.
Schatzberg, Michael. 1988. *The Dialectics of Oppression in Zaire.* Bloomington: Indiana University Press.
Sekese, Azariele. 1981. *Mekhoa le Maele a Basotho.* Morija, Lesotho: Morija Sesuto Book Depot.
Shanafelt, Robert. 1989. "Talking Peace, Living Conflict: The Mental and the Material on the Borders of Apartheid." Ph.D. diss., University of Florida, Gainesville.
Spiegel, Andrew, and Emile Boonzaier. 1988. "Promoting Tradition: Images of the South African Past." In *South African Keywords,* ed. Emile Boonzaier and John Shalp, pp. 40–57. Cape Town: D. Philip.
Taussig, Michael. 1984. "Culture of Terror—Space of Death: Roger Casement's Putumayo Report and the Explanation of Torture." *Comparative Studies in Society and History* 26:476–97.
United Nations. 1983. "South Africa Condemned for Aggression against Lesotho." *United Nations Chronicle* 19: 14–18.
Wallman, Sandra. 1972. "Conditions of Non-Development: The Case of Lesotho." *Journal of Development Studies* 8 (2): 251–61.
Weisfelder, Richard. 1976. "The Decline of Human Rights in Lesotho: An Evaluation of Domestic and External Determinants." *Issue* 6: 22–33.
Work for Justice. 1990 (September). "Police Kill Teen-agers." 26: 1–2.
World Almanac and Book of Facts: Crime Rates by Region, Geographic Division, and State. 1989. New York: Newspaper Enterprises.

8

The National Language Question and Minority Language Rights in Africa: A Nigerian Case Study

F. NIYI AKINNASO

An extended debate is currently under way in Nigeria concerning the choice of a "national" language and the status of minority languages. On 23 March 1990 the executive secretary of the Nigerian Educational Research and Development Council (NERDC) announced the government's plan to embark on a language survey to prepare the country toward the adoption of what was variously described as the "national language," the "official language," and the "lingua franca" (*Guardian* 25 March 1990: 2; *New Nigerian* 26 March 1990: 15). The aim of the survey, which was to begin in April, was to determine which of Hausa, Igbo, and Yoruba would qualify for this status. These three languages had been officially recognized as "major" languages in both the National Policy on Education (NPE) of 1977 (revised 1981) and the Constitution of the Federal Republic of Nigeria of 1979 (revised 1989); they were to be taught in the nation's schools and would supplement English as the languages of legislative debate in the National Assembly, in the government's official publications, and in network news broadcasts.

But this is not the first time that the Nigerian government has made a move toward linguistic unification. On 21 November 1961—a year after independence—a bill came before the Nigerian Parliament urging that Hausa be adopted as Nigeria's lingua franca. On that occasion an Esan-speaking member of Parliament, Chief Anthony Enahoro, championed the course of more than 350 minority language groups in Nigeria when he declared: "As one who comes from a minority tribe, I deplore the continuing evidence in this country that people wish to impose their customs, their languages, and even more their ways of life upon the smaller tribes. My people have a language, and that language was handed down through a thousand years of tradition and custom. When the Benin Empire exchanged ambassadors with Portugal many of new Nigerian languages of today did not exist. How can they now, because the British (have) brought us together, wish to impose their language on us?" (cited in Dyewale 1977: 81).

This statement has a much wider context in Nigeria's political history in general and in the country's language politics in particular. Within this wider context, Enahoro's statement raises the fundamental issue of language as a right, advocating the rights of language minorities to participate in social, educational, economic, and political processes in *their own* country in *their own* languages. Partly as a result of Enahoro's speech, the bill failed in 1961 and the matter of a single indigenous lingua franca was officially shelved.

While the tone of Enahoro's speech was new, the message and the sentiment behind it were not. The speech grew out of more than a decade of agitation by linguistic minorities for recognition and greater political participation. Nor was the failure of the Hausa bill on this occasion a turning point in the fight for language and political rights of minorities. Rather, the turning point was the incorporation of specific human rights provisions in the Nigerian Constitution in 1958 on the recommendation of the Willink Commission of Inquiry, otherwise known as the Minorities Commission. This commission was set up in 1957 to look into the basis of political conflicts between language minorities and the dominant group in each of Nigeria's three major regions, conflicts that escalated as independence became more and more a reality. The conflicts arose from the fear or perception by linguistic minorities that the three major ethnolinguistic groups—Hausa in the north, Yoruba in the west, and Igbo in the east—would dominate and oppress them upon the attainment of independence from Great Britain. Consequently they began to demand the creation of more states essentially based on ethnolinguistic groupings.

Today, thirty years after independence, there are twenty-one states in Nigeria, representing the end product of a long process of political evolution set in motion and fueled by language minorities in various parts of the country. A brief sketch of Nigeria's political development is necessary as a background against which to measure the present political and sociolinguistic situation.

From Regionalism to Statism

Before colonization in the nineteenth century, Nigeria was a sprawling territory of apparently unrelated ethnolinguistic groups, each with its own distinctive language, history, and traditional patterns of religious, social, economic, and political organization. Because most transactions were carried out within the ethnic group, there was no need for a language policy and language rights was not one of the problems to be dealt with. However, once the colonial government brought the various groups together under the same political organization, the emergence of various movements on behalf of minority language rights became inevitable.

During the early years of colonization, the country was ruled as three distinct political units: the Northern Protectorate, the Southern Protectorate, and Lagos Colony. From the point of view of the colonial administration, the recognized language in the north was Hausa, while Yoruba and Igbo (the British called it Ibo) were the recognized languages in the south (i.e., including Lagos Colony). The merger of Lagos Colony with the Southern Protectorate in 1906 was inevitable in view of the geographical, cultural, and linguistic affinities with the western part of the protectorate. Thus there were two major political units when the protectorates were amalgamated into one nation in 1914.

However, a three-unit political arrangement resurfaced again in 1939, although in a different form and for quite different reasons. Partly in recognition of major ethnolinguistic differences between the Igbo and the Yoruba peoples in the south, the Southern Protectorate was split in 1939 into the Eastern and Western provinces, each with its own lieutenant governor. This arrangement was given constitutional backing in the Richards Constitution of 1947, which divided Nigeria into three regions: Northern, Eastern, and Western. That constitution also introduced the first official language policy, recommending the use of Hausa in the Northern Region and English in the south (i.e., Eastern and Western regions) and in national administration. However, the use of Hausa as the official language of the north was reversed in 1954, when English was named the official language of all regional and national administrations.

The amalgamation of the protectorates in 1914 opened up a complicated ethnolinguistic landscape and heightened intergroup contact that became more stressful as different groups had to compete for access to limited resources and social rewards. The eventual restructuring of the country into three regions gave political prominence to the three dominant ethnolinguistic groups: the Hausa/Fulani peoples in the north, the Igbo-speaking people in the east, and the Yoruba-speaking people in the west. But between the major ethnic groups, especially in the middle belt and the delta areas in the south, were caught hundreds of minority ethnolinguistic groups whose distinctiveness from the larger groups was hardly initially recognized by the colonial government.

Eventually, however, it became impossible for the government to ignore the linguistic minorities. As independence became more and more a possibility they began to demand separation from the dominant groups, the most prominent agitation coming from the Edo, Esan, Urhobo, and other linguistic minorities in the Western Region who wanted to be separated from the dominant Yoruba group. On the recommendation of the Willink Commission, the colonial government decided to maintain the status quo until independence in 1960. The new independent government eventually granted the separation in 1963, leading to the creation of the Midwestern Region. Four years later, regionalism gave way to statism as the then military government carved twelve states out of the existing four regions. While the declared intent was to improve national consciousness and political integration, the fragmentation of the regions increased the possibilities of political autonomy for hitherto unrecognized minorities. The consequence was increased demand for more recognition by other minorities still locked within the new states. Thus the number of states increased from twelve to nineteen in 1976 and from nineteen to twenty-one in 1987. The number of local government councils has correspondingly increased from just over 100 in the early colonial days to 453 in 1989. While ethnic and linguistic loyalties are critical factors in the creation of the new states, it is at the level of local governments that the isomorphism between linguistic and political boundaries is most pronounced, as virtually all the local government boundaries coincide with language or dialect boundaries.

One of the major consequences of the creation of new, often smaller, political units is that the new units provide a basis for the development of new identities and loyalties, thereby making it possible for many of the languages previously neglected in the larger units to be used in new networks and for new functions. Thus, while Hausa, Igbo, and Yoruba continue to enjoy the high status accorded them since colonial days, many more languages have come to national consciousness and several others have become very prominent in state and local government contexts.

However, while the creation of new political boundaries, often along language cleavages, has led to the emergence of hitherto unknown languages on the political and educational scenes as well as in the mass media, the current debate in Nigeria concerning official language policy, especially the drive toward the selection of a single "national" language, stands to undermine the status of minority languages and may lead to a serious political crisis, as it did in India. There is a dual need for a serious examination of the political and language situation in Nigeria and an assessment of the language rights of minority groups, especially their rights to social, religious, educational, economic, and political participation in their own languages. This chapter examines Nigeria's language policy against the background of the nation's history and sociolinguistic situation, assesses the country's language rights record, raises some critical issues, and provides some directions for the future. While concentrating on the Nigerian case, the discussion also provides historical and comparative perspectives.

A Dual System of Rights

The study of language rights in Nigeria must be viewed against the people's perception of what human rights are. It is therefore necessary to state at the outset that a dual system of rights is maintained in Nigeria, as in other African nations: (1) precolonial, traditional conceptions of rights embedded in local customs and (2) postcolonial, Western conceptions of rights as contained in the Universal Declaration of Human Rights. While the latter system of rights is a creation of colonial constitutions, the former is embedded in the customs and traditions of the people and underlies day-to-day social interactions. Moreover, in the Western conceptions human rights are considered universalistic, being applicable to all human beings irrespective of their geographic location. By contrast, in local tradition and custom human rights exist within the context of particular groups. Comparing Western and traditional Yoruba conceptions of human rights, Marasinghe points to another critical difference that makes the survival of traditional conceptions of human rights more enduring:

> . . . it is important to recognize that the values we (Westerners) embody within our own conceptions of human rights are identical with the value system which traditional societies endeavor to protect through their conceptions of human rights. But there is one difference: While our conceptions are guaranteed to the extent to which our rulers guarantee them through tightly drafted constitutional documents, theirs become institutionalized as an essential part of their own social organization which guarantees their existence in society. This makes their conceptions of rights less vulnerable and more permanent than ours. (Marasinghe 1984: 43–44)

Today both Western and traditional conceptions of human rights coexist among the Yoruba, as among other ex-colonial groups, leading to conflicting perceptions of what human rights are. In general but by no means exclusively, traditional conceptions of human rights predominate in most informal transactions within the family and the kin group, especially in the rural areas, while Western conceptions of human rights are usually evoked in formal transactions, especially in the urban areas. I shall not distinguish between the two systems of rights in the following discussion of language rights because of the centrality of language to formal and informal transactions in all areas of national life and, more importantly, because of the fundamental importance of language rights in both traditional and Western conceptions of human rights. In order to appreciate the importance of language rights to educational and civic participation in Nigeria, it is necessary to review the language situation in the country. It is to such an appraisal that I now turn.

The Language Situation in Nigeria

A description of Nigeria's language situation calls for a multilayered analysis if the complexity of the linguistic landscape is to be fully understood. At one level of analysis, it can be said that there are three major types of languages in Nigeria. First, there are three exogenous languages—English, French, and Arabic—each with its own distinctive history, uses, and functions. Second, there are the indigenous languages, usually said to be about four hundred in number (Hansford, Bendor-Samuel, and Stanford 1976), sharing a total population of nearly 110 million speakers (recent UNESCO estimates). Third, there is a "neutral" language, Pidgin English, which is a hybrid of exogenous (mainly English) and indigenous (mainly southern Nigerian) languages (for more detailed discussions of the language situation in Nigeria, see Adetugbo 1978, 1984 [English]; Akinnaso and Ogunbiyi 1990 [Arabic]; Agheyisi 1984 [minority languages]; and Akinnaso 1988, 1989 [all languages]). At another level of analysis, it would appear that the languages are hierarchically ordered, while revealing contrasting and overlapping characteristics as well as functions. A brief examination of the three language types is sufficient to reveal the salient features.

Exogenous Languages

Each of the three exogenous languages—English, Arabic, and French—has its own history, uses, and functions. The first of these languages to arrive in Nigeria was Arabic, which accompanied Islam and trans-Saharan trade into the northern territory of present-day Nigeria in the ninth century A.D. Although initially restricted to religious contexts, Arabic soon developed into the language of judicial and political administration, of social and commercial interactions, and of literacy and scholarly activities and remained so until well into the nineteenth century. Despite its decline, Arabic remains the predominant language of Islamic worship and Koranic pedagogy and it continues to be taught as part of Islamic religious education in Koranic schools and in some Western-type schools (for further details on the rise and fall of Arabic in Nigeria, see Akinnaso and Ogunbiyi 1990).

The decline in the status and functions of Arabic was caused by the increasing status and functions of English, which came into the country first as the language of traders in the sixteenth century, later as a missionary language in the eighteenth century, and then as the colonial language in the following century. Finally, it was adopted as the nation's official language by the middle of the present century. Today English is the de facto official language of Nigeria, being the predominant language of government and the bureaucracy, education, (higher) commerce, mass communication, international trade and politics, and science and technology. Moreover, it is used as the language of interethnic communication among the educated elite. English is thus the most important language in Nigeria today in terms of status and range of functions (for further details, see Adetugbo 1978, 1984).

French, the least popular of Nigeria's exogenous languages, lacks the historical root and the range of functions that the others have had. Consequently, it has the fewest number of users and the least appeal to learners, its main uses being limited to diplomatic and educational contexts and border communication with neighboring Francophone countries. French is essentially a foreign language in Nigeria, taught only for the above purposes in some schools and universities.

While English and French could be classified as second and foreign languages, respectively, the classification of Arabic is problematic. To be sure, Arabic was once an important second language in Nigeria; but it yielded that status to English at the turn of the century. However, the shift from Arabic to English is not complete, partly because Arabic still dominates Islamic worship and Koranic pedagogy and partly because a dialect of Arabic has survived as the mother tongue of a small population in northeastern Borno state. Consequently, while Arabic may be classified as a foreign language, in contradistinction to English, speakers of Shuwa Arabic in Borno state regard it as an authentic indigenous language. Between the two extremes, however, many Muslims consider Arabic as a second language and argue that they and their children learn Arabic with the same zeal and enthusiasm with which English is learned.

Indigenous Languages

Nigeria's indigenous languages vary greatly in their demographic, functional, structural, and spatial characteristics. Using number of speakers, range of functions, extent of development, use in formal education, degree of official recognition, etc., as criteria for classification, the languages display a tripartite classification. The terms of the classification are both conceptual and real. While the terms "national," "regional," and "minor" are cleverly avoided in policy documents, policymakers and the Nigerian public conceive of Nigerian languages in these terms. More importantly, as we shall see later, federal and state governments confer statuses on the languages on the basis of this classification and allocate resources for their development accordingly.

The highest category consists of the three "major" languages: Hausa (about 22 million speakers), Yoruba (about 20 million), and Igbo (about 17 million). This means that the three languages are spoken by about 53 percent of the population. Native speakers of Hausa are distributed unevenly across eight northern states, whereas Yoruba and Igbo native speakers are respectively distributed, albeit unevenly, across six states in the west and midwest and four states in the east and midwest (for more detailed statistics, see Akinnaso forthcoming c). These three languages have a double classification, for they join nine others to form the second category of "regional" languages. The nine other languages are (figures in parentheses indicate speaker population in millions): Fulfulde, also called Fula(ni), (8.71); Efik (5.43); Kanuri (4.2); Tiv (2.56); Ijo (2.15); Edo (1.8); Nupe (1.23); Igala (1.12); and Idoma (0.9). All together, these nine languages are spoken by about 27 percent of the population. The remaining 20 percent speak as many as 380 or more local languages that form the third category of small-group, "minority" languages (for an account of the problems and prospects of this category of languages, see Agheyisi 1984). Since the creation of states, some of these minority languages have come into prominence within their respective states or local governments. Nevertheless, well over 250 minority languages are still yearning for recognition and lack orthographies.

The distribution of the numerous minority languages presents a highly complicated linguistic landscape in which more than fifty languages are spoken in some states (e.g., Gongola and Plateau), whereas other states (e.g., Imo and Oyo) are virtually linguistically homogeneous. On the whole, more than two-thirds of the minority languages are spoken natively in the northern parts of the country, while the remaining languages cluster largely around Bendel, Rivers, Cross-River, and Akwa-Ibom states in the south.

The patterns of contact between Nigerian languages have been greatly influenced by historical, religious, political, commercial, and geographical factors. For example, geographical contiguity, trade, the ideology of "northernization," the Islamic religion, the use of Hausa as a regional official language during the colonial period, and the association of the language with the Hausa-Fulani social and cultural elite conferred both utilitarian values and prestige on Hausa, thus attracting many northerners to learn it. Furthermore, in varying degrees throughout the federation, the shifting nature of political boundaries since colonial times has continued to alter and redefine patterns of contact between minority and majority languages (Agheyisi 1984; Akinnaso forthcoming b).

However, while linguistic minorities in the north accept and use

Hausa as a lingua franca, no indigenous language in the south gained such a status except Efik, whose geographical spread is essentially limited to only two states, Cross-River and Akwa-Ibom; its adoption as a lingua franca in these states was aided by missionary and colonial literacies that provided instruction in Efik in the second half of the nineteenth century. There are various reasons for the differential patterns of sociolinguistic development between the north and the south. On one hand, the numerous factors that promoted the spread of Hausa in the north were absent in the south. Christianity did not provide the kind of common religious heritage and binding web that Islam provided in the north, for local religions and customs persisted in the south, with elaborate traditions maintained around kingdoms, chiefdoms, clans, and local shrines—traditions that are embedded in language and other forms of symbolism and jealously preserved by various ethnolinguistic groups. In particular, the rich heritage of the Benin Empire of the Edo-speaking group, situated in the middle of the south, served as a counterforce to the powerful Yoruba kingdom to the west and the relatively acephalous, yet powerful, Igbo social organization to the east. The relatively large size of these three groups and political rivalry among them have made language domination by any one group impossible. Besides, Pidgin English developed into a lingua franca during the early years of European contact, first in the coastal areas, later throughout the south, and lately the entire country. By the time the ethnic groups in the south began to interact politically, the English language had been acquired by the nationalist politicians of the time and so provided a lingua franca among them.

Pidgin English

While English continues to perform "high" language functions in Nigeria, Pidgin English has almost taken over the role of lingua franca in informal domains. From its origins in the early days of European contact to the present stage of creolization in parts of Bendel state, Pidgin English has developed from a mere trade language to the most popular medium of intergroup communication in various heterogeneous communities throughout the country. While commercial centers continue to provide the typical settings for its routine use, Pidgin English is also widely used in public institutions and service centers. It has also made significant inroads into the print and electronic media; there are now regular newspaper columns, news broadcasts, and various entertainment programs in Pidgin English. Furthermore, Pidgin English is also used in billboard advertisements, in newspapers, and on radio and television all over the country. A language once confined to the coastal areas, Pidgin English has now spread all over the country and even beyond. Of particular concern to educators and policymakers today is the gradual adoption of Pidgin English as a lingua franca in many educational institutions, especially federal government colleges, which, as a rule, admit children from different ethnolinguistic backgrounds. However, it remains stigmatized in official domains because it is still viewed as a "corrupt" form of language, is largely associated with illiterate and "uneducated" users, and poses a threat to standard (Nigerian) English that is taught in schools and used in formal settings. Consequently, Pidgin English has had no place in the nation's language policies, despite its widening influence. There is a sharp contrast in importance and value, for instance, between Pidgin English in Nigeria and Tok Pisin, a Melanesian pidgin, which has been elevated to the status of official language in Papua New Guinea.

Language Hierarchy

The three types of languages described above form an interesting five-tier system of language hierarchy when such factors as degree of official recognition, prestige, extent of development, contexts, and range of use are taken into consideration. This hierarchy is, of course, heuristic rather than official. Although the terms of the classification derive from official and public perception of the languages, none of the terms is actually used in policy documents.

At the top of the hierarchy is English, the official language of the nation. Although Hausa, Igbo, and Yoruba are recognized as official languages alongside English in the constitution and as "major" languages in the NPE, they are generally also regarded as national languages, next in rank to English. The third category is the group of regional languages. The list of these languages varies from twelve to more than twenty, depending on what factors are considered. For one thing, the national languages have a dual classification, being also considered regional languages in their respective native states. Moreover, as indicated above, the list of regional languages has swelled by the creation of new states and local government councils that has brought a number of hitherto unrecognized languages into prominence. For example, Kaduna state alone is now said to have five regional languages: Fulani, Gwari, Jaba, Kaje, and Kurama. Some of these languages had little or no chance of rising to this status when Katsina, a predominantly Hausa-speaking state, was part of the old Kaduna state. The fourth category, local languages, consists of the more than three hundred minority languages, with speakers ranging from a few to several thousands or even a million and above. The fifth and last-ranking language in the hierarchy is Pidgin English, which is generally regarded as neutral, although the recent emergence of a population of children in parts of Bendel state for whom Pidgin English has come to function as a mother tongue calls the neutrality of the language to question. Of course, the above analysis does not reflect Arabic and French, which may be regarded as languages for special purposes, the former for Islamic worship and Koranic pedagogy and the latter for diplomatic relations and foreign language learning.

It should be noted that each language is not an island unto itself nor are the ranks as rigidly compartmentalized as the above description seems to suggest. While it is true that some of the languages perform certain exclusive functions, considerable functional overlap exists among many of them. For example, like English, the national and regional languages perform specific "high" functions, being used as media of instruction at specific levels of education and in certain forms or levels of mass communication. Similarly, depending on geographical location, two or more of English, Pidgin English, Hausa, and Efik are in constant competition as the language of interethnic communication. Furthermore, in various communities throughout the country individual and societal multilingualism exists, promoting constant interaction among the different languages and speech repertoires. Consequently, a great deal of borrowing exists, especially from English and Arabic to various Nigerian languages and from one Nigerian language to another.

This complex linguistic landscape explains the centrality of languages to social, educational, and political life in Nigeria today. Language is not only the source of individual identity but also the basis for social, cultural, educational, and political life. Political units (states, local government councils, and sometimes cities and towns), cultural troupes (e.g., musical and theater groups), communication networks (television and radio stations), and the print media are all essentially divided along linguistic lines. Even markers of identity, such as personal names, are distinguishable by language. It is no wonder, then, that language loyalties override most other questions that form part of the body politic. The emphasis on language in national development planning should therefore occasion no surprise. For present purposes, the critical question to ask is, to what extent are the language rights of ethnic minorities accommodated within the nation's language policies and development programs?

Language Policy and Language Rights

Two important themes underlie Nigeria's language policy: the desire to achieve unity—i.e., national integration—and the recognition of diversity—i.e., cultural pluralism and the rights of individual citizens and groups. The integrative policies are reflected in (1) the requirement that three major Nigerian languages (Hausa, Igbo, and Yoruba) be used, in addition to English, in the National House of Assembly (Nigerian Constitution, Section 53) and (2) the requirement that every schoolchild learn at least one of these three languages, in addition to his or her mother tongue and, of course, English (NPE, Section 1:8).

Recognition of linguistic diversity and language rights, on the other hand, is reflected in three related policies: (1) the proviso that in addition to English each state may select one or more Nigerian languages spoken in the state for the purposes of conducting the business of its House of Assembly (Nigerian Constitution, Section 95); (2) the requirement that the mother tongue or the language of the immediate community be used in early primary education (NPE, Sections 2:11[3] and 3:15[4]); and (3) the additional provision in the revised constitution that "[g]overnment shall promote the learning of indigenous languages" (Section 19[4]). For convenience, I shall henceforth refer to these three policies as the "rights" policies. Reinforcing the "rights" policies is the notion of equal opportunities reflected in the constitution under the term "federal character," defined as "the distinctive desire of the peoples of Nigeria to promote national unity, foster national loyalty and give every citizen of Nigeria a sense of belonging to the nation" (Section 277).

The general implications and impact of Nigeria's language policies have been discussed elsewhere (Akinnaso 1988, 1989, forthcoming c). The focus here is on the implications of the policies for the preservation and maintenance of minority language rights. In this regard, it is interesting to note that the "rights" policies reflect two important orientations toward language. First, these policies manifest a language-as-resource orientation that sees minority languages as potential resources not only for their users but also for the nation as a whole. Second, the policies reveal a language-as-right orientation that sees minority languages as a right to which their speakers are entitled. As argued elsewhere (Akinnaso 1989, forthcoming b), both orientations are congruent with the ideologies of linguistic pluralism, which sees linguistic diversity as a national resource, and vernacularization, which emphasizes the development and maintenance of indigenous languages. More importantly, both orientations converge in the initial mother tongue education policy, which has come to be the cornerstone of the national policy on primary education. It is this policy more than anything else that guarantees the right of every Nigerian to literacy education in his or her mother tongue (for a fuller discussion of the mother tongue education policy, see Akinnaso forthcoming a).

It is important to note, however, that the "rights" policies did not evolve overnight. As indicated at the beginning of this chapter, the foundation was laid with the emergence of a powerful movement in the south on behalf of minority language rights, leading to the establishment of the Minorities Commission in 1957 and the subsequent incorporation of specific human rights provisions in the constitution in 1958. The powerful speech by Enahoro before Parliament in 1961 marked another milestone because it cautioned the government about the possible dangers of linguistic unification policies that fail to recognize the language rights of minorities.

The government took decisive steps to recognize minority language rights in 1977, 1979, and 1989, when the three "rights" policies were enunciated. In addition, the government also recognizes the plight of linguistic minorities in the creation of political units. But perhaps the most decisive step for language development was the reorganization of the Language Center, which was established in 1971. In July 1980, the federal government reconstituted the status and role of the Center and redesignated it the National Language Center (NLC). Although the major mission of the NLC is to implement language-related policies formulated at the national level, it is specifically charged with the statutory responsibility of promoting Nigerian languages and encouraging efforts already made to foster them at state level and at various research institutions.

These efforts have yielded interesting results for language minorities. The mother tongue education policy enunciated in 1977 encourages literacy in traditional tongues, leading to the provision of orthographies for various minority languages (for details, see Akinnaso forthcoming a). In Rivers state alone, for example, at least twenty-eight local languages have been developed for use in primary education (Agheyisi 1984: 247). On the whole, it is estimated that approximately one hundred Nigerian languages now have orthographies of varying degrees of standardization. Much of the success of these efforts is owed not necessarily to the NLC but to the activities of various agencies, including state ministries of education, state-owned and voluntary arts and culture organizations, the NERDC, languages and linguistics departments in the universities, associations of teachers of indigenous languages, and various boards and committees (e.g., the Local Language Committee of Niger State) working on the development of various minority languages.

The additional provision in the revised constitution of 1989, ensuring government support for the learning of indigenous languages, reinforces the possibility that all Nigerian languages will be developed and maintained. The controversy that led to the inclusion of this provision is particularly instructive as it mirrored the minority languages movement during the 1961 parliamentary debate on linguistic unification. First, like the 1961 bill, the motion before the Constitution Review Committee (CRC) was a call for linguistic unification, although the emphasis was on promoting three major languages—Hausa, Igbo, and Yoruba—instead of just one. Second, it was a coalition of CRC members from minority language groups that not only defeated the motion but also led the committee to recommend an unqualified pluralism that the government later accepted (for reports on the debate, see *Newswatch* 20 March 1989: 13–18).

The legislative language policy of 1979 that makes it a constitutional requirement for each state to select its own language(s) of legislation made it possible for the legislative houses to select appropriate local languages, although for political reasons these efforts have been much less successful than those in the educational domain (Brann 1985; Akinnaso forthcoming c). For example, linguistic fragmentation and the absence of a clearly dominant language in some states have mitigated against the choice of a local language. However, the fact that some states could not choose a local language for the purposes of legislative debate does not mean that local languages are not being developed for official use in other domains. In each of the linguistically heterogeneous states several local languages have been developed for use in primary education and the mass media.

Although the federal government, through the "rights" policies, recognizes the validity of efforts to develop and preserve the linguistic and cultural heritage of the various ethnolinguistic groups, it is at state and local government levels that the efforts are actually being made. Thus in mass communication, for example, state governments have jumped at the "rights" policies by making use of the mass media in promoting broad-based community awareness in various local languages. Accordingly, state-owned radio and television stations broadcast a variety of programs in local minority languages and even dialects. Such programs include news broadcasts, traditional performances (music, drama, storytelling, festivals, and rituals), announcements of local events, advertisements, and music requests. Similarly, many local newspapers and several occasional publications have sprung up in different states, each promoting one local language or the other. Not even Pidgin English is excluded from performing these functions (Akinnaso 1989).

In local government administration, the ability to speak the local language, especially the appropriate dialect(s), is often the best guarantee for access to political participation, job opportunities, and other social rewards. Although records are normally kept in English, business meetings and negotiations, mobilization tours, campaign rallies, and even customary court proceedings are often conducted in the appropriate local language or dialect. In a sense, then, states and local government councils provide a territorial dimension in the exercise of language rights by bringing into prominence all the languages and dialects within their territories. True, the Nigerian government has never considered the possibility of language districting as in Canada and Finland (see McRae 1978), but language has always been an important factor in the creation of political units—regions, states, and local government councils.

The local languages reign supreme in the traditional government domains headed by obas, emirs, and chiefs. Although Western conceptions of human rights are embedded in the statutes that regulate the conduct of traditional governments, traditional conceptions of human rights underlie most transactions. The emphasis on the importance of the local language in traditional government should therefore occasion no surprise, for the local language is considered central to the exercise of traditional rituals as well as traditional civil rights and obligations. This recalls a recent case, the much-publicized competition for the post of the sultan of Sokoto. One of the reasons given for the rejection of a top contender for the post was his reply in English to a memo written in Hausa, the supposed official language of the emirate. Although there were other political considerations at work, this particular case highlights the importance of the appropriate vernacular in local, especially traditional, politics.

Language as an Instrument of National Integration

We have seen that due consideration is increasingly being given to minority language rights in the formulation of language policies in Nigeria. Where attempts have been made at outright linguistic unification, the bill or motion to bring such policies into being has been soundly defeated. Yet the integrative policies mentioned earlier are needed in order to avert possible centrifugal effects that might result from a multilingual policy that encourages each group to use its own language without due consideration for (a) unifying national language(s).

There are other compelling political reasons for the integrative policies. First, like other ex-colonial nations, Nigeria is eager to replace English with an indigenous official language, as the persistent use of the colonial language continues to hurt the sense of dignity and self-respect as an independent nation. In a sense, then, the integrative policies represent a struggle against linguistic colonialism. Second, it would appear that Nigeria is working toward a language policy that would emphasize an indigenous language that all members of the nationality could identify with as "our" language and could then use to contrast themselves with members of other nationalities (Fishman 1968). Incidentally, this reenacts the trend in the Western world of the mid-nineteenth century, when language became accepted as the most important single defining characteristic of nationality (Inglehart and Woodward 1972).

Unfortunately, however, such integrative policies tend to undermine minority language rights because their call for integration into a unified national culture necessarily contrasts with the affirmation of cultural and linguistic pluralism entailed in the "rights" policies. While it has been possible for language minorities to tolerate the officialization of Hausa, Igbo, and Yoruba as "major" languages, it is not likely that agreement will ever be reached on the choice of just one of these languages as the "national" or "official" language.

It is worthwhile to note the sociolinguistic reasons why the officialization of the three major languages has been tolerated so far. First, the additive numbers and spread of speakers, range of functions, and degree of development of the three major languages make them tower above the remaining languages put together. It is estimated that at least 70 percent of the total Nigerian population speaks one of the three major languages as a first or second language. Furthermore, each of the three languages has had over a century of development and use in literacy education. Given such a situation, acquiescence is the most politically expedient response from language minorities.

Second, the wording of the policies that confer higher status on the three languages is very cautious and imprecise and no systematic guidelines for action have so far been provided, thus making it difficult for the government to enforce the policies. So far, the only status term used in policy documents in reference to the three languages is the term "major" (NPE, Section 1:8). The policy in question sounds more like a general statement of principle and has a futuristic ring about it: "the Government considers it to be in the interest of national unity that each child should be encouraged to learn one of the three major languages other than his own mother tongue." The constitution cleverly avoids using any status term at all, stating only that "The business of the National Assembly shall be conducted in English and in Hausa, Igbo and Yoruba *when adequate arrangements have been made therefor*" (Section 53; emphasis added). I have italicized the temporal clause to emphasize that the implementation of the policy in regard to the three Nigerian languages is presented as a matter for the future. At the moment, then, the general attitude to the integrative policies seems to be "let's wait and see." This attitude of indifference partly explains the general lack of implementation of the integrative policies (see Akinnaso 1988, 1989, forthcoming b; Fakuade 1989).

However, no matter how vaguely it is couched, any policy that confers "national" or "official" status on any single Nigerian language is bound to be seriously resisted. Any chosen language—even Hausa, which allegedly has the largest number and widest spread of speakers—will be in the minority, while speakers of the remaining languages are likely to form a coalition to oppose it. Indeed, if Hausa is chosen as the national language, it will readily be construed as an attempt to establish the political hegemony of the north over the south by placing the latter at a linguistic disadvantage, thus replicating the situation in India, where Hindi, a northern language, was promulgated as the national language. The resultant strife may be even more severe than it was in India. Such strife can be averted only if Nigeria can learn from the experiences of ancient, medieval, and contemporary nations in Africa and elsewhere in dealing with matters of national language and minority language rights.

Historical and International Perspectives

For most of recorded time, multilingual societies have been the rule rather than the exception (for detailed historical reviews, see Inglehart and Woodward 1972; Guy 1989). In the ancient world all major states and empires, including Egypt, Babylon, Persia, China, and the Roman Empire, were multilingual. For example, the Roman Empire encompassed speakers of Italic, Greek, Celtic, Basque, Slavic, Semitic, and Germanic languages, among others. Equally multilingual were the medieval and early modern states, ranging from the Ottoman, Russian, and Austrian (later Austro-Hungarian) empires to the precolonial states of the Aztecs in Central America, the Benin in West Africa, and the Mogul in Southeast Asia. In none of these ancient, medieval, and early modern states was the principle of "one nation = one language" successfully pursued, although one or more languages emerged as linguae francae in many empires. In the case of the Roman Empire, for example, not only did Latin emerge as a lingua franca, but it eventually took root as a native language in many areas outside its Roman homeland and developed into the language of learning in medieval Europe. These developments took place without the Romans ever promulgating a language policy that would give preeminence to Latin. In those empires where attempts were made to impose a language on the people, linguistic minorities have revolted, often leading to a reversal of such policy, official recognition of the language of the revolting group, or the granting of independence to such a group. Thus, although social, economic, and political factors were also at work, language loomed large as a factor in political conflicts and in the subsequent division of most empires into distinct nation-states (for example, see Inglehart and Woodward [1972: 366–70] for an account of the role of language in the eventual dissolution of the Austro-Hungarian empire).

The same multilingual picture still obtains in the modern world, not only in the postcolonial nations of Africa and Asia but also in Europe, Australia, and elsewhere. The situation in the former Soviet Union is particularly instructive. In recognition of high multilingualism within the Union, Soviet language policy accords official status to several dozen languages. While the Russian language is spoken by about 50 percent of the population (of 280 million), each constituent republic uses its local indigenous language as its official language, for local education, commerce, industry, broadcasting, cultural affairs, and so on. Moreover, minority languages are recognized, developed, and maintained within each republic. Moscow's reaction to the current dispute over Nagorno-Karabakh is particularly instructive (Guy 1989: 51). Armenians in Nagorno-Karabakh, located within the Azerbaijan Republic, are complaining that their language and culture have been suppressed by the Azerbaijanis (whose language is related to Turkish). Moscow's proposal, involving official status and enhanced institutional support for the Armenian language and culture in Nagorno-Karabakh, shows that what is seen as the solution is official recognition for linguistic minorities rather than insistence on a single unifying language.

Even where attempts have been made to apply the principle of "one nation = one language," the geographical reality of language distribution has frustrated the efforts. For example, in their bid to apply the monolingual model in adjusting political boundaries in Europe after World War I, the treaty makers of Versailles were forced to throw in the towel when dealing with Eastern Europe, where they had to leave German speakers in Czechoslovakia, Turks in Bulgaria, Hungarians in Romania, and so on, while creating Yugoslavia with half-a-dozen different "official" languages. As Inglehart and Woodward (1972: 358) observed, the treaty makers were thus forced to show "an unprecedented respect for the rights of linguistic minorities." In none of these nations today can the problem of minority language rights be swept under the carpet.

Elsewhere, especially in Africa, the linguistic situation became even more complicated after European colonial expansion in the eighteenth and nineteenth centuries. The erstwhile British and French empires became probably the most linguistically complex political entities in history, making the problem of minority language rights a much more serious political issue. In these ex-colonial nations, language policy issues are further complicated by the imposition of colonial languages at the expense of indigenous languages, which were not developed at all in the French colonies, while only a limited number were developed in the British territories. This notwithstanding, ex-colonial nations have been very cautious in their language planning efforts, especially in regard to the national language issue, partly because of the multiplicity of languages to choose from and partly because of the fragility of the political situation.

Three different methods have been adopted in choosing a national language in these nations. At one extreme, a few languages, usually those spoken by relatively large populations, are promoted to national status and taught in the schools. Thus, two such languages are recognized in Kenya, three in Nigeria, four in Zaire, five in Senegal, and six in Guinea. At the other extreme, some countries, such as India, attempt to hazard the attendant tension by naming one of the indigenous languages as the national and official language. Between the two extremes is a third approach—the choice of a relatively "neutral" language as the official language, the most illustrative case being the choice of Swahili, a trade language, as the national and official language in Tanzania.

There is, of course, no magic solution to the national language question, as each country must be mindful of the constraints within which options must be examined (see Foster forthcoming). These constraints typically include the nature of the colonial heritage, including the language policy pursued by the former colonial regime; the degree of linguistic fragmentation within the nation-state; the extent and effects of ethnic, religious, and economic cleavages between groups; the existence of a lingua franca that may be acceptable as the national language; the extent of development of the local languages; the people's attitudes toward particular languages; and the financial strength of the nation. The combination of these factors explains, for example, why Pidgin English is stigmatized and remains a low-status lingua franca in Nigeria, while in Papua New Guinea Melanesian pidgin bids fair to become the national language. The case of Swahili in the East African nations of Tanzania and Kenya is even more instructive. Both countries appear to have much in common: multilingualism, including a multiplicity of Bantu- and Nilotic-speaking populations; a common colonial heritage; and a common lingua franca, Swahili. Despite these shared features, however, the efforts to elevate Swahili to national language status were differently received in the two countries: the attempts in Tanzania have been successful and those in Kenya are almost certain to fail because in the latter situation religion and ethnicity weighed more heavily in the considerations than in the former.

Some Future Directions

The above findings and discussion provide three lessons for Nigeria and for other African nations as well. The first important lesson has to do with the need to confront the burden of history and contemporary social realities. In view of the historical legacy of English; its contemporary importance in education, science and technology, international politics, world trade, and the global information economy; and its relative neutrality—the fact that no indigenous ethnic group in the country can claim it as its native language—what role, other than the symbolic, will an indigenous national language play in Nigeria? If English is going to remain as the de facto official language, as it still is even in India and Tanzania, why risk the political tension that may attend the promulgation of an indigenous language as the national official language?

This leads to the second lesson, namely, that Nigeria must consider the relative weights of the various constraints that may affect the choice of a national language. These constraints include the country's north-south dichotomy along with other coinciding cleavages such as religion; marked differences in educational development; and differential contribution to the national economy. Already, the north-south dichotomy has precipitated a civil war and numerous military coups, including the Orkar coup of 22 April 1990. This set of factors will weigh very heavily in the choice of any of the three major languages now in contention. When all these factors are properly considered, it will be very clear that maintenance of the status quo is the safest political choice.

Third, as Nigeria is the most populated and most linguistically diverse nation in Africa, the rights of its minorities to their languages must be an important consideration in any language policy decision. Up to now it would appear that Nigeria has had a tolerable language rights record even though the existing "rights" policies have yet to be fully implemented, the majority of the minor languages still awaiting development. There is need to maintain and strengthen this record. In this regard, the following suggestions would be useful.

On the premise that "[a]n intelligent awareness of the tensions which would result if one language were given preference may prevent language from becoming a serious basis of cleavage" (Inglehart and Woodward 1972: 376), I would suggest that the issue of a single, indigenous, national language in Nigeria be permanently shelved. Instead, attempts should be made to implement the existing policies, with some modifications. First, the language hierarchy outlined earlier should be officially recognized and resources allocated accordingly to the development of all the languages. Second, while actively promoting the implementation of the integrative policies, the federal government should also support the implementation of the "state" policies, especially the development of minor, local languages. In this regard, Nigeria can borrow a leaf from Australian and Soviet language policies. Third, a committee should be set up to appraise existing language policy pronouncements against the background of the history, political situation, and linguistic landscape in Nigeria. For political expediency, such a committee could be named the National Committee on Languages and charged with the responsibility of providing a comprehensive policy to be known as National Policy on Languages, rather than National Language Policy. To date, no comprehensive policy statement on languages has been formulated in the country, the few language policy pronouncements that have been made originating only in the context of other, more centrally defined national concerns, such as the formulation of a national policy on education and the drafting of a constitution for the country. In drawing up a comprehensive policy on languages in Nigeria, the appropriate committee will surely benefit from case studies such as this one.

In conclusion, no matter how the Nigerian authorities decide to tackle it, issues of language usage are bound up with the country's political agenda and with human rights. Clearly, then, further research into language policy in Nigeria, as well as elsewhere in Africa, will throw light on human rights consciousness as this develops and crystallizes into political action. Nothing expresses the plural basis of African nation-states so much as the continent's linguistic diversity; therefore this quality and the way it is handled will be a bellwether of the African concern for the rights of peoples and groups for many years to come.

References

Adetugbo, A. 1978. "The Development of English in Nigeria up to 1914: A Sociohistorical Appraisal." *Journal of the Historical Society of Nigeria* 9: 89–104.
———. 1984. "The English Language in Nigerian Experience." Inaugural lecture delivered at the University of Lagos, 21 March. Lagos: University of Lagos Press.
Agheyisi, R. U. 1984. "Minor Languages in the Nigerian Context: Prospects and Problems." *Word* 5: 235–53.

Akinnaso, F. N. 1988. "Language Education Opportunities in Nigerian Schools." *Educational Review* 40: 89–103.

———. 1989. "One Nation, Four Hundred Languages: Unity and Diversity in Nigeria's Language Policy." *Language Problems and Language Planning* 13: 133–46.

———. 1990. "The Politics of Language Planning in Education in Nigeria." *Word* 41: 337–67.

———. 1991a. "On the Mother Tongue Education Policy in Nigeria." *Educational Review* 43: 89–106.

———. 1991b. "Toward the Development of a Multilingual Language Policy in Nigeria." *Applied Linguistics* 12: 29–61.

Akinnaso, F. N., and I. A. Ogunbiyi. 1990. "The Place of Arabic in Language Education and Language Planning in Nigeria." *Language Problems and Language Planning* 14: 1–19.

Brann, C. M. B. 1985. "Language Policy, Planning and Management in Nigeria: A Bird's-eye View." *Sociolinguistics* 15: 30–32.

Fakuade, G. 1989. "A Three-Language Formula for Nigeria: Problems of Implementation." *Language Problems and Language Planning* 13: 54–59.

Federal Ministry of Information. 1981 [1977]. *Federal Republic of Nigeria National Policy on Education*. Lagos: Federal Ministry of Information.

———. 1989 [1979]. *Constitution of the Federal Republic of Nigeria*. Lagos: Federal Ministry of Information.

Fishman, J. 1968. "Nationality-Nationalism and Nation-Nationism." In *Language Problems of Developing Nations*, ed. J. Fishman, C. Ferguson, and J. Das Gupta, pp. 39–52. New York: John Wiley and Sons.

Foster, P. Forthcoming. "Literacy and the Politics of Language." In *Literate Systems and Individual Lives: Perspectives on Literacy and Schooling*, ed. A. Purves and E. Jennings. Albany: State University of New York Press.

Guy, G. R. 1989. "International Perspectives on Linguistic Diversity and Language Rights." *Language Problems and Language Planning* 13: 45–53.

Hansford, K., J. Bendor-Samuel, and J. Stanford. 1976. "The Index of Nigerian Languages." *Studies in Nigerian Languages* 5. Zaria: Ahmadu Bello University Press.

Inglehart, R. F., and M. Woodward. 1972. "Language Conflicts and Political Community." In *Language and Social Context*, ed. P. P. Giglioli, pp. 358–77. Harmondsworth: Penguin.

McRae, K. D. 1978. "Bilingual Language Districts in Finland and Canada: Adventures in the Transplanting of an Institution." *Canadian Public Policy* 4.

Marasinghe, L. 1984. "Traditional Conceptions of Human Rights in Africa." In *Human Rights and Development in Africa*, ed. C. E. Welch, Jr., and R. I. Meltzer, pp. 32–45. Albany: State University of New York Press.

Oyewole, Y. 1977. "Toward a Language Policy for Nigeria." *Odu* 15: 74–89.

9

Education and Rights in Nigeria

AJUJI AHMED and RONALD COHEN

Human rights depend on education. Whether rights are restricted by practice or belief to a single group or extended to include humanity as a whole, they must be transmitted through education across generations to ensure their authority. In the terms described in chapter 1, the widening of the moral universe to make rights an aspect of species membership is something that must be protected by its incorporation into the learning process and institutions that play a role in that process. The courts, the mass media, the religious institutions all contribute. But the educational system is of central importance for its major contribution in reproducing the values of the culture. This means that in formal school settings future generations of adults must receive instruction in how and why rights are universal.

Just as important to human rights is the right of all people(s) to equal access to the opportunities for personal and/or group advancement through the acquisition of complex skills and to positions of power and privilege. In the contemporary world such access is highly correlated with educational qualifications. Many rights deemed "human" cannot be activated without universal acceptance of, and commitment to, some measure of equal and universal access to education. The knowledge and skills derived from education sort people in modern societies into those who receive greater or lesser rewards for their efforts. Any commitment to the right of individuals and groups to seek access to resources and rewards based on their abilities means there must be an implementable right to education, since its absence makes distributive justice impossible. Without education as a right, equality is an inoperative and unrealizable ideal.

Beyond this democratization of social mobility lies mass participation in modern social life. However they are conceived, human rights in an isolated village or group of villages can be handled by public opinion, traditions, and local political and judicial authority in face-to-face interactions. Once society becomes as complex as the modern state, then the bulk of social, economic, and political activity occurs beyond the level of interpersonal relations. Understanding social life as abstraction, along with major events reported by the media or through hearsay, and the place of the self and one's own group within it requires some knowledge of the society, its geography, economy, political organization, and history. For people to have any conception of what their rights are, or who they share them with, in a vast and anonymous social order, they must be given the rudiments of a common educational background that expands their experience of local society into a national and even a global one.

In the United States, the founding documents and the Constitution imply equal educational opportunities by placing the highest value on a generalized concept of equality. This has always been interpreted to mean that education is an obligation of governance and a right of citizenship. In England and Wales, recognition of the need to break up age-old distinctions of rank and privilege through the provision of education to all classes is relatively recent. Educational policies since the Balfour Act of 1944 have been aimed squarely at more equal access to education. Similarly, the rehabilitation of the educational system in France after World War II was based partly on the ideology of the Revolution—liberty, equality, and fraternity—and partly on recommendations of the Algiers Committee that called for the extension of the famous revolutionary slogan to French education. In the former Soviet Union and Eastern Europe, equal access to education has been a carefully monitored process designed to provide as equal an access as possible to knowledge and scarce resources and rewards (Holmes 1985). In general, then, the post–World War II period in Europe witnessed a strong growth in the development of democratized educational opportunities as part of the rights-conscious reconstruction of these societies. By the mid-twentieth century, education had become a right rather than a privilege in the industrialized world.

Three decades later the Banjul Charter on Human and Peoples' Rights (1981) endorsed the provisions of the earlier UN document, the

Universal Declaration of Human Rights. However, it also added special clauses designed to include and sanction specifically African customs and beliefs that emphasize collective goals and ideals instead of concentrating solely on individual rights. On the other hand, there is widespread and growing awareness of the need to apply the necessary political will to preserve and protect (individual) civil and political liberties and rights. But how far the reality has matched the aspiration is problematic. If the peoples of the African continent are ever to achieve their ideals, then the issues raised by the problem of human rights along with its causes and results must be squarely faced.

In more specific terms these same ideas have also influenced educational ideology and policy. In all the international meetings and fora convened to discuss the issue, the goal is to make human rights universal rather than confining them to any particular moral universe limited by ethnicity or statehood. The UN Universal Declaration of Human Rights incorporates the notion that the individual human being has an inalienable right within all nations and among all peoples to the general set of rights listed in the document. More importantly for our purposes, the document clearly states that all individuals and states shall "strive by teaching and education to promote respect for those rights and freedoms " (*Yearbook of the United Nations* 1948–49: 535). Thus the major international instrument promulgating universal human rights mandates that human rights education must be included within the curricula of all signatories. It is therefore an obligation of all governments to see to it that schools teach about human rights and that the message reaches as wide a proportion of their youth as possible. Moreover, access to such formal education is mandated to be as open and as equal as possible. Article 26 of the Universal Declaration states that all persons have the right to a free and compulsory education, at least in the elementary stages. The document goes on to say that technical and professional education must be made available to the general public and that higher education must be equally accessible to all on a merit basis.

These ideas and their objectives have been accepted by the developing nations of Africa. Many of them added human rights clauses to their independence constitutions or did so in succeeding decades. As early as 1961, the ministers of education of the new African states met in Addis Ababa and outlined a blueprint for ensuring the right to free and equally available education. All present at the conference agreed that this policy was to be implemented within two decades of their

(1961) meeting (UNESCO 1961). Three decades later, it is doubtful that any country in Africa has actually fulfilled that promise, or is even likely to do so in the next two to three decades. Why this should be so, how education as a scarce resource is more and less justly and adequately distributed, and how it delivers on its obligation to teach pupils about human rights are the subjects of this essay. Although the scene is Nigeria, the conditions described generally apply across the continent as a whole.

Education in Nigeria

Non-Western Education

There are three fundamentally distinct educational systems in Nigeria. Although we are concerned primarily with only one—the formalized Western-style institution—it is important to view it in relation to the entire gamut of educational activities. These separate systems are the indigenous, the Koranic, and the formal European-style schools. In the rural areas, where the majority of the population lives, children learn the skills and rules of adult community membership in their homes and through participation in local activities. In the southern parts of the country such learning was often supplemented in the past through age-based groups of boys being instructed by community adults. Apprentice systems are widespread for a large variety of occupations. Over half of the entire population is still educated this way. Rights of the person in terms of property, judicial process, personal security, degrees of freedom of choice in terms of occupation, marriage, gender, and moral responsibilities to and for others are transmitted at this level. All of these traditions are deeply affected by ethnicity and only penetrated by more widespread or universal principles when the rights involved bring other than local legal systems and conflicts into play. In effect, rights education is still deeply influenced by the age-old adaptation of local groups to their social and physical environments. When wider laws apply, such as national-level land registration and transfers to nonlocal or absentee owners, or compulsory education for girls who by local rights traditions should be married off rather than attending schools, then conflicts result that are not easily resolved.

About half of the population of Nigeria is Muslim. For this group education has always been a religious duty implying a minimal understanding of prayers, the Arabic alphabet, and basic principles of law and morality. A few students go on to more advanced studies, which includes theology and jurisprudence at one of the more advanced centers of Islamic learning in the northern part of the country. From this semiformal training and from participation in community life, people learn about inheritance rights, rights to due process, laws of evidence, privacy, gender rights, marriage and divorce, and duties to civil and religious authorities.

Such education has entered the more formal systems in two ways: by bringing Islamic teachers into the Western-style schools and by creating private parochial schools that attempt to meet the requirements of government education but emphasize Islamic religious beliefs as well. The use of Islamic teaching in public primary schools in northern Nigeria was begun before independence. In a study of the effects of schooling in the 1960s, Peshkin (1971) noted that the Islamic class stressed morality, rights, and duties and was by far the most popular part of the school curriculum. The parochial schools are limited to the larger cities and are for the most part attended by children of the traditional and some of the modern Islamic elite who feel that parochial education ensures religious and moral instruction for their young rather than having it weakened in the public school system.

For the Christians, including the syncretist movements, there are Sunday schools and a few religious-based schools that have survived from the older missions. Like their Muslim counterparts, these schools stress morality and the rights and duties of church members to one another and to religious and civil authorities.

With only a few notable exceptions, all of these non-Western-style educational formats tend to impart an understanding of human rights from a less than universal perspective. Thus indigenous village rights and rules are based on local ethnic traditions and not easily extended to nonethnics. Both Islamic and Christian teachings are theologically committed to a universalist ideology of morality and human rights, but in practice both have always viewed nonbelievers as apostates outside the moral universe of the religious community—and behaved as if such were true. Thus insults and even violent outbreaks between Muslim and Christian students in secondary school settings have occurred as recently as the 1980s. Essays written on religion by college students indicate widespread contempt and a lack of respect for each other's religious beliefs and even civil and political rights among the different religious groups. At the official level, however, equitable treatment and protection of religious rights is maintained. On university campuses, whether the majority of students are Muslim or Christian, the rights of both groups are protected.

Exceptions occur among educational efforts and groups that crosscut these more deeply ingrained cleavages. One of these is that of apprenticeship in the modern job sector. Regardless of ethnicity, religion, or regional background, apprenticeship to crafts in the modern occupational sector transcends older, more parochial views of rights. Thus truck or taxi driving, building trades, and many service jobs are similar throughout the country. Although recruitment to such trades is influenced by ethnicity, the rights and duties associated with craft and union membership have led to more universal notions of rights and common interests based on a common job experience. Similarly, the feminist movement (discussed below) crosscuts older divisions, uniting women under the banner of gender rights that transcend ethnic and religious differences. So far this movement is confined to university-trained women and is located mostly on university campuses among a small group of activists.

Western-Style Education

The major goal of formal education has always been the production of workers for the salaried job sector. In Nigeria's early colonial period this sector included interpreters, tax collectors, clerks, and junior clergy, along with a host of junior positions required to help senior British officials administer in government and trade. Later on, in the 1930s and 1940s, positions began to open for local administrators, school principals and inspectors, army and police officers, judges, lawyers, customs officials, and lower-level managers who could be trained to take over branch offices and eventually large sectors of international trading organizations. The higher-level educational requirements for this second group created a cadre of highly educated men and women who, as ministers, teachers, writers, and ultimately as leaders in the independence struggle, were agents of great social and cultural change and began setting the agenda for the destiny of the country. Starting out as a means of obtaining helpers for colonial rule, education soon produced its own goal, that of developing leaders and officials with the skills and values to govern their own country. And by the end of World War II, these leaders had convinced the colonial power that education's main purpose was to produce "men and women with the standards of public service . . . which self-rule requires" (Colonial Office 1945). This purpose lived on after independence. The country's new leaders and their expatriate advisers assumed that the achievement of independence required an accelerated pace of economic development to match the new political status of the country. Education was seen primarily as the means of production for the medium- and high-level manpower required to achieve more rapid economic development—in other words, as investment in the production of social capital (Ashby 1964).

In contrast to these economic goals, human rights did not feature prominently either as subject matter in the curricula of the schools or as an issue of equal access. In the early years the Colonial Office's *Memorandum on Education* (1925) responded to outside criticism (Lewis 1962) by expanding access to education, instituting the use of local vernaculars in the lower grades, and including course materials on "moral instruction" implemented through religious teachings and, later on, instruction in civic duties. Notions of human rights were absent.

Also absent was the issue of individual versus group rights, so prominent in contemporary human rights discussions. Theoretically, in much of the contemporary discussions a stress on individual rights is said to be tied to Western traditions, while an emphasis on group or collective rights is supposedly rooted in African cultures. However, the European missionaries argued early on for their *collective* right to preach to Muslims in the schools. Thus the Church Mission Society (Anglican) wrote a letter to the governor in the early 1920s complaining of a lack of access to teaching in the north. This was based on the claim that it was the missionaries' right to teach about their religion and the right of Hausa Muslims collectively to receive the Christian message since this knowledge was the only way African peoples could achieve the "highest blessings that can come to any nation" (cited in Fafunwa 1974: 118). In any event, the colonial government did not agree. For them the main focus of educational policy remained centered on the problem of skilled labor supply. Furthermore, they were duty bound by earlier agreements not to allow Christian proselytizing in Islamized areas. No matter what groups demanded it or by what logic—collective or individual—the safeguarding of human rights did not constitute a significant part of formal education for many years.

The selective factor eventually turned out to be local concerns and needs. The civil war of the late 1960s (to 1970) introduced Nigerians to some of their own simmering rights problems in a traumatic and tragic manner. The intolerance and violence of ethnic and communal groups against one another made it clear that if the nation were to survive its citizens must be taught to respect the rights of others within the rule of law and an emergent political culture of security for all persons and groups defined by both citizenship and a common humanity. Education was to contribute its share by actively promoting the intercultural understanding of Nigerian societies and instructing students on the rights of all citizens (see Nigerian Educational Research Council 1972). Curricula in all schools, especially at the lower grades, were to stress the idea of a united, democratic country that fostered justice for all and the notion of a legally protected egalitarian society that fostered opportunity for citizens no matter what their creed, ethnicity, and location by birth or residence. Experience had shown that rights were not just a matter of signing international charters and covenants. The matter was much more serious. Bloodshed and resource-gulping modern warfare and reconstruction of precious infrastructures were the costs of not coping with the rights issue as a national priority.

Another innovation was that of the National Youth Service. Begun in the early 1970s, this program is compulsory for all university graduates. Before they can obtain employment they must give a year of service to the country, which for most means that they are sent to some part of the nation well away from their home area and must carry out some community service functions in a quasi-military organization. For the majority of students this is the first time they will have been outside their home regions working closely in a cross-cultural setting among fellow citizens whose customs and languages are foreign. The results have yet to be assessed through systematic studies, but it is clear to participants and those familiar with the program that it does lead to an appreciation of the differences among one's fellow citizens, reveals their common humanity and creates a sense of unity across barriers hard to breach in any other way than that of personal contacts and work experience.

As for the schools today, many of the ideas of the UN Universal Declaration are included in their curricula. Courses on Nigerian cultural variation and geography and on the rights of all citizens are presented even at the primary school level. There are, however, no studies to show whether or not such efforts have accomplished the goals of creating a more sensitive and tolerant population dedicated to upholding human rights. What evidence we do have suggests that there is still much intolerance among students and nonstudents alike. As already noted, outbreaks between Christian and Muslim students, although not widely reported, occur regularly in secondary-level boarding school settings. Parents away from their home areas who wish to have their children sit examinations for entrance to one of the more prestigious federally funded secondary schools regularly send their youngsters back home because of what they believe are local biases against "outsiders." The fact that people plan their lives to take into account regional and ethnically defined restrictions on their rights and willingly admit this to friends indicates that rights are at the very least at issue. Teaching about rights in schools must be supported by practices outside the school environment; otherwise education is effectively masked and subverted.

In summary, as of the early 1990s education about rights issues in Nigeria has not come nearly as much from formal schooling as from experience and conflicts in politics, organizations, the mass media, literature, labor unions, and the pulpit. Much rights-related education is correlated with educational institutions in the form of student organizations, teacher and faculty unions, demonstrations, strikes, and national political culture that accompanies such activities in the media. These activities extend well beyond the scope of this chapter, but it is important to note that Nigerian literature has always stressed moral and human rights issues and local novelists are widely read and even used in secondary and postsecondary curricula. In secondary and postsecondary history and social science classes, ideologically oriented materials are regularly introduced that stress emancipation and rights of the world's exploited peoples. Because this curricular material enters at the more advanced levels of education, it affects only a tiny minority. On the other hand, university students have been in the vanguard of those demanding greater protection of human rights. The Nigerian Union of Students has had a respectable twenty-five-year history of struggling with rights issues, culminating in the 1980s judgments in favor of the University of Maiduguri students who took the university administration to court for having them rusticated and fined for property damage during student demonstrations in 1984. Although the students did in fact perpetrate the damage, their successful argument that the university deprived them of their right to due process because as plaintiff it investigated, prosecuted, and judged their case is a milestone precedent in rights protection for the country as a whole. Women's rights and rights of workers, of students, of religious minorities, of immigrants, and so on are emphasized primarily in organizations devoted to their furtherance. Religious education stresses moral duties, and, to a lesser extent, the rights of persons and groups. It is clear, then, that using the public educational institutions to further awareness and formal understanding of universal human rights agreements or even of the African Charter on Human and Peoples' Rights is not a well-developed part of normal education in the country.

The Right to Education

The UN Charter of Rights assumes that the national education system is the agency through which the understanding and acceptance of all universal human rights shall be promulgated and recognized. It is also assumed that once in place education will be equitably provided, that all children will benefit, providing entire generations of maturing adults with an appreciation of universal human rights. Unfortunately, the capacity of a national system of education to perform these functions is dependent on the economic, social, and cultural realities of individual countries and the role of education in their national life. This includes most importantly the distribution of educational resources and whether education itself is considered a right to be provided to all groups. In more systematic and realistic terms, the goals of the UN Charter are constrained by elite blueprints for the satisfaction of goals other than equitable access to educational resources. Why this should be so can be seen in the way educational policy has been developed and carried out in Nigeria, a country that shares many characteristics with other ex-colonial nations.

As noted above, education in Nigeria has been guided historically by authoritarian and elitist principles of governance and the persistent dominance of development as the primary goal of society. In policy terms this means a commitment to statism (cf. Wunsch and Olowu 1990). Nurtured by colonialism and taken on uncritically by the independent nation's leaders, statism reflects an ideology of development that assumes the need for government-led actions to transform the existing order of things through improvements across all sectors of national life. For our purposes this materialized in the assumption that the function of education was to produce the necessary "manpower" for development. Indeed, from the late 1940s onward education was viewed even in the Colonial Office in terms of its contribution to the long-term prospect of political independence seen in the supply of "men and women with the standards of public service and capacity for leadership which self-rule requires" (Colonial Office 1945). In effect, then, education in Nigeria led ineluctably from low-level job training as helpers to higher-level skills and more responsible, more important jobs. And this development is correlated with the growth of the independence movement and the recognition of the right of Nigerians to self-determination.

The history of Western-style education explains its orientation and the access problem. Although the first mission school was founded in 1843 by Methodists, it was the Church Mission Society (Anglican) that pushed forward in the early 1850s to found a chain of missions and schools, followed quickly in the late 1850s by the Roman Catholics. Other missions—Presbyterian, Methodist, and others—soon pushed into the middle belt. An education department was founded in southern Nigeria in 1887 and began setting curricula requirements and administering grants to the mission societies. By 1914 (when north and south were unified into one colony) the south had fifty-nine government primary schools, ninety-one mission primary schools, and eleven secondary schools (all but one, King's College in Lagos, run by the missions). The 1,100 primary school pupils in the north were dwarfed by 35,700 pupils in the south, and there were no secondary schools in the north. By the 1920s the pressure for places in southern schools led to increased numbers of independent schools financed by local efforts and the sending of favorite sons overseas for more advanced training.

In 1916 Lugard, first governor of the unified colony, set up a school inspectorate that was to emphasize regular examinations as the major criterion for assessing school progress (Fafunwa 1974: 111). Although grants to mission schools were no longer to be based solely on examination results, examinations remained centrally important in government schools. Discipline, buildings, and adequacy of teaching staff were to be inspected as well, but the most points given to a school's performance went to the numbers and rankings of its examination results. This stress on examination results as the basis for judging schools and their products is still dominant in the 1990s. The job market supports the system by using examination results as a basic qualification for employment in government and the private sector. Thus undergraduates must receive an "upper second" in their final grade to be considered for government jobs.

By 1950 the country had developed a three-tiered system of primary, secondary, and tertiary education based on the British model allowing wide participation at the bottom, sorting into academic and vocational training at the secondary level, and reserving tertiary education for a small elite group destined for leadership.[1] On the eve of independence in the late 1950s, Nigeria had gone through a decade of exceptional educational growth leading to a movement for universal primary education in the Western Region. From 1947 to 1957, primary school enrollments in the north went from 66,000 to 206,000; in the west, from 240,000 to 983,000; and in the east, from 320,000 to 1,209,000. Secondary-level enrollment went from 10,000 for the country as whole in 1947 to 36,000 in 1957; 90 percent of this rise occurred in the south. Given the central importance of formal education, it soon moved into position as "the largest social programme of all governments of the federation" (Idachaba 1985: 33), absorbing as much as 40 percent of the budgets of the state governments. Thus by 1985 there were approximately 12 million primary school pupils in attendance at 35,000 schools; some 3.7 million students attending 6,500 secondary schools; and about 125,000 postsecondary students attending 35 colleges and universities. The pressure on the system is so intense that projections suggest as many as 800,000 postsecondary students by the end of the l990s (Ahmed 1993), with a correlated growth in numbers and size of all educational institutions to match this estimate.

Universal primary education (UPE) became official policy for the federation as a whole in the 1970s. Complete implementation has not yet been achieved, but the pressure was on throughout the 1980s to complete the task even under conditions of economic recession. The statistics reflect this growth. From 1947 to 1957 the country tripled its primary school pupils, going from 7 percent to 21 percent of the school-age population. By 1985, with a population estimate of 23 million between the ages of five and fourteen, approximately 47 percent of the age cohort were attending primary school, more than double the percentage of the cohort and four to five times the actual numbers of pupils involved since independence. Although growth slowed down and actually decreased in some rural areas in the late 1980s, it is projected that by the early part of the next century UPE will be virtually completed.

Growth at the secondary and postsecondary levels has been even more dramatic. In 1957, secondary-level education was available for approximately one-half of one percent of the population aged fifteen to twenty-four. By 1985 this negligible figure had jumped to 22 percent of the secondary-level age-group. Higher education also grew rapidly. In the early 1960s there were approximately 4,000 students at six institutions (Ibadan, Ife, Lagos, Ahmadu Bello, University of Nigeria, and Institute of Technology, Benin); this figure rose to 19,000 by 1971 and to 30,000 by 1975 at these same institutions. There are now thirty-five polytechnical institutes, military colleges, state and federal universities, and colleges of education and of agriculture with an estimated enrollment of 150,000 to 200,000 in 1990–91. Demographically this amounts to under one percent of the college-aged (twenty-four to twenty-nine years old) cohort of the population. In sum, by the early 1990s about half of the primary-school-age children are in attendance; about one-fifth of the secondary-level age-group go to some kind of secondary-level school; and under one percent of the postsecondary age-group actually attend such institutions.

These numbers reflect three kinds of unequal access. First, even though there has been an enormously accelerated growth in education, the south's half of the population has three to four times more secondary schools per state. There are more than 150 secondary schools in almost every southern state; all northern states have less than 100, and many have less than 50. Most of the southern states each have well over 100,000 secondary school students; most northern states have under 30,000. Postprimary education is many times more available for those in the southern portions of the country. Second, although teacher training has also grown, it has not been able to keep up. And in those areas where there are the most secondary school students (Bendel, Cross River, and Imo), the pupil-teacher ratio is the most unfavorable, averaging seventy-six students per trained teacher as opposed to thirty to fifty students per teacher for most of the country. On the other hand, the trend is clearly upward for the entire country from figures that show much lower ratios of school attendance for the 1960s. Thus, increased numbers in the schools has meant overcrowding and less favorable pupil-teacher ratios. Third, the educational pyramid is lopsidedly male. One or two southern states have equal numbers of boys and girls in primary school, but for the country as a whole in 1980 primary schools were less than 40 percent female; secondary schools less than 35 percent female; and postsecondary schools less than 15 percent female (up from 12 percent in 1970). Higher education is primarily for men. There are therefore regional inequalities and gender inequalities, and, most insidiously, as time goes on the quality of education cannot keep up with the pressure to increase the numbers of students. Those who go to school today receive a much poorer education than those who went earlier on.

Because access to education has been declared a universal human right, the data above can be discussed from that point of view. The governments involved (both state and federal) have announced policies aimed at providing universal and open education for all. However, the inequalities associated with much longer and greater educational access in the south mean that compensatory efforts must be made to give northerners equal chances. This has not been done. Instead capital investments in facilities and in teacher training have been equalized by state from the federal purse—freezing the prior inequities and worsening the pupil-teacher ratios in the south, where attendance figures are much higher. These inequities interacting with the colonial legacy of elitism, which restricted access to upper levels of education, and qualifications resting almost solely on examination results have had dire results.

The British ideology of education exported to Nigeria can be characterized as elitist and Neoplatonic. Schools and colleges were to be highly selective. The fortunate few who found their way into the system were to be refined in character and intellect, then recruited into leadership roles in government and business. The curriculum and recruitment were to emphasize and implement this highly selective "thin stream of excellence and narrow specialism" (Ashby 1964). In many parts of the country this reflects the traditional stratification in society at large that defined the right to education to be a claim based on hereditary status rather than citizenship, human rights, or merit. This Neoplatonic worldview assumes that because individuals are in effect unequal, social order should be based on such inequality. The ideal society within such a view consists of a class of leaders and a class of their followers. Each is hereditarily defined and predestined for his or her position. Therefore the most desirable social order is one in which people practice and support these traditional inequalities. And society is "just" when natural (i.e., human) rights reflect this natural class structure through educational institutions that nurture and maintain it.

The real and recognized conflict over rights and education comes in opposition to the restrictiveness of both indigenous and colonial views on the one hand and the view that education is a universal right on the other. Exacerbating this conflict is that of educational qualifications as a means to power and privilege. Stemming from the independence struggle and expanded by the civil war is the widespread belief that for Nigeria to be both independent and stable, education must be shared equitably across all of society's varied groups and individuals. At first, increased access to education was part of the rhetoric of independence leading quite logically to demands for universal education and the opening up of secondary and higher-level institutions. This was meant to challenge the British view that Nigeria had not the trained personnel to be granted its independence. Since then, and more importantly for its effects on educational policy, access to higher tiers of the educational pyramid has been viewed as the enabling capacity for indigenization; the official policy of all postindependence regimes is to replace foreign personnel with Nigerians as soon as possible. Later, however, this same issue of access to top jobs was accelerated and strengthened by the national unity ideology emerging from the civil war. This has produced a widely but still not universally accepted idea that *all* Nigerians must have equal access to education and those positions of power and privilege legitimately restricted through qualifications and credentialing.

By and large indigenization has been successful. Both government and the private sector set up training programs for higher-level managers and technicians from the late 1950s onward that soon brought Nigerians to the forefront in all of the highest-level jobs in both the public and private sector. Within a decade after independence it was difficult to find expatriates in anything but advisory or consultant capacities in both the public and the private sectors. Both private and public education expanded rapidly to produce the competences necessary.

As with any crash program there were difficulties. By the early 1970s more than half of the higher-level jobs in the entire country were in the hands of men under the age of forty.[2] The Gorsuch *Report on the Public Services* (1961) noted that statistically speaking the average federal public servant was aged thirty to thirty-five, had secondary school education, and was Yoruba. The seasoning and experience that go with slower maturation and competition with others for promotion were all too often not available. Educational opportunities and ethnic nepotism made for numerical dominance of southerners. Worse yet, it influenced the development of a national political culture that decried such nepotism while practicing it and created strong pressures for equal access to jobs to anyone fortunate enough to obtain the necessary educational credentials. When these positions filled up in a flush of indigenization euphoria, pressure for the formation of new states (i.e., more jobs among coethnics), new parastatals, and new universities filled the political dialogue of the country. For a time government was able to get a breather from the pressure for jobs by supporting new states and therefore entire new sets of bureaucratic offices.

But the bubble had to burst. A country cannot go on creating jobs paid for by the public purse in order to accommodate an ever-growing stream of graduates. In Nigeria southern educational advantages were offset by northern dominance of top jobs in the federal civilian government up to 1966, and by regional administrations that provided a separate tier of government above the states and below the federal level that could exert national influence and be responsive to regional interests and ambitions. The first serious eruptions took place in late spring of 1966. Suddenly and without any consultation the new Ironsi military government declared the country a unitary state, abolishing regional administrations at the stroke of a pen. All future appointments would be made on a strict merit basis using educational qualifications by the southern-dominated centralized military government. Within days of the decree riots broke out in the north, several led by students, against southerners living in the region. Northerners quite logically saw the decree as a means of biasing all future appointments and promotions in government toward the more educated southerners, jeopardizing northern aspirations and power. The violence of June 1966 was the first of several outbreaks and subsequent disagreements that led eventually to the civil war. Education is more than manpower training. Educational inequities leading to regional and ethnically lopsided elite recruitment sow the seeds of serious social and political problems. The frustrations and fears associated with such biases foster deep grievances and fears that have the potential of destabilizing the plural state itself.

This pressure to provide for equitable elite recruitment underlies the tremendous effort to invest in and increase the capacity of the educational establishment. That helps explain the growth. But rapid expansion without the required resources of instruction, teacher training, equipment, libraries, laboratories, buildings, and incentives has corroded the quality of instruction being delivered. As long as the country was growing apace fueled by rapidly expanding parastatals, by new states popping into existence, and by burgeoning government departments and expanding business firms underwritten with oil revenues, then the growing numbers of graduates could be absorbed, even though competition was fierce for the best positions. But as pressures for top jobs increased and the job market tightened in the 1980s, the ingrained criterion of examination results as the primary sorting device for access to schools, universities, and ultimately jobs led to rapid growth of education, watering down its quality. In addition, widespread corruption and cheating among both faculty and students took place at all levels, but especially at secondary and postsecondary institutions since job entry depends so highly on examination results. Economic hardship among teaching staffs produced increased attention to moonlighting activities in noneducational work. Added to this was the shortage of books and educational materials in the country, the lack of any incentive for research and writing, and the use of out-of-date notes, equipment, laboratories, and the like, with few or no replacements when things wore out. Unfortunately, nothing is being done to rectify the situation. The teaching of English, which is the language of instruction beyond primary school, has reached such poor levels of quality that university faculty now complain they cannot understand the written work of their students. One hopes that the publication of critical works and international attention to this crisis will turn things around before the country loses a large portion of its educated labor force.

As long as scarce resources are so closely tied to credentials rather than job performance, recruitment criteria will have a downward pressure on the quality of education being provided in the country as a whole. Making a scarce service into a human right cannot guarantee the quality of the service delivered. And this is not simply a matter of watering down the rights of students and their families. For ultimately the country's development depends on the quality as well as the quantity and equitable distribution of education. Tragically, however, insatiable pressures to distribute this scarce resource along with growing scarcities of well-trained teachers and good facilities have resulted in the deterioration of education itself. This in turn leads back to educational stratification, including private education and foreign schools for the elites, which brings the problem of equitable distribution full circle. Public education as a human right implies sufficient quality to sustain its utility as a resource. Given access to education as a human right, then the inevitable pressures for democratization that follow pose a constant danger because access alone cannot ensure that quality remains constant or improves as supply increases more rapidly than actual resources allow. Unfortunately, this issue has not been seriously dealt with in Nigeria, as well as in many other places. But it is a problem whose time has come. Nigeria and indeed all Third World countries cannot continue to decrease the quality of education and at the same time hope to promote and produce competent and productive graduates required as the basic social capital for development. In this sense rights and what is appropriate for the achievement of national welfare and prosperity all begin to converge, indicating their inextricable interdependence.

Conclusion

Human rights and education are related in two ways: through the inclusion of rights knowledge in the development of curricula and through access that reflects the right of all persons to an education. These in turn help to keep rights issues robust in the social life of peoples and to enable all humans to strive for positions and rewards in society that should be open and available to all. In Nigeria rights education was part of the parochial education of local cultures but not of the formal colonial-inspired Western schooling. It has entered the curricula of schools through literature, through the predilection of specific teachers, and as a means to achieve national unity after a deeply scarring civil war.

Access to Western-style education has been restricted by the colonial experience and British beliefs that the very best education is the preserve of a small elite. In Nigeria the Western-style schools are more numerous and entrenched in the southern Christian areas. This inequity has not been redressed even with independence and has led to conflict and instability in the society over time. The enormous expansion of education after independence has not abated but has led to a serious decrease in the quality of public education available—which means that the demand for education can help to create a new kind of scarcity, that of a good education, and a new problem, the possibility that the pressure for increased access can lead to the loss of social capital in the society as a whole.

In the end, then, rights to social services such as education, medicine, representative government, and an accessible judicial system may very well be rights that all persons in contemporary society should or must possess. But the quality of such services is also a defining feature of the rights involved. Without this protection, rights deteriorate into a trick played on individuals and groups by leaders more devoted to drumming up support than to achieving human rights. One of the great tragedies of modern life is the disappointment of so many millions who, having fought to obtain the dignity and promise implied in the human rights struggle, finally arrived at the goal only to find the goalposts moved.

Notes

1. The statistical material on education has been calculated from Idachaba (1985); that on women from Agheyisi (1985). Although these numbers may not be exact, the inequalities and growth rates they demonstrate are so great that there is very little doubt about the validity of the main points being made.
2. Personal communication from Sir Kashim Ibrahim to Ronald Cohen.

References

Agheyisi, R. U. 1985. "The Labour Market Implications of the Access to Higher Education in Nigeria." In *Women in Nigeria* (prepared for publication by an editorial committee). London: Zed Books.
Ahmed, A. 1993. *Educational Reform in Nigeria*. Boulder, Colo.: Lynne Rienner.
Ashby, E. 1964. *African Universities and Western Tradition*. Cambridge: Harvard University Press.
Colonial Office. 1925. *Memorandum on Education*. London: HMSO.
———. 1945. *Report of the Commission on Higher Education in the Colonies* (Cmd 6647). London: HMSO.
Fafunwa, A. B. 1974. *History of Education in Nigeria*. London: George Allen and Unwin.
Gorsuch, R. B. 1961. *Report on the Public Services*. Lagos: Government Printer.
Holmes, B., ed. 1985. *Equity and Freedom in Education: A Comparative Study*. London: Allen and Unwin.
Idachaba, F. S. 1985. *Rural Infrastructures in Nigeria*. Ibadan: Ibadan University Press.
Lewis, L. J. 1962. *Phelps-Stokes Reports of Education in Africa*. London: Oxford University Press.
Nigerian Educational Research Council. 1972. *A Philosophy for Nigerian Education: Report of the National Curriculum Conference*. Ibadan: Heinemann.
Peshkin, A. 1971. *Kanuri Children*. New York: Holt, Rinehart and Winston.
UNESCO. 1961. Addis Ababa Final Report.

Welch, C. E. 1984. "Human Rights as a Problem in Contemporary Africa." In *Human Rights and Development in Africa*, ed. C. E. Welch and R. I. Meltzer. Albany: State University of New York Press.
World Bank. 1988. *World Development Report*. Baltimore: Johns Hopkins University Press.
Wunsch, J. S, and D. Olowu, eds. 1990. *The Failure of the Centralized State*. Boulder, Colo.: Westview Press.
Yearbook of the United Nations. 1948. New York: United Nations.

10

Academic Freedom in Africa: A Right Long Overlooked

GORAN HYDEN

It is something of a paradox, amidst the growing volume of literature on human rights in Africa, that none deals with the specific question of academic freedom as a right. This is even more puzzling given the serious infringements this right has suffered in most African countries in the postindependence era. More recently, however, there appears to have been a change in the situation. Declarations in support of the importance of academic freedom were passed by the Association of University Teachers in Zimbabwe in 1989 and by delegates from autonomous staff associations in six institutions of higher learning in Tanzania in May 1990 (Dar es Salaam Declaration 1990). Both these documents, while emphasizing the social responsibility of academic teachers, assert that members of the academic community hold certain rights and freedoms with respect to both the state and the administration of educational institutions. The documents go even further to underscore the importance of the right to self-government within institutions of higher learning. Although their jurisprudence differs (Shivji 1990), the two declarations bear much in common with the Lima Declaration on Academic Freedom and Autonomy of Institutions of Higher Education (World University Service 1987), adopted in response to what the organizers viewed as an alarmingly widespread tendency to undermine, restrict, or suppress academic freedom and autonomy of institutions of higher education in Third World countries. Coinciding with these tendencies and drawing on the local initiatives that they set in motion in various African countries, the Council for the Development of Economic and Social Research in Africa (CODESRIA)—Africa's social science research council—organized a symposium in Kampala, Uganda, in November 1990 on "Academic Freedom, Research and the Social Responsibility of the Intellectual in Africa" primarily with a view to moving ahead on this set of issues.

With all these developments now in place after a long public silence on academic freedom in Africa, there is reason to take stock of what has happened since independence to explain the relative neglect of this issue and its resurgence in the early 1990s. More specifically, in this chapter I will examine the peculiar conditions under which academic freedom was first established, subsequently undermined, and finally resurrected. In so doing I will try to illustrate the dilemmas confronting African intellectuals and thus highlight the particular challenges they face. References will also be made to the deliberations in the 1990 Kampala symposium.

This chapter is primarily about academics. Because they are a subgroup of intellectuals I will sometimes also refer to them as such. I am aware that the use of this term raises many definitional problems. Who is an intellectual? How free from social attachments is such a person? Attempts to answer these questions have led to much controversy. For example, Karl Mannheim provides a rather exclusivist definition. To him, the intellectual is socially unattached and therefore capable of transcending ideological disputes that polarize society (Mannheim 1948). In this perspective, the "superstructure" of ideas constitutes the autonomous sphere within which intellectuals move. Antonio Gramsci, by contrast, views the intellectual in an inclusivist fashion. Because every human being presumably has a worldview—and thus criteria for social and ethical behavior—he or she is potentially an intellectual but never autonomous, always organically linked to specific economic and social class interests (Hoare and Smith 1986). Writing in the Gramscian tradition, Feierman (1990) has recently described how ordinary "peasant intellectuals" helped shape the political discourse in Tanzania both before and after independence.

For my purposes in this essay, I take a middle position between the exclusivist and inclusivist stands, suggesting that the intellectual be defined in terms of degree rather than kind. Thus I define an intellectual as a person who is significantly engaged in thinking about ideas and nonmaterial problems using the faculty of reason. Knowledge of a specific subject or the possession of a degree does not, by this definition, automatically qualify a person to be an intellectual.

Similarly, a person without academic qualifications may be an intellectual provided that person utilizes his or her thinking capacity and possesses sufficient knowledge of his or her subject of interest. A classic example of a person who lacked academic qualifications yet was one of the leading intellectuals of his time is the British philosopher Herbert Spencer. Following Alatas (1977), I believe intellectuals manifest the following social characteristics: (1) they are recruited from different social backgrounds, though in differing proportions; (2) they are to be found supporting or opposing various cultural or political movements; (3) their occupations are for the most part nonmanual (for example, they may be writers, lecturers, priests, poets, scientists); (4) they tend to remain distant from the rest of society, often forming networks of their own; (5) they are interested not only in the purely technical side of knowledge but also in ideas about religion, the good life, art, nationalism, the planned economy, culture, and the like; and (6) intellectuals, in contrast to others, tend to be concerned with the general and transcend the immediate, day-to-day concerns of most people. Logically and operationally this means that all intellectuals are dependent on the right to freedom of speech and the right of association. When such rights are curtailed, they can survive only by going underground or into exile, hoping, as intellectuals in Eastern Europe did, that one day they can effectively regain their rights from there.

The Rise of African Intellectuals

In order to understand fully the predicaments of African intellectuals, it may be helpful to draw some comparisons with the position of intellectuals elsewhere. In places like ancient Egypt, Greece, Rome, and China, they originally rose to prominence in the context of patrimonial regimes, often sponsored—and utilized—by persons with power. In this respect, they were organically tied to ongoing social and economic processes. Whether in monasteries or castles, secret societies or palaces, they helped shape the dominant culture. This "high" culture, of which the intellectuals were a privileged part, was a world of its own, way above the parochial and profane peasant culture of the day. In those days, there was no inclination toward populism. Peasant culture was outright avoided and often despised. This differentiation was, of course, the product of a class society. In precapitalist Europe, intellectuals were satisfied with this role as advisers and entertainers of the ruling class. It gave them both social comfort and a sense of importance they were reluctant to trade for anything else.

Things began to change with the victory of capitalism. New and impersonal standards of evaluation were being introduced as part of this system. The bourgeoisie redefined the social parameters of everyone in society, including the intellectuals. Many intellectuals found themselves supporting the emerging capitalist class, but others were alienated by the "nakedness" of the system that this class was busy putting into place. A particularly important trait of the new order was the emergence of a predominantly instrumental or calculative rationality, which became the dividing issue among the intellectuals of the nineteenth century. In one group were those who saw this rationality as the foundation stone of a better and more efficient society. No one captured the full dimensions of this promise better than Max Weber. In an opposing group, of whom Marx and Engels were the most prominent, were those who realized the emancipatory potential of the new order but believed that the bourgeoisie had no interest in realizing it; hence the need for a social transformation that would catapult the working class, led by an "enlightened" revolutionary cadre of intellectuals, into power. In still another group were those intellectuals, especially in Germany, who, as a result of the growing rationalization of society, responded by advancing essentially romanticist and populist ideas, i.e., the assumption that the irrational has a place side by side with rationalism in any society.

As the outcome of an expansionist capitalism in Europe in the nineteenth century, colonialism brought to Africa a social order that was replicated on what existed in Europe. It provided Africa not only new avenues of social mobility but also the social contradictions to which the system gives rise. Thus, as the workers eventually gained strength in Europe, so did the "counterhegemonic" culture of this class and its intellectual representatives. This divided the Africans along three lines: those who accepted and adopted the culture of the colonial rulers; those who sided with the exploited classes and their representatives in Europe; and those who identified with neither but argued the need for the resurrection of an African culture.

For a long time, European rulers could count on the loyalty of those Africans that they had educated. Being inducted into the "high" culture of their colonial masters was not only a privilege but also a challenge that many enjoyed because it provided opportunities for upward mobility that were not negligible, especially in Francophone colonies where this incentive was most systematically exploited. Thus, even if only a very tiny percentage of the population benefited from these opportunities, those who did found themselves thrown into a whole new world of ideas, the vistas of which appeared to be unbounded. To be sure, many of the first African intellectuals had to fight against racial prejudice, and gaining recognition was often difficult. Yet intellectual pioneers such as Casely-Hayford and Cheik Anta Diop proved that Africans, in spite of their late recognition, were as capable as anyone else of making a contribution to global knowledge. One result of this was the eventual creation of institutions of higher learning in Africa. The British were first among the colonial governments in establishing such schools in Kampala (Makerere) in the late 1920s and in Ibadan in the 1940s. As the vice-chancellor of Makerere, Dr. Senteza-Kajubi, pointed out at the Kampala symposium, Makerere was established in an "aristocratic culture," where the assumption was of a "loyal institution in search of learning." This loyalty was, of course, secured through a close connection with the universities back in Britain. University dons were recruited from Britain, curricula modeled on and degrees conferred by universities there (Mazrui 1975). More importantly, however, there was deep respect for intellectual pursuits associated with these imported institutions. These early institutions were important in helping the emerging African elite overcome parochial divisions and develop new ideas about their societies.

The significance of this point was felt even more strongly outside the academic walls. Although colonial rule was autocratic and paternalizing, the system provided a few pockets of opportunities here and there that Africans soon took advantage of. Many of these opportunities resulted from contradictions between the essentially liberal regime back home and the denial of such rights to people in the colonies. If the European powers were serious in their "civilizing" mission and insisted that their values were not only superior but also universal, then why and how could they deny these rights to Africans? This was the question that many African intellectuals began to ask themselves as colonial rule proceeded, but with little evidence that the European masters were going to grant these rights voluntarily to colonial subjects.

One group sided with those in opposition to capitalism in Europe. Where the opportunity existed, these Africans were encouraged to start local branches of trade unions and radical political parties in their own colonies (Hodgkin 1960). European counterparts often served as advisers and helped provide financial support. The more difficult it was for the Africans to operate in their own colonies, the closer became the ties to these European organizations. Thus in Portugal, for example, where liberalism itself was very weak, there was least recognition of the extension of political rights to Africans. The result was that the political space for a democratic and nonviolent end to colonialism was almost nil. It is not a coincidence that African intellectuals from the Lusophone colonies became especially dependent on underground Portuguese opposition movements and had to resort to armed struggle as they launched their own struggle for independence.

Where political openings did exist, as in the British and French colonies, Africans were able to take advantage of the contradictions between liberal promise and practice and could thus often "shame" their colonial masters into accepting changes in their political status. Africans realized that their best chance of making political gains was to adhere to the rules of liberalism—to defeat the colonial master on his ideological homeground, so to speak. The question they had concerned tactics: how closely should they accept and imitate the reigning ideologies of European radicals? Some became very effectively inducted into socialism or communism without much questioning of the consequences these paradigms had for the gaining of new political rights. Others maintained that their credibility as African nationalists rested on their ability to develop a Pan-Africanist position that reflected the cultural uniqueness of the continent. Whichever position prevailed in any given colony, there was a lively public debate on these issues both in the colonies and in the metropolitan countries. The participants in these debates were African intellectuals for whom the shaping of Africa's future was a historical challenge. It is no coincidence that the literature dating back to the years immediately before and after independence devoted considerable attention to the role of African intellectuals: their ideas, their strategies, and the question of their social reproduction (see Shils 1960; Apter 1964; Coleman 1965). Political ideas were taken seriously and were openly debated in magazines (in, for example, *Transition* and *East Africa Journal* in East Africa), many of which were quite critical of the African political leaders. Development strategies were also publicly debated and intellectuals, both within and without the ranks of government, participated. Much attention was devoted to the African university, the principal mechanism for producing fresh generations of intellectuals to serve the needs of the new nation. A British scholar, Sir Eric Ashby, was a pacesetter in this debate (Ahmed 1993) by pointing to the key role African academics had played in the nationalist struggle and the need, therefore, to reshape the African university so that it would emphasize the cultural liberation of the African mind (Ashby 1964). Political leaders like Nyerere (1966) and many others joined in this debate. Despite differences of opinion, the debates took place within a strikingly broad consensus that the African university had to do more than its counterpart in the developed societies. It had to serve as a spearhead for national development.

The Curtailment of Academic Freedom

There was a definite measure of global optimism and innocence about the prospects for progress in the new states in the early 1960s. Only a small number of very conservative analysts questioned the ability of African states, with foreign assistance, to make rapid strides forward. Even these analysts underestimated the extent to which the new power configurations and the widely embraced developmentalist ideology of the global community were going to prove harmful to Africa's ambition to make social and economic progress. Most importantly for our purposes, it is clear that no one in those days paid much attention to the significance of civil and political rights to this ambition. Although such rights had played an important role in the struggle for political independence, these rights, including those pertaining to academics, were consistently ignored in the first two decades of independence in most African countries.

This process may be analyzed at two different levels. The first is the cultural or ideological; the second, the political or structural. The African leaders adopted a "mobilizational" approach to development that assumed that the answers to the challenges of the new states were held only by a small clique of officials. Members of the international community took an "apolitical" stand, arguing that they were only in the business of "development." As a result, nobody cared about process issues, i.e., the ways by which decisions were made. Political leaders were allowed to hijack the public agenda for their own ends and build political structures that reinforced this monopolization. Let us examine these two sets of issues more closely.

The Suppression of Public Discourse

The main thrust of African nationalism was to discredit the institutions and policies imposed on the African societies by the colonial governments and at the same time restore the honor and prestige of things local and customary. In short, as many African leaders expressed it at the time, it was a matter of reestablishing an African identity to their countries. On this virtually everyone was in agreement, Africans as well as expatriates. What no one seemed to recognize were the potential implications this would have for the protection of basic civil and political rights.

The anticolonial orientation of African nationalists meant that they adopted a romanticist and populist stand on political matters. They demonstrated an open distrust for the economic and the analytical. Although they welcomed expatriates to serve as planners and advisers in key government institutions, they left little scope for the analytical mind when it came to actually making policy. They also espoused a strong belief in the superior moral worth of ordinary people, of the uneducated and unintellectual. Even well-educated and intellectual leaders like Nyerere in Tanzania took pleasure in publicly ridiculing the educated whenever they showed any doubt about the wisdom of his own leadership. The simplicity and wisdom of customary African ways of doing things became the hallmark of political strategies not only in Tanzania but all over the continent. As the nameless masses were rediscovered and folkways established as the source of linguistic and cultural creativity, the legitimacy of the academic was being undercut. This antielitist stand was received positively in most circles, both in Africa and elsewhere. The assumption was that the potential of the people had been ignored by the colonial authorities. Any attempt to realize it through political means was therefore acceptable.

While welcoming the social energy that this new political mobilization was expected to generate, the international community engaged in its own business of devising the formal mechanisms that were deemed necessary to implement ambitious national development plans. Given the sensitivity to any interference in national matters that African leaders understandably showed immediately after independence, the international community, especially the donor agencies, refrained from any open political criticism of the way the recipient governments conducted their affairs. With the exception of instances where the national interest of the donor country was in question, the international discourse on development was apolitical. Following a positivist tradition in Western societies, it was reduced to technicalities and confined to ends-means analyses of development projects and plans evolved by the recipient governments.

African leaders found no problem in accommodating this kind of policy advice. It did not challenge the way governments conducted their affairs. The apolitical nature of the stance of the donors gave the African leaders plenty of leeway to bring about the political changes deemed necessary to enhance their own power. One such change that went largely unquestioned by Africans and outsiders alike was the introduction of one-party governments in virtually all countries on the continent. Whether introduced by force or not, this change was justified in the name of national unity: the need for everyone to work together toward the same development goals. The fact that unity was confused with uniformity never became the subject of public criticism. The result was a serious devaluation of the concept of civil and political rights, with many African officials—and intellectuals—referring to the latter in a derogatory fashion as "Western" and "imperialistic."

Another change that went largely without debate and criticism was the transformation of the university into an instrument of national development. For understandable reasons, most observers were sympathetic to the notion that in countries where the educated few constituted a privileged elite, the university, as a public institution, could not and should not play the same role as in developed societies. One African intellectual, Yesufu (1973: 40), expressed this point by emphasizing that the African academics could not pursue knowledge for the sake of it but only for the amelioration of the conditions of the ordinary people of the continent. The African university must therefore be differently motivated than similar institutions elsewhere. African academics were largely supportive of this concept, as were donors who insisted that if they were to support research, it had better be "applied," i.e., serving the objectives of national development as defined in their own or governmental documents. Throughout the 1960s and 1970s, few African academics argued the need for attention to "basic" as opposed to "applied" research. Even fewer came out in defense of the civil and political rights that were being eroded by this unfortunate combination of political populism and apolitical developmentalism.

The Monopolization of Political Power

Particularly harmful for intellectual freedom was the monopolization of political power that African leaders embarked on in the wake of national independence. Some of this may be understood with reference to the need for a strong political center at a time when a new nation-state is being welded together. The strong dependence on external resources to supplement domestic efforts also called for a centralized approach to governance. None of these factors, however, served as the driving force behind the process of power monopolization. Doing so was the need for the African leaders to establish a domestic foundation for their exercise of political power. What this meant was that they considered themselves to have a right, as leaders, to use public means to establish such a foundation. In short, political activity became a means of acquiring economic wealth and social prestige that in turn could be dispensed so as to build up and sustain political loyalties in a context in which affective relations rather than ideological differences tended to prevail.

This point may not be fully appreciated without reference to a comparison with other societies. Despite claims by some Marxists to the contrary, African countries could hardly be described as class societies at the time of independence. Ruling positions had been occupied by Europeans. Although they had nurtured an African elite, the latter did not possess the material resources nor the cultural self-confidence to walk directly into the shoes of their colonial predecessors and act as a ruling class. Their challenge, as suggested above, was to lay the foundation for political rule. The generation of African nationalists that took over at independence was a loose assemblage of community leaders, more or less effectively welded together into a national liberation coalition by their sense of a common enemy. The principal cleavages below this surface of national unity were ethnic or religious, not economic. It was the ability of individual leaders to conceal these cleavages through personalized agreements of reciprocal rights and obligations that kept the country together, especially after the notion of a colonial—or neocolonial—threat had lost its persuasive power as a mobilizing factor. But this highly personalized form of rule was delicate and could not tolerate the principled discourse that ideology gives rise to. Hence, a major concern for African political leaders after independence was to limit public scrutiny and debate of political affairs. Using a variety of means, including co-optation, intimidation, and occasionally persuasion, these leaders were converting politics into a prerogative of a small clique of privileged individuals. Shivji's (1991) account of this process in Tanzania, which contributed to the debate about the country's political future, is instructive and, I believe, quite typical of what happened in most countries in Africa after independence.

The transformation into a one-party regime, which in Tanzania was a de facto consequence of the preindependence elections, encouraged the gradual evolution of the ruling party as an organ associated with the state rather than with civil society. It became a "state-party," as Shivji puts it, which derives its authority from law, as opposed to a political party, which derives its legitimacy from the people. The state-party was increasingly compelled to rely on coercion rather than persuasion to achieve its ends. In this process, the material and financial basis of the party also changed. It could now draw on substantial subsidies from the state and indirect "contributions" from the growing number of parastatal institutions that were established. Party membership fees and voluntary contributions from well-wishers and sympathizers ceased to be important sources of revenue. Both political and administrative work in the party was increasingly being carried out by paid officials rather than by volunteers or cadres who do so because of commitment to a cause. In practice, the organizational structure of the party became almost identical with that of the state. It adopted such mundane paraphernalia as cars with special party plates, party flags, and state police outriders. All this meant that the party ceased to be not only a political party as we know it in democratic contexts but also a regular ruling party. The self-perception of the state-party, which it energetically tried to enforce on the Tanzanian population, is not simply that of a ruling party staying in power but that of a supreme political organ that holds the last word on the social good and the political truth. This means that one of the main objectives of a political party—to get into government—is transformed into a singular goal of monopolizing politics.

This objective has been pursued single-mindedly in most African countries in the first three decades of independence with often catastrophic consequences for civil society—and thus the civil and political rights of individuals. I am suggesting that a major reason for this trend across Africa has been the absence of real class power. Instead of clinging to private wealth as rulers typically have in other parts of the world, African leaders have clung to public resources, turning them into means for the enhancement of their own political power. This privatization and monopolization of political power has rendered these leaders extrasensitive to public criticism and they have as systematically as possible taken steps to discourage it. The result is that there has been virtually no debate of major public policies, let alone of the constitutional and legal principles that should guide the conduct of politics. It is with this kind of political reality that academics and other intellectuals in Africa have had to contend for almost thirty years.

Consequences for the Intellectuals

In the early years after independence, African intellectuals felt an affinity with the objectives of the nation-state. Many accepted positions in political and administrative positions in government, not merely because of good salaries but also because of a genuine commitment to the nationalist cause. But this recruitment of intellectuals into official positions of the state, which continued almost unabated through the 1960s and 1970s, depleted civil society of its strength. Only to the extent that these intellectuals in government were ready to take independent positions was there going to be much of a public discourse on matters of state. For a while some tried to bring different perspectives to bear on policy, but with the consistent trend toward greater reliance on affective relations rather than ideas and reason, the scope for such interventions rapidly declined. Those who persisted found themselves in political detention or were in some instances killed. The latter happened in the late 1960s to two East African intellectuals, one on the political right—Tom Mboya in Kenya—and the other on the political left—Kassim Hanga in Tanzania. These assassinations and detentions in the first decade of independence pretty much discouraged intellectuals from sticking their necks out.

The almost inevitable consequence was a growing self-censorship among African intellectuals, an attitude that was very much lamented—and sometimes criticized—in the Kampala symposium. A few remained adamant and continued to criticize their societies. Writers like Ngugi wa Thiongo in Kenya were eventually forced into exile. Many of these intellectuals ended up in Europe and North America. Given the distance from their homelands and the relative openness of these societies, the exiles were capable of continuing their intellectual pursuits but were unable to exercise much influence back home. On the other hand, those who decided to stay on the African continent faced their share of problems. As temporary guests in other countries they soon learned that they had to be very careful because the political security services of African governments often collaborated. Thus they were not only effectively silenced but also constantly exposed to the risk of being deemed "superfluous" or "undesirable" by the host-country authorities. Tiyambe Zeleza of Malawi (1990) provided a very insightful account of these issues in Kampala.

The case of those intellectuals just discussed must not be confused with that of many other African academics who have left their home country for economic reasons. During the late 1970s and 1980s a good number of university teachers in countries suffering economic decline moved to what participants in the Kampala symposium referred to as "greener pastures," notably in southern Africa, where job opportunities have been available and remuneration considerable, at least by African standards. Most of these academics ended up in the small universities of Botswana, Lesotho, and Swaziland, but some ventured as far as the "homeland" universities in the Republic of South Africa. The latter move was seen by many as having added insult to the injury already inflicted on African intellectuals.

If political co-optation and intimidation gradually reduced the number of true intellectuals and silenced any autonomous voices in African countries in the first two decades of independence, the situation changed in the 1980s. The promise of a better life for themselves and their families that many Africans, intellectuals included, had accepted in exchange for their political freedom had not materialized. As the secretary-general of CODESRIA, Thandika Mkandawire, stressed in Kampala, this barter produced neither more food nor more products. On the contrary, the economic decline that became increasingly evident in the 1980s, and forced many governments to succumb to demands by the international finance institutions for shrinking the public sector, seriously added to the already existing sense of insecurity among the intellectuals. For many, the policies imposed by the International Monetary Fund and the World Bank were seen as a rape of their countries. It is not surprising, therefore, that together with the oppressive African governments, these two institutions came under particularly heavy criticism in the symposium.

The educational sector has been severely hit by the cutbacks governments have ordered. People have been asked to carry a heavier burden themselves through various cost-sharing measures. University students have been forced increasingly to finance their studies with loans. With the prospect for a job on graduation very dim and salaries for those few who actually obtain one very low, the loan burden appears especially heavy. Existing university teachers find no difficulty in sympathizing with the students' cause. Their own salaries have been reduced to a trickle of what they used to be before inflation and devaluation made them "unlivable." For the bulk of Africa's academics today, moonlighting is a necessity and typically provides the bulk of their annual income. Such parallel activities stretch from farming, chicken breeding, and cattle raising, on one end, to lucrative international consultancies, on the other. The material conditions of the African intellectuals have deteriorated so much that it is surprising that there are any left at all.

Events in the past couple of years, however, indicate that Africa's intellectuals are very much alive and ready to wage a war for their rights. The growing impatience among both academics and students in various countries in Africa is evident in a rapidly increasing series of strikes and demonstrations aimed at the corrupt and ineffective authorities of their countries. This has escalated the number of clashes between these groups and the national security forces. CODESRIA had compiled press clippings of such incidents for the Kampala symposium, and both Amnesty International and the London-based Africa Watch had prepared reports on the detention of academics in various African countries. Judging from the reaction that this material generated in the symposium, there is growing evidence that Africa's intellectuals are not going to take the consequences of one-person and one-party rule lying down, even though as a result of this decision many expose themselves to great personal risks. Symposium participants were treated to vivid eyewitness accounts of some of the worst slaughters that have taken place in recent years, e.g., the incident in Lubumbashi, Zaire, in May 1990 in which a large number of students—according to some sources as many as 150—were killed by security forces storming the campus.

While this growing unrest among students and teachers in institutions of higher learning has gained momentum from the political reforms in Eastern Europe and the calls from Western donors for African governments to be more respectful of civil and political rights, it began before it was evident that the communist systems of Eastern Europe—the model for many African leaders—were going to collapse. Much of the drive for political reform among Africa's intellectuals draws its inspiration from domestic contradictions, and it would be wrong to attribute it primarily to the wave of liberalization taking place elsewhere in the world. The fact that many tend to do so, however, is indicative of the dilemmas that African intellectuals face today.

The Dilemmas of Africa's Intellectuals

As the African intellectuals step up their battle for rights that enable them to play a more constructive role in society, they are faced with dilemmas that their counterparts in other regions of the world are not likely to encounter. Three such dilemmas became particularly apparent in the Kampala symposium. First, how can intellectuals perform their role without alienating the "masses"? Second, to what extent can they be both nationalists and universalists? Third, how can they become advocates for democratic rights without appearing merely to echo the voices of the international donor community?

The first of these dilemmas refers to the notion that intellectuals operate in what Mahmood Mamdani (1990: 1) described as the interface between manual and mental labor. Whether or not we accept his class-based argument about the "organic" role of intellectuals, it is evident that the principal task of the intellectual is to construct an image or model of society—a lens, as some would say, through which reality may be observed. In so doing the intellectual is inevitably engaged in "objectifying" that reality. The end product is a cognitive map, created through a set of symbols that signify and highlight certain aspects of society more than others.

The sphere in which intellectuals operate separates their discourse from day-to-day or practical discourse in which the majority of the people participate. This alienation from the "masses" is a consequence of intellectual activity in any society, but it becomes particularly problematic in African countries, where intellectuals have been educated in foreign languages and where for historical reasons vernaculars still lack the conceptual diversity needed to comprehend a range of contemporary phenomena. This shortcoming has forced African intellectuals to retain their discourse in languages to which the ordinary people are not privy. One consequence has been that political leaders, weary of critique from intellectuals, have effectively been able to criticize them of being strangers to the problems of the people.

This raises the question of language rights (discussed more fully by Akinnaso in chapter 8). What difference would it make if intellectual discourse were to be conducted in an African language? The experience of Kiswahili in Tanzania suggests that the use of a vernacular—or a lingua franca developed out of a series of related vernaculars, as is the case with Kiswahili—does increase communication between the elite and the people. But languages are more than mere means of communication. They are embedded in cultures and as such are reflective of a broad range of values associated with a given society. Thus, while steady progress has been made in constructing new words for a large number of phenomena—mainly technical and official—for which there was no equivalence in Kiswahili or the local vernaculars in the past, the culture associated with the language still limits the intellectual discourse to narrow and often parochial parameters. It enables the intellectual to be more closely in touch with the people, but the use of Kiswahili limits his or her ability to stay in touch with, let alone appreciate, intellectual developments elsewhere. Which is more important has always been, and continues to be, a matter of dispute among African intellectuals. For example, Ngugi wa Thiongo believes that the only effective means of communication with the masses is the local vernacular. In this argument he has been proven right, at least in part, by the fact that the Kenyan authorities banned his plays in Kikuyu—the vernacular—but have never prohibited his books in English, which are freely available in stores throughout the country. On the other side is the late Okot p'Bitek, who satirized the African elite, including his fellow intellectuals, for not appreciating their roots, yet found it necessary to communicate in English in order to get his message home. Therefore, whichever way African intellectuals turn will exact costs: emphasizing the need for staying in touch with the masses limits the intellectual horizon and outreach because of the limits and the parochial character of the culture; stressing the global character of intellectual discourse, on the other hand, distances them from the particular problems facing the masses.

This dilemma has been reinforced by the fact that intellectuals have not really been allowed to operate in civil society. As suggested above, political leaders have either co-opted them into the state realm or silenced them through suppression. This has also had a bearing on their ability to deal with the second dilemma: how far can they be both nationalists and universalists? The political leadership in African countries has never allowed a debate of nationalist issues. These leaders have taken for granted that they know what is in the best interest of the new nation; hence it has been left to officials in state-parties to decide these matters unilaterally. This means that the nationalist rug has been pulled out from under the intellectuals' feet. While retaining their ambition to be relevant to the nationalist cause, they have been compelled to seek other platforms from which to argue their points.

In the context of the anticolonial atmosphere that has continued to dominate African countries, it is not surprising that African intellectuals have been more inclined to turn to Marxism and not to liberalism for ammunition. The class argument has served their cause well, even if it has had little to do with the "objective" conditions in Africa, primarily because it is directed at the social establishment and contains the call for an overhaul of existing social relations. Many African intellectuals have implicitly or explicitly maintained that because their argument is not conservative, it can't be "foreign" in societies striving for social transformation, and it therefore gives them the legitimacy they need to criticize corrupt and oppressive rulers in Africa. The fact is, of course, that the political circumstances are a good deal more complex. First of all, Marxism is no more indigenous to Africa than is liberalism or capitalism. Hence it has not been difficult for political leaders to claim that Marxist intellectuals are espousing "foreign ideologies." What is more, with the delegitimization of this school of thought in the very countries where until recently it was most strongly embraced, the African intellectuals still adhering to it appear to be out on a limb. Even here, therefore, whichever way they turn they find themselves up against big obstacles.

This brings us to the third dilemma that was very much in the forefront of the debates in Kampala: how to advocate democracy without appearing merely to echo the words of the West? With no opportunity to embrace nationalism fully as their cause and with the decline, if not death, of Marxism, the options for African intellectuals have been severely circumscribed. They have had little choice but to adopt gradually the language of the liberals: civil and political rights, which until recently were scorned by African leftists, are now part of their discourse, as the Kampala symposium bore evidence of. But how can they accommodate themselves in the same ideological arena as Western liberals? Although the space in this arena is crowded and the risk of confrontation great, the African intellectuals seem to have found three modes of coexistence.

The first, which is typical of the ideological left, is to redefine the liberal-democratic agenda by advancing the argument that true democracy does not stop with the strengthening of civil society; it must embrace the people and their social movements. In the Kampala symposium, this point was made by several speakers, though nowhere was it more strongly articulated than in the writing of Mamdani. The dilemma that he and others advocating this argument face is that there are no real social movements in African countries today. They used to be there in the colonial days and in some countries, like Ethiopia and Liberia, where the incumbent elite was being challenged by popular movements from within. In other places, the conditions for the emergence of social movements are very adverse as long as politics remains based on affective relations rather than real policy issues. Mamdani's references to the revolutionary strength of Meison (All-Ethiopia Socialist Movement) in Ethiopia and MOJA (Movement for Justice in Africa) in Liberia (Mamdani 1990: 10–12), while relevant as sources of inspiration to the political left, are not easy to replicate in Africa today, even if political reforms allow the introduction of more than one political party.

The second position has aimed at trying to keep some distance from the donor institutions so as to demonstrate the continued independence of the African intellectuals. This approach was very much in evidence in the symposium; a couple of presenters (see Ali 1990) related anecdotes of how African academics have been "forced to adhere to the agenda of expatriate consultants." Most of the attention was paid to the potential and real influence that powerful institutions like the World Bank have among African academics, although the donor representatives present came from "friendly" agencies (the Rockefeller Foundation, the Swedish Agency for Research Cooperation with Developing Countries (SAREC), and the Norwegian ministry of foreign affairs). A particularly insightful paper on donor relations with African academics was provided by David Court (1990). That paper, like many comments from the floor, suggested that the predicament facing both donors and academics is much more complex. No one disputes the fact that today donor agencies, particularly those with large funds, exercise influence over the African policy agenda in a way that they were never able to do in earlier decades. In this respect, the concern expressed by many African intellectuals is understandable: their agenda is in danger of being "domesticated" by outsiders, many of whom have little interest in and patience for empathizing with the predicament of African intellectuals.

The third position, which was also articulated at the meeting in Kampala, essentially amounts to an acceptance of the values of the West. Some Africans may have arrived at this position by way of resignation—having explored all other alternatives and found no other way forward. There is, however, also a growing constituency of African academics who have embraced liberalism more positively. Civil and political rights have come to occupy a more important position in their minds as a result of the oppression and tyranny that they have witnessed in so many places on the continent since independence. As the demands for political reform are growing, they find themselves in the forefront, often siding with outsiders against their own governments. For example, Ali Mazrui mentioned in his presentation to the symposium that he had advised the World Bank to introduce "social democratic indicators" by which it and other donors could hold African governments accountable for their behavior toward their own people. Not all participants agreed with Mazrui that this was a priority—in fact, it was viewed by some as playing into the hands of already powerful donors—and African leaders themselves are, of course, very uneasy about any such political conditionalities. Yet most African governments have so little credibility left, either among their own people or in the international community, that it is very unlikely that they can escape such conditionalities in the years ahead if they wish to continue receiving financial support from the West. For some in the symposium, this prospect appeared as a threat of recolonization. For others, however, it was merely a long-awaited recognition that democratic rights are an integral part of development (as Rhoda Howard argues with reference to women in chapter 5) and that African governments cannot expect to be treated any differently from governments in other parts of the world.

Conclusion

The CODESRIA symposium in Kampala, around which much of the discussion in this chapter has been built, is important for several reasons. First, it signifies the return of the development debate to the role of intellectuals that was once so prominent in Africa. Second, it indicates the readiness of the African intellectuals to examine more closely their own problems. For instance, symposium participants adopted the Kampala Declaration on Intellectual Freedom and Social Responsibility and vowed to institute a Pan-African mechanism for monitoring and disseminating news about violations of the rights of teachers and students as well as other intellectuals. Third, it marks the evolution away from a predominant concern with issues only of political economy and so-called development rights, which used to be so dominant as recently as just a few years ago.

"Intellectuals need freedom like the fish need water," argued one participant (Prah 1990: 4). One can add that symposium participants went a step further by insisting that "development requires freedom like fish require water." It was appropriate, therefore, that Ali Mazrui offered a friendly amendment from the floor to Kwame Nkrumah's famous call to his fellow African nationalists that they should first acquire political power so as to obtain the benefits that come with progress. In Mazrui's words, the maxim of the 1990s ought to read: "Seek ye first the kingdom of the mind, and everything else will be added unto ye."

No one at the conference, however, was so naive as to assume that political recognition of the rights that allow intellectuals to make their contribution to the development of society will come easily. Even with a measure of *glasnost* now present in most African countries, political reform is likely to be slow and difficult. Democracy requires a degree of civility and public tolerance of different viewpoints, a characteristic that African societies so far have showed little evidence of being able to generate and accommodate. Similarly, at least some African intellectuals need to internalize that what is important in a democracy is not the claim to possession of the truth but confidence in the process of arriving at it.

References

Ahmed, A. 1993. *Education Reform in Nigeria*. Boulder, Colo.: Lynne Rienner.

Alatas, Syed Hussein. 1977. *Intellectuals in Developing Societies*. London: Frank Cass.

Ali, Ali Abdel Gadir. 1990. "Donors' Wisdom vs. African Folly: What Academic Freedom and Which High Moral Standing?" Paper presented at the Symposium on Academic Freedom, Research and the Social Responsibility of the Intellectual in Africa, Kampala, 26–29 November.

Apter, David, ed. 1964. *Ideology and Discontent*. New York: Free Press.

Ashby, Eric. 1964. *African Universities and Western Tradition*. Cambridge: Harvard University Press.

Coleman, James S., ed. 1965. *Education and Political Development*. Princeton, N.J.: Princeton University Press.

Court, David. 1990. "Universities and Academic Freedom in East Africa 1963–1983: Random Reflections from a Donor Perspective." Paper presented at the Symposium on Academic Freedom, Research and the Social Responsibility of the Intellectual in Africa, Kampala, 26–29 November.

Feierman, Steven. 1990. *Peasant Intellectuals.* Madison: University of Wisconsin Press.
Hoare, Q., and Geoffrey N. Smith, eds. 1986. "Introduction to State and Civil Society." In *Selections from the Prison Notebooks of Antonio Gramsci.* London: Lawrence and Wishart.
Hodgkin, Thomas. 1960. *Nationalism in Colonial Africa.* New York: New York University Press.
Mamdani, Mahmood. 1990. "The Intelligentsia, the State and Social Movements: Some Reflections on Experiences in Africa." Paper presented at the Symposium on Academic Freedom, Research and the Social Responsibility of the Intellectual in Africa, Kampala, 26-29 November.
Mannheim, Karl. 1948. *Ideology and Utopia,* trans. Louis Wirth and Edward Shils. London: Routledge and Kegan Paul.
Mazrui, Ali. 1975. "The African University as a Multinational Corporation: Problems of Penetration and Dependency." *Harvard Educational Review* 45, no. 2 (May): 191-210.
Nyerere, Julius K. 1966. "The University's Role in the Development of New Countries." Opening address, World University Assembly, Dar es Salaam, Tanzania, 27 June.
Prah, Kwesi. 1990. "African Academics, Politics and States of Unfreedom." Paper presented at the Symposium on Academic Freedom, Research and the Social Responsibility of the Intellectual in Africa, Kampala, 26-29 November.
Shils, Edward. 1960. "Intellectuals in the Political Development of the New States." *World Politics* 12, no. 3 (April): 329-68.
Shivji, Issa G. 1990. "The Jurisprudence of the Dar es Salaam Declaration on Academic Freedom." Paper presented at the Symposium on Academic Freedom, Research and the Social Responsibility of the Intellectual in Africa, Kampala, 26-29 November.
———. 1991. "Debate Must Focus on Democracy." *Daily News,* Dar es Salaam, 7 January.
World University Service. 1987. *The Lima Declaration on Academic Freedom and Autonomy of Institutions of Higher Education.* Geneva, Switzerland.
Yesufu, J. M. 1973. *Creating the African University.* Ibadan: Oxford University Press.
Zeleza, Tiyambe. 1990. "The Intelligentsia and Academic Freedom: The Question of Expatriate African Scholars in African Universities." Paper presented at the Symposium on Academic Freedom, Research and the Social Responsibility of the Intellectual in Africa, Kampala, 26-29 November.

11

The Challenges of Domesticating Rights in Africa

GORAN HYDEN

A principal objective of this book is to transcend three limitations that have characterized much of the literature on human rights in Africa: the emphasis on textual analysis of leading documents, the dichotomization between "Western" and "African" rights, and the focus on adherence by individual countries to universal rights. The emphasis throughout is on the "constitutive" dimension of human rights in society, i.e., the processes by which they are being brought about and institutionalized. The contributors to this volume deal with both domestic and global forces that help shape rights and rights consciousness on the African continent. For example, Okoth-Ogendo, Howard, and Shanafelt draw attention to how Africa's position in the international order has affected the articulation of a certain stand regarding what rights are important and what weight to give to "rights" in relation to "development." Ahmed and Cohen, Akinnaso, Hansen, and Hyden point to various domestic arenas in which rights issues have already emerged or are beginning to emerge. Language and education rights are potentially explosive in Africa's plural societies. Obvious violations of the rights of groups like refugees and academics have already given rise to a new social consciousness. Rights, then, are dynamic and, once out in the open, potentially explosive.

What we believe is particularly significant about the African continent in the early 1990s is the extent to which human rights are rapidly imposing themselves on the domestic political agenda of individual countries. For three decades Africans have either ignored the rights question (and often referred to it somewhat derogatorily as an expression of Western imperialism only) or satisfied themselves with a focus on the collective rights of Africans vis-à-vis the international community. With these limitations now giving way, the role of human rights in African politics becomes much more pertinent and relevant than before. That is why I wish to return in this concluding chapter to the question of how human rights might be domesticated in African politics and how they may be sustained in socioeconomic circumstances that are likely to remain difficult in the years ahead.

The presentation is divided into three sections. The first deals with the relationship between rights and politics in Africa over time. Beginning with a look at precolonial Africa, it traces this relationship through the colonial and postcolonial periods. The second section places the contemporary African scene in a comparative context and discusses various rights perspectives and their impact on governance. The third section addresses, with specific reference to Africa, the question of the universality of rights in the context of a global order where the notion of state sovereignty prevails but is increasingly being challenged by perceived global interdependencies.

Rights and Politics in Africa: A Historical Overview

Drawing on Cohen's point in chapter 1 that rights emerge from public discourse about fairness claims and Nagan's argument in chapter 4 that decision-making processes condition the place of human rights in the public order, I argue in this chapter that politics is the ultimate arbiter of the place accorded to rights in society. It is not a coincidence that the concept of human rights is, as Donnelly (1982b) stresses, an artifact of Western civilization. The fact that the Judeo-Christian tradition has become the harbinger of rights on a global scale has less to do with the moral superiority of the particular rights derived from this tradition than with its ability to institutionalize political processes within which a rights discourse can be meaningfully conducted. Particularly important is the consistent use of reason to redefine the public realm and thus overcome the limitations and rigidities inherent in specific customs and traditions. Western civilization has become what might be called a "supertradition" that remains resilient and constantly influential because of the flexibility that reason gives to its values, not because of a presumed superiority of any one of the values it espouses. The systematic application of reason to the basic questions of how individuals should relate to each other and to their rulers helps create rules that are divorced from particular interests. As a result, political space is created within which fairness claims can be made with reference to "rules of the game" that individual actors can evade only at considerable cost. It is this aspect of Western culture that makes it so controversial to people of other backgrounds who are used to accepting tradition without question and for whom the scope for alternatives is therefore limited. It is with this perspective in mind that I will now examine more closely the relationship between rights and politics in Africa over time.

Precolonial Times

Following the point above, one can argue that each culture contains specific sets of rights and duties that are understood by its members. In this sense rights are universal. The difference between one society and another is the extent to which rights can be contested in public. It is only where rights shift from being latent to becoming manifest that we are ready to speak of the existence of rights.

In chapter 2 Fernyhough does an excellent job of putting to rest the argument that rights in precolonial Africa were exclusively collective or communitarian. To the extent that this argument (cf. Legesse 1980; Wai 1979; and Marasinghe 1984) portrays Africa as made up only of communal forms of social organization, in which membership constitutes the basis for rights, it conveys a one-sided, if not totally incorrect, image of the continent. Fernyhough demonstrates that in many precolonial societies, particularly those that had evolved rudimentary state structures of their own, social contradictions sometimes caused rebellions. These challenges to communitarian values are little known, but it is reasonable to assume that they helped redefine social relations and thus the contents of rights. Certainly there were precolonial societies, e.g., the Ashanti in Ghana, where a rudimentary "constitutional monarchy" had evolved. In these places, kings and other officials could not do whatever they pleased; they had to adhere to rules that had become sacrosanct in the community.

I must question, however, Fernyhough's claim that civil and political rights were established in these precolonial societies. First of all, it is not clear that rebellions and other forms of challenges to existing norms led to the extension of new rights that were individual as opposed to communitarian. It is reasonable to assume that as often as they may have caused a redefinition of rights, tradition was invoked to restore the same old rights. In short, although oral history may throw additional light on this issue, there is little in what we now know of precolonial Africa that indicates the existence of a rights discourse in public. Even if it existed, which I do not dispute, custom prevailed and prevented the emergence of a more open-ended debate about the content of various rights. The absence of a written tradition in many precolonial societies reinforced this reliance on custom rather than reason. It is therefore not surprising that rights in precolonial Africa were more often latent than manifest and typically "frozen in time." That is also why the efforts by some scholars—and politicians—to portray African rights in the contemporary context as exclusively "communal" have a definite ring of surreality about them.

The absence of a written law that could be reinterpreted in the context of changing circumstances may in fact have been the principal reason why human rights in precolonial Africa remained latent and really never developed into abstract systems of rule. As Milne (1986: 115) argues, "law can deliberately create new rights but custom cannot." Even if that may be an exaggeration, there is little doubt based on historical evidence that law differs from custom in that it is potentially more innovative. Thus we can conclude that while the rights situation was most likely much more complex than the current debate on African rights has suggested so far, there was little, if anything, in the way African societies ruled themselves that encouraged the growth of rights consciousness, let alone rights discourse.

Colonial Times

A peculiar legacy of precolonial Africa was the persistence of relatively rudimentary technologies for tilling the land and therefore the prevalence of what Goody (1971) refers to as the rule over people rather than land. While this precapitalist mode of production did not rule out the rise of state structures, it had the effect of encouraging patrimonial rather than bureaucratic forms of governance. While the latter encourages the rise and predominance of a rule orientation, the former feeds on clientelist relations, where an affective rather than a legal dimension is determinant.

This system became subject to great pressures as European countries extended their power and control over Africa in the late nineteenth century. Although Africa had been stratified by both domestic and external forces prior to this date, colonization in the late nineteenth century brought with it the capitalist system of production. The result was the gradual reorganization of production on the land along lines that reflected the internal dynamics of this economic system. Even though scholars differ on the extent to which capitalism under colonial rule actually changed African society, there is little doubt that colonial rulers brought to Africa a different system of governance. It was not any more democratic than what Africans had experienced before, but it was rule oriented, thus inserting between the European officials and the African population a new social detachment. In precolonial times, Africans in need had been able to call on their ruler at any time, but in the system established by the Europeans they had to accept not only queuing for their turn but also the possibility that their need could not be met because it did not fit government priorities.

Given this situation, it is not surprising that African reactions to colonial rule led to rebellion and frustration. The confrontation between African and European values in the early days of colonial rule had the effect of making the local population, especially those interacting with their colonial masters, develop new fairness claims that would not necessarily have come about otherwise. At least as far as human rights goes, colonial rule did "shake up" the Africans and forced them to think in new terms. Thus, while they were kept in bonds during the whole colonial period, a new social and political consciousness grew out of that experience. The relatively "naked" character of domination that prevailed in many colonies, backed up by the notion that Europeans were culturally superior and therefore engaged in an historically necessary "civilizing mission," forced on the African population the discrepancy between the promises of civilization and its political practice.

This transparent discrepancy, which Africans experienced in many situations (Hodgkin 1960), had two consequences that are of significance to the discussion here. The first was that Africans discovered the opportunities inherent in the Western system of governance as practiced in Europe. They learned how people were treated as citizens with equal rights and began to argue that these rights ought to be extended to colonial subjects as well. As the nationalist movements in Africa began to gather momentum after World War II, this argument served as a principal catalyst. The irony of these nationalist struggles, however, was that while the Africans were demanding civil and political rights (e.g., one man, one vote; freedom of association; and freedom of speech), the total denial of such rights during the colonial period turned this demand into a collective expression. These more specific rights were simply overshadowed by the fundamental call for self-determination or independence. Thus, while these specific rights served a useful purpose of shifting European opinion in favor of the plight of the colonized peoples, they were never effectively internalized by sufficient numbers of Africans to become irreversible rules. To the extent that a new rights consciousness had evolved, it was one directed against domination by outsiders.

The other consequence was that Africans never really developed a respect for and loyalty to the public realm established by the colonial masters. The arena of public policy-making had always been dominated by the Europeans. A few Africans had been incorporated into this system. Some had become its trusted and efficient servants. Still, these numbers were very few and the colonial state—the core of this public realm—was too closely associated with exploitation and repression among too many Africans to allow a respect for the civic institutions inherited from the colonial masters to evolve (Ekeh 1975).

Postcolonial Times

The first couple of decades of independence in African states were understandably characterized by a search for a new identity—one that gave these countries back some of their "Africanness." The deliberate strategy of the continent's nationalist leaders was to identify the cultural elements that they perceived as peculiar to Africa. Prominent spokespersons for this generation of leaders, notably Kwame Nkrumah, Sekou Toure, and Julius Nyerere, emphasized such features as the "classless" structure of African society and its communitarian as opposed to individualist foundation. In doing so, these influential nationalists set the stage for much of the debate on human rights in Africa that was to follow, beginning in the 1970s. It has been reviewed at some length by Fernyhough and alluded to by several other contributors in this volume, so there is no reason to go over it again. Suffice it to say at this point that whatever the merits of this outlook on human rights, it reflected very much the predominant thinking in Africa until recently. To be sure, there were those, particularly in neo-Marxist circles, who refused to identify with this perspective, but their position was to downplay the significance of rights by viewing them as "bourgeois inventions." In this climate, then, African politicians and intellectuals found it difficult to recognize the importance of civil and political rights as perceived elsewhere in the world, particularly in the West. They preferred to stress the exceptional nature of the African case.

This orientation was reinforced by their perception that as stragglers in a global race for progress, Africa's new states could not afford to consider individual rights with the same degree of concern as countries that were more developed and had the "luxury" of nurturing pluralism. Development demanded national unity and invited a stress on duty rather than on rights. In the early years after independence, many Africans shared this perspective. They were ready to make the sacrifice to build the new nation. It is difficult to say how long this outlook was spontaneously embraced by these Africans, but it is clear that it was long enough to provide African governments with a rationale to build up a strong political apparatus that could be used for development—but also for control of citizens who did not share the ideology pronounced by the leadership. In short, African leaders could justify their move toward greater authoritarianism in the name of development. Neither the continent's own intellectuals nor others, notably the donor agencies, commented much on this trend in the 1960s and 1970s. The former were preoccupied with defending Africa against what they perceived as neocolonial machinations. The latter tried to stay out of official comments on the internal affairs of any African country. Therefore, frequent human rights violations—for example, detention without trial—were committed but largely overlooked as long as they did not threaten national development or upset specific foreign governments by hurting their interests.

A third factor that contributed to the neglect of human rights in the early years after independence was the plural or multiethnic composition of African societies. The colonial powers had drawn up the national borders with little or no consideration of how these grouped or separated local peoples. The artificiality of these borders became another excuse for strengthening the state apparatus to enable it to keep the fledgling nation-state together. As a corollary, rights of individuals or minority groups were seen as potentially subversive, i.e., encouraging tendencies toward secession.

Together these powerful factors laid the foundation for authoritarian rule in postindependence Africa. The basic tenets were contained in the Charter of the Organization of African Unity that heads of state adopted in 1963. They paved the way for a trend in which it became natural for African governments to see themselves as absolved from rights concerns at home. The fact that the few attempts to monitor civil and political rights were conducted by Western-based organizations like Amnesty International could be used by these governments to conjure impressions of foreign support for "traitors" or "secessionists."

These factors are also important in understanding why African leaders subsequently came to emphasize "development rights" in particular. This so-called third generation of human rights is a direct outcome of the African experience and was launched in the optimistic days of the 1970s when OPEC had hiked up oil prices and the world was talking of the need for a new international economic order. Development was no longer merely a demand but a right that poor countries could and should claim from the rich nations. Such rights made sense to African governments and it is no coincidence that they have met with more support in those circles than anywhere else.

The evolution of this new set of rights had the effect of providing African governments with a legitimate foundation for engaging in "rights talks" without having to concede acknowledgment of civil and political rights for citizens of their own countries. To be sure, they had continued to be concerned about extending such rights to Africans in countries still under colonial occupation or white minority rule, but they had managed throughout most of the 1970s to keep this effort separate from the question of applicability to their own countries. This was feasible as long as these governments were seen as making a genuine effort to develop their countries and care for their citizens in a social or economic sense. The opportunity to operate with two separate rights standards began rapidly disappearing in the late 1970s as a result of the liberation of the Portuguese colonies and, above all, the rise to power of tyrants like Idi Amin, Macias Nguema, and Emperor Boukassa. Their blatant violation of even the most basic rights as well as their extensive use of torture and political assassinations became too much for many other African leaders, who realized the costs of such misdeeds to the rest of the continent.

The emergence of civil and political rights for individual citizens on the public agenda in African countries dates back to those grim days when the above-mentioned dictators could kill at will and it appeared the value of human life was totally lost. The African Bar Association, often in conjunction with the International Commission of Jurists, began organizing seminars on rights in various parts of Africa in the 1970s, and partly as a result of these efforts the first indigenous human rights associations began to operate in those days. Particularly important were the mainstream churches, notably the Catholics, Anglicans, and Presbyterians, in fostering this concern among local people. These fledgling efforts by lawyers and church activists were also important in getting the human rights issues on the OAU agenda. They proposed a human rights charter for Africa at the OAU meeting in Banjul in 1979 and continued to be involved in drafting the Banjul Charter on Human and Peoples' Rights, which was adopted by heads of state at a meeting in Nairobi in 1981 (Peter 1990; see also chapter 3 of this volume).

It was only in the late 1980s that the Human Rights Commission conceived in the Banjul Charter became operational. With limited powers of investigation and no right to prosecute, the Commission is a toothless tiger, but it has had the effect of legitimizing a broader debate on human rights and raising the prospect that—at least in the future—Africans themselves may take steps against violators of human rights (Kannyo 1984). So far, however, nothing has happened along such lines. The most encouraging thing in the 1980s was the spontaneous emergence of a public debate among Africans of the place of human rights in society and a recognition that civil and political rights were not a "luxury" but often a precondition for development. The broadening and deepening of this discourse is reflected in several volumes to which not only outsiders but also Africans have made significant contributions (Welch and Meltzer 1984; Forsythe 1989; An-Na'im and Deng 1990).

This debate has gained extra momentum in the early 1990s as more and more African countries have been swept by the winds of change created by political reformation in Eastern Europe and the Soviet Union. In a very short period of time the thrust of rights discourse in Africa has moved from an almost exclusive focus on the rights to development to a focus on rights as prerequisites for development. This was apparent at the conference on academic freedom in November 1990 to which reference is made in chapter 10. It is also evident in the increasingly frank debates about democracy that are currently taking place in many African countries. If these debates are anything to go by, it is likely that the Banjul Charter will soon be perceived as belonging to a past era. At a minimum, one can expect that demands for strengthening the Charter in the direction of greater protection of individual rights—especially those that relate to democratization—will evolve. In sum, the very first steps toward domesticating the whole range of human rights in Africa and placing them on the public agenda are now being taken. The rest of this chapter is devoted to the question of what the challenges are in translating this ambition into practice.

Rights and Governance: A Comparative Perspective

What has happened in Africa in the last few years is quite remarkable in that a far-reaching process of democratization has been set in motion in the midst of a serious economic decline. Africans talk genuinely of a "second liberation" (Hammarskjold Foundation 1987), yet they experience growing economic hardship. At first this seems contradictory, but what is often not fully understood is that the "discovery" of rights has an emancipating effect regardless of what the prevailing economic conditions might be. As Alexis de Tocqueville wrote, "There is nothing which, generally speaking, elevates and sustains the human spirit more than the idea of rights. There is something great and virile in the idea of right which removes from any request its suppliant character, and places the one who claims it on the same level as the one who grants it" (cited in Minogue 1977: 34). What we are witnessing in much of Africa, then, is the sense of elation brought about by the growing self-recognition that civil and political rights apply to Africans as much as to any other people of the world. But keeping this excitement alive depends on how successful African countries will be in solving their economic difficulties and how helpful the rest of the world will be toward Africa. The rights seed has been planted in soil that is still in need of improvement.

There are many challenges confronting African countries today, but there is growing recognition that they are institutional or, more specifically, related to the way these countries are being governed (World Bank 1989). The most striking is the weakness of civil society, i.e., the paucity and lack of strength of voluntary associations that bring citizens together in public action across primordial lines. The state-centered approach to development that African countries adopted with full support by the international community after independence has created a situation in which society has been reduced to a social desert. Instead of being encouraged to engage in public action for development, Africans have been left to fend for themselves in the informal sector or seek favors by attaching themselves to political patrons who might help them make social or economic gains. This has created a dual legacy that most likely will prove difficult to overcome. The first is a growing reliance on personalized rather than institutional leadership (Lemarchand 1972; Jackson and Rosberg 1982). Clientelist and patrimonialist forms of relations have come to dominate African politics. As I have suggested elsewhere (Hyden 1983), exchange of favors has taken the place of impartial principles, the economy of affection the place of the rule of law. The second is the gradual decline in loyalty to and belief in the ability of the state to solve societal problems. People have withdrawn into their local communities and seek solutions to their existential problems without waiting for the government to do anything. This may be interpreted as a positive sign—after all, people are at long last taking issues into their own hands. It would be wrong, however, to be too excited about this trend. First of all, the ability of local people to do things on their own is limited—a lot of problems are too big for them to solve by themselves. As a result, only small issues get tackled. Second, there is a tendency for people to depend on what are essentially "parochial" forms of organizations. These are very localized in character and difficult to extend beyond narrow cultural boundaries. They may help solve local problems but they add little to the growth and strengthening of civil society.

This estrangement of state institutions from society and the ensuing parochialization of social relations can be found throughout Africa but have been particularly evident in countries that adopted a socialist strategy of development and, in the process, reduced the opportunities for people to interact socially in new ways in the marketplace. Structural adjustment may help restore such interaction, and there is reason to believe that economic liberalization, if it is made to work, will enhance the prospects for political liberalization and thus for the strengthening of civil society. The growing concern for civil and political rights will itself contribute to this process.

The study of how rights consciousness emerges and how rights get institutionalized is as important a part of the study of human rights as is the monitoring of their implementation. Rights evolve in particular circumstances. Their content and the intensity with which they are being defended or advocated are related to prevailing political practice. Therefore it may be helpful to place the African situation in a comparative perspective and assess the prospects for a stricter adherence to civil and political rights in African governance by indicating how rights and duties tend to be treated in different regime types.

The distinction between rights and duties has always been treated as important in political theory. Debates continue in scholarly journals about their "correlativity" (e.g., Singer 1964; Braybrooke 1972; and Donnelly 1982a). In Western theory rights and duties are usually regarded as two sides of the same coin. One person's right is someone else's duty. Thus a "right" is a sphere of autonomy, guaranteed by law, within which a person may act in accordance with his or her conception of the good. A "duty" is the legal demand on another person or persons to respect that sphere of autonomy. In practice, however, this correlativity is rarely total and societies do tend to differ in terms of their relative emphasis on "right" as opposed to "duty." A rights orientation tends to be most pronounced in societies where the principle of exchange guides social action. Thus it is not a coincidence that rights tend to be strongly developed and duties more problematic in capitalist systems like the United States. A recent debate suggested that the sense of duty in America has declined so much in recent years that a "Bill of Duties" may become necessary to supplement the Bill of Rights (Lasch et al. 1991).

A certain balance between the two tends to be achieved in some countries, such as those in Western Europe, which allow free economies but where relatively small and homogeneous populations constitute real communities to which people feel loyal. The utilitarian logic that permeates American society is here tempered by a sense of obligation to the nation. It comes naturally and it is informed by respect for other human beings, at least those making up the same community. Patriotism in these countries does not require a manifest pride in the constitution or the flag. While many Europeans raise their flag to indicate that they are at home, Americans typically do so to display support for a national cause.

This need to mobilize a sense of duty around symbolic targets is important in understanding the predicament of countries like the former Soviet Union and Yugoslavia. Communism was viewed in both places as a superior social order based on the hegemony of strong central institutions (notably the vanguard party and the state) to which people were expected to display their highest level of respect and obligation. Here, then, individual rights were ignored and duties emphasized. Yet when it became apparent that these central institutions failed to deliver expected benefits and continued to complicate life, people's loyalty shifted away from these "man-made" institutions toward the ethnic or religious communities of which they had always been a part but whose significance had been overshadowed by the power and control exercised by the party and the state. By ignoring the rights dimen-

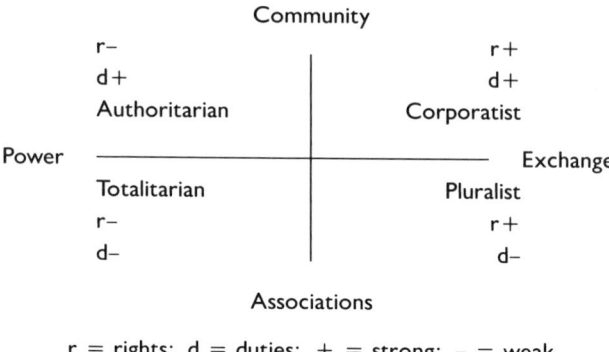

r = rights; d = duties; + = strong; − = weak

Figure 1. Rights, Duties, and Regime Types

sion and "placing all their eggs" in the duties basket, the governments of these countries helped create the state of disintegration in which these countries find themselves today.

The difference between totalitarian and authoritarian regimes is that the latter relies more on existing communities than on central institutions with "imperial" ambitions. Thus there may be more of a "fit" between the leadership and the expectations held by the community, even if governance is nondemocratic. Many countries that today are democratic or are undergoing democratization have emerged from authoritarian rule. The rich literature on the transition from authoritarianism in Latin America (e.g., O'Donnell, Schmitter, and Whitehead 1986) provides many illustrations of how different this process is from what the East Europeans are engaged in today. In the Latin American countries, duty has always been emphasized and often successfully upheld at the expense of rights, but the fact that leaders have typically shared the community values with their followers is probably one reason why authoritarian rule so often has given way to more democratic forms of governance without major upheavals. It is also significant that whenever authoritarian (notably military) rule has become too brutal (as in Argentina and Chile), a genuine sense of outrage has developed and rights consciousness has grown in leaps and bounds. Thus any negation of the reciprocal expectations that exist between leaders and followers contains the potential for regime change in countries where authoritarian rule prevails. The relationship between rights, duties, and regime type is summarized in figure 1.

The prevailing regime type in Africa resembles the authoritarian type. As so much recent research (e.g., Rothchild and Chazan 1988; Wunsch and Olowu 1990) has demonstrated, a predominant feature of African politics is the prevalence of informal over formal systems of governance. African politics is conducted with less emphasis on institutions than on the personalized relations to which the persistence of a communitarian logic gives rise. Furthermore, African politics has been characterized more by reliance on power than on exchange; state rather than market has been the preferred mechanism of governance. It would be wrong, however, to assume that the situation is necessarily the same everywhere. For the purpose of understanding what the opportunities might be for domesticating human rights in Africa, it is important to identify some of these differences and assume not one but several possible future scenarios.

Let us return to the question of "cultural fit" between rulers and ruled. The hypothesis alluded to above is that wherever rulers are drawn from the same community as the ruled, it is possible to balance rights and duties more easily than in contexts where such a correspondence does not exist. The case of Botswana seems to bear this out. Botswana is a country that is dominated by one single ethnic community, the Tswana. It is also a place where colonial penetration was modest; customary institutions were retained under British rule. Although the country's economy has been diversified, particularly after independence, to rely on the production and export of precious minerals, the local cattle economy has continued to provide the principal source of livelihood for the people of Botswana. In addition to being one of Africa's most successful economies, the country is also one of the most democratic. Ever since independence it has allowed a multiparty system. In the 1980s it has continued to open up by allowing the development of independent newspapers (Holm and Molutsi 1992). What is more, leaders generally respect constitutional rules; they do not overstep the boundaries of the public mandate they have been given. As a result, Botswana is remarkably free from arbitrary arrests, corruption, and other violations of the reciprocal expectations that exist between rulers and ruled.

The case of Lesotho, however, places Botswana in a comparative perspective. Both nations are dominated by a single community—in the former, the Sotho. Both were subject to modest colonial penetration and both are located in southern Africa, dependent on the economy of the Republic of South Africa. Still, Lesotho is a country where efforts to introduce local democracy have been aborted by leaders who have placed their own interests above those of the community. As a result, as Shanafelt discusses in chapter 7, the rule of law has been undermined and political violence allowed to take its place. How do we explain this difference? One possible explanation is materialist: large numbers of Sotho males have become migrant workers in South Africa, while the Tswana have remained flourishing cattle owners. While Botswana has been able to reduce its dependence on South Africa by developing alternative export markets, Lesotho has become increasingly dependent on that country. But economic dependency and other economic variables are not always correlated to democracy in the same way and other explanations are possible. One is that democratic governance, once allowed to develop, breeds its own success. Respect for rules and tolerance of other views grow inconspicuously but in ways that strengthen the foundation of democratic governance. "Rights talk" works.

The importance of the governance factor can also be seen in other examples. What is astonishing about Africa is how few revolts the continent has witnessed as a result of the tremendous rise in cost of living that most countries have experienced in the 1980s and 1990s. To be sure, riots have occurred, but they have been relatively isolated, confined to the privileged (e.g., students and teachers) rather than the underprivileged urban strata. More serious has been the breakdown in the social order caused by malgovernance. As political leaders like Samuel Doe of Liberia and Siad Barre of Somalia turned increasingly toward their own kith and kin and disregarded the welfare of other citizens in the country, loyalty to their regimes began to dwindle. As the code of political conduct derived from the notion of reciprocity between rulers and ruled was blatantly violated, the bonds that had held the country together gave way to more narrowly defined (clan, ethnic, religious) loyalties.

This argument has a wider applicability in Africa. It is necessary to enable us to understand how it is that African countries are currently entertaining democratic ideals while undergoing economic stagnation. The conventional wisdom, as laid out in many studies (Lipset 1960; Needler 1968; Banks 1970; Bollen 1979; Lipset, Seong, and Torres 1990), is that democracy is almost exclusively correlated with economic growth. The current efforts to democratize governance in Africa, which are affecting most countries (Africa Demos 1993), draw their strength not from the economic performance of these countries but from pent-up frustrations with their autocratic rule. Thus, as the case of Africa shows, there is a need to add another hypothesis to the study of democratization. It is the opposite of the first: the more people have experienced various forms of malgovernance (arbitrary arrests, blatant favoritism at the expense of others, and other types of breaches of reasonable fairness claims), the stronger the desire and commitment to establish respect for civil and political rights.

It would be wrong to assume, however, that such desire and commitment will always last long enough to enable the successful institutionalization of such rights. In many countries in Africa, the changes in regime structures that are required are quite considerable. Therefore it is important to identify some of the intervening variables that cannot be ignored in future studies of rights and governance in Africa. Three factors are of special significance: the weakness of the civic public realm, the transient nature of social relations, and the tendency to endure rather than challenge hardship.

One of the most apparent weaknesses of the African political systems is the weakness of the civic public realm (Ekeh 1975; Jackson and Rosberg 1982; Rothchild and Chazan 1988). Individual citizens have little or no loyalty to the institutions—civil or military—that have been set up for the purpose of governing their country. Instead, their immediate loyalty tends to be toward a primary social organization such as their home community. In some cases, this loyalty has a religious as opposed to a secular basis. This has led to a paradox of governance: instead of taking advantage of this strong community orientation, African governments have done everything since independence to curb or destroy it. They have viewed it as potentially subversive, as undercutting the effort to build a new nation-state. One of the few countries in Africa that has tried to grapple with this issue in a constitutional fashion is Nigeria, where a federal mode of governance has been attempted as a way of addressing the centrifugal pressures inherent in African society. It is in this context that issues such as educational quotas (discussed by Ahmed and Cohen in chapter 9) or the right to a third language—a vernacular (addressed by Akinnaso in chapter 8)—have arisen. The "costs" and "benefits" of reversing the past trend are now being cautiously assessed in some other countries, and a recent study (Wunsch and Olowu 1990) makes a strong case for the need to allow greater decentralization of authority to local-level institutions of governance.

Greater attention to human rights and the need for the rule of law will in and of itself help build a better understanding of the importance of a civic public realm that is respected by those who enter and operate within it. "Rights talk" makes a contribution to the formation of an institutional superstructure that is truly civic and stands above primary social organizations, yet gives people a chance to practice local governance. Two scenarios may be hypothesized here. The first is that recognition of the importance of a civic public realm and, by implication, respect for the rule of law will be most immediate in situations where conflict between religious or other groups in society is very pronounced (e.g., Sudan and South Africa) but where the task of creating such a realm is also most difficult. Success is possible, but only if there is a willingness to avoid extreme approaches and engage in a "positive-sum" game involving a reciprocal give-and-take of crucial issues affecting one's own community. The second scenario applies to other countries where the conflicts between communities are less sharp and have been successfully managed since independence in an informal manner, relying more on personal patronage than on constitutional rule. Bringing about rights awareness in such societies may prove more difficult; individuals do not automatically identify the advantages of a different system of governance when the existing one seems to work, at least from their personal perspective. Personal rule, however, has its definite limits, particularly when seen from the national or macroeconomic perspective. It does not foster the evolution of institutions that can run society. The success of governance is totally dependent on the personal qualities of the individual ruler. Thus, perhaps somewhat paradoxically, consciousness about the importance of legal and constitutional rights is more likely to develop in countries where the personal ruler is arbitrary and autocratic rather than benign and benevolent. It may be no coincidence that human rights are much more openly discussed and known in Kenya and Uganda, where violations have been many over the years, than in Tanzania, where they have been relatively few and certainly not blatant.

Another feature of the African scene that cannot be ignored when talking about the prospects for the domestication of human rights relates to the transient nature of social relations among people. As Kopytoff (1984) argues, Africans have tended to be "frontier men," but very different from those in the Americas. Africans have had the wish to migrate in search of new opportunities, but this ambition has been focused on discovering new social attachments. Even though Africans have in the end always returned to their original homestead—if no earlier, certainly at the time of burial—the African culture is not "feline," as he suggests. There is no strong attachment to a particular place. Instead, individuals develop social networks in which the exchange of positive sentiments—the essence of the economy of affection—serves to cement relations among people. Such relations, however, are typically fleeting: they serve a particular purpose at a particular time but are often abandoned in favor of other, more rewarding relations as circumstances change. Even relations of domination are of this kind. They are based on the control of other persons rather than control of material resources. This is perhaps the strongest argument against the use of "class" to describe relations of domination in Africa.

But what are the implications of this phenomenon for the domestication of rights? Two aspects of this cultural orientation are of particular importance. One is that the concept of private property lacks a strong foundation in African culture. Even today, in spite of many decades of capitalist penetration, the basic principle of private property rights, which is so fundamental to that system—and to the emergence of civil and political rights—is only beginning to be understood and embraced. This reluctance to recognize the principle of private property as fundamental to the establishment of social order has its parallel in the public sector, where respect for public property, as understood in Western culture, is equally faint. Thus it can be hypothesized that wherever economic policies encourage the evolution of a "bourgeois" culture, the prospects for the institutionalization of civil and political rights are greater than where the policies fail to do so.

The second aspect is the role affection plays in African culture. In contrast to Western societies, where affection has been domesticated in the private realm and where, as a result, individuals expect to show emotions, in Africa it straddles both the private and the public realm. There is nothing embarrassing in the use of affection in any of the realms, but it is done without display. Showing sentimentality—as Westerners do without restraint in public—is to Africans a sign of weakness in the context of the private relations between two persons. Demonstration of affection in official contexts is often viewed as a sign of pride and arrogance. The result is that affection is everywhere, yet always reduced to a covert status. Here it may be hypothesized that civil and political rights will be most easily realized in societies where the prevalence of relations of affection are being effectively questioned as useful in the public realm and hence increasingly confined to the private realm. A trend in such a direction is already under way in certain circles, notably among the educated elite.

The tendency to endure rather than challenge hardship is another factor in African culture that cannot be ignored. This "stoic" feature manifests itself particularly in situations where the difficulties are imposed by outside and anonymous forces. For example, the orientation that many refugees show to their predicament is, as Hansen discusses in chapter 6, one of coping at any cost—preferably, when circumstances permit, in a way that allows them to avoid being captured by official authorities and placed in settlements. But even other categories of people demonstrate extraordinary endurance in taking hardship. Again, when they find ways of coping with it, they use their "exit" rather than their "voice" option, i.e., they evade rather than challenge the authorities to do something for them.

This is not to suggest that Africans always take matters "lying down." They are extremely sensitive to any harm that is inflicted by other persons who break the code of reciprocity that helps maintain social order. Thus the transparent fashion in which colonial rulers violated such norms gave rise to strong anticolonial sentiments among people at large. Similarly, in postcolonial days the use of the voice option has been invoked only in instances when rulers or patrons have abandoned their commitment to treat their subjects or clients fairly. The problem with these responses is that they have been fleeting and at least up to now have not resulted in the institutionalization of organized venues for preempting similar clashes in the future. It seems that participants in these confrontations have taken for granted that the code of reciprocity is so deeply entrenched in the local culture that somehow social peace and order will be automatically restored. The "institutionalized suspicion" that in Western tradition has led to the evolution of systems of checks and balances—and thus fostered rights consciousness—has so far not been considered necessary by Africans. Thus, a hypothesis would have to include reference not only to whether people adopt the exit or the voice option but also to whether in the latter case there is evidence of awareness about the need for institutional checks and balances. Such awareness is widespread in countries like Nigeria but still far from accepted in other countries, although the current democratization wave appears to give it a boost.

This list of intervening variables is neither complete nor fleshed out here but is meant to be indicative of the kind of questions or propositions that can be developed for meaningful research on rights and governance issues in Africa in the 1990s. The suggestions above are derived from our "constitutive" approach to the study of human rights, which invites the researcher to focus as much on the process of rights formation as on their implementation.

Universal Rights and State Sovereignty

This book suggests that although rights violations in Africa are still frequent and there are many constraints to the institutionalization of the rule of law, progress has been made in the latter direction, particularly in the past few years. One major reason for this is that the international climate has changed dramatically as a result of the ending of the Cold War and the strong wave of democratization in Eastern Europe. While the notion that "democracy has no enemy anymore" may be exaggerated, there is reason to believe that the current prodemocracy move in literally every corner of the world is enhancing the process of universalizing civil and political rights to an extent hitherto unknown. This raises anew the question of how global efforts to institutionalize these rights can be combined with a legitimate respect for the principle of state sovereignty.

African countries have so far been particularly sensitive to any encroachment on state sovereignty. The Organization of African Unity has used this principle to preempt the temptation of one African government meddling in the affairs of another, but it has also been applied to prevent a closer examination by outside agencies of such things as human rights violations. The extent to which this principle should be allowed to reign, however, has increasingly come into question as civil strife or civil war afflicts individual member countries, as in Ethiopia, Liberia, Somalia, and the Sudan. Mass killings, if not outright genocide, have been associated with these conflicts. Other Africans as well as outsiders believe that silence or nonintervention in these circumstances is morally repugnant. Where does one draw the line between a legitimate and a nonlegitimate intervention to protect human rights?

In order to answer that question it may first be necessary to ask whether states are capable of moral responsibility. Michael Walzer (1980) is at present probably the most eloquent defender of the notion that states, like individuals, should be treated as free persons, the pursuit of whose objectives requires the noninterference of others (Vincent

1986). In Walzer's perspective, states are worthy of respect because they provide collectively for the purposes of individuals. The common tradition of a country shapes a common life that it is the function of the state to protect against the outside world (Walzer 1977: 54). The scope for just interventions in Walzer's theory is very limited. A repressive government should be allowed to get away with such acts as long as it can demonstrate that it is in accordance with the domestic tradition that the state is presumed to protect against outsiders. If a Muslim government applies with vengeance the *sharia* law, which in the view of many outsiders would be seen as oppressive or barbaric, others cannot justify an intervention as long as Islam is the single or overwhelmingly dominant religion in the country.

Contrasting this conservative approach to state intervention is the position taken by Hansen in chapter 6. He questions the basis on which states in Africa can claim sovereignty. He believes that individuals and groups should be allowed to get in the way of the relations of states in order to reduce their inclination to do harm to people. In short, Hansen rejects the idea that states are capable of acting in a morally responsible fashion.

An increasing number of Africans have been inclined to take a similar, if not identical view, out of frustration with the postindependence governance experience on the continent. A. M. Babu (1991: 31), one of the continent's most respected intellectuals, writes that most people who are speaking on behalf of Africa are not really representative of the people; they are in power simply by denying the democratic rights of their opponents. Their views are not authentic; they have alienated themselves from the local cultures by not allowing others to define the orientation of state policies.

This new questioning of the basis of state sovereignty in the African context is providing a rationale for outsiders to become increasingly vocal on how African states should conduct their affairs. These outsiders include not only the human rights organizations like Amnesty International and Africa Watch but also other nongovernmental organizations and governments representing donor countries. Although Rhoda Howard, both in chapter 5 of this volume and elsewhere (Howard 1989), criticizes Canada for engaging only in cosmetic or symbolic gestures of criticism of human rights violations, whether in South Africa or elsewhere on the continent, there is little doubt that outside organizations have moved their positions forward with respect to their readiness to openly criticize autocratic tendencies in African politics. Forsythe (1989) concludes his recent work on human rights and development by suggesting that the future of human rights in developing countries rests on action by nongovernmental organizations who are ready to "stick their neck out" to criticize governments for violating such rights.

Donor countries have long recognized the role of human rights in development assistance, but, as some observers (Rehof and Gulman 1989; Magnarella 1990) have noted, it is only more recently that they have tried to operationalize these ideas. The question is, of course, how far they should go in order to be helpful to this cause in Africa. If they come across too strong, they may cause a backlash. OAU Secretary-general Salim Salim is on record as having said that Africa would not allow the outside world to dictate how the continent should be run. Nelson Mandela, while on a state visit to Kenya, told his host—President Daniel arap Moi, one of Africa's most insistent autocrats—that Western countries have no right to teach Africans about democracy. African scholars attending the Kampala conference on academic freedom (reported on in chapter 10) expressed a similar sentiment when they argued for the need for Africans themselves to be in charge of the democratization process.

But cannot donors be of some assistance in this process? Babu believes that Western countries can and should be more forthright in demanding African adherence to human rights conventions as a prerequisite for providing aid, and Mazrui (see chapter 10) argues that donors should develop "social democratic indicators" to assess African progress toward constitutional forms of democratic governance. While these viewpoints are understandable in the African context today, it is also necessary to recognize the limitations inherent in any outsider's attempt to promote the domestication of human rights in Africa. People can never be forced to become democratic or to respect human rights. This process is ultimately dependent on the effectiveness of domestic social forces. Outsiders can at best help to set standards and provide encouragement but are, and should be, confined to a backseat in this venture. As Richard Schwartz (1990: 382) concludes in a recent book on human rights in Africa, every society can learn from other societies effective ways of implementing rights, but in the end it is up to every local culture to give specific content to the formulation and implementation of such rights. The universalization of human rights is possible without necessarily abrogating such principles as state sovereignty and cultural integrity, but it requires much more attention to the issues of how rights develop in different cultures and how they get on the public-policy agenda.

These issues constitute a rich and varied research program that this book has only begun to sketch out but that needs further development and refinement as researchers in different disciplines engage in scholarly investigations that enable us to understand better the factors at play in the process of domesticating human rights in the African context.

References

Africa Demos. 1993. Newsletter issued by the African Governance Program, the Carter Center of Emory University, Atlanta.
An-Na'im, Abdullahi Ahmed, and Francis M. Deng, eds. 1990. *Human Rights in Africa: Cross-cultural Perspectives*. Washington, D.C.: Brookings Institution.
Babu, A. M. 1991. Struggle for Democracy. *Africa Events* 6, no. 12 (December): 30–31.
Banks, Arthur S. 1970. "Modernization and Political Change: The Latin American and AmerEuropean Nations." *Comparative Political Studies* 2 (2): 405–18.
Bollen, Kenneth A. 1979. "Political Democracy and the Timing of Development." *American Sociological Review* 44 (3): 572–87.
Braybrooke, David. 1972. "The Firm But Untidy Correlativity of Rights and Obligations." *Canadian Journal of Philosophy* 1, no. 3 (March): 351–63.
Donnelly, Jack. 1982a. "How Are Rights and Duties Correlative?" *Journal of Value Inquiry* 16: 287–97.
———. 1982b. "Human Rights and Human Dignity: An Analytic Critique of Non-Western Conceptions of Human Rights." *American Political Science Review* 76 (2): 303–16.
Ekeh, Peter. 1975. "Colonialism and the Two Publics in Africa: A Theoretical Statement." *Comparative Studies in Society and History* 17 (1): 91–112.
Forsythe, David P., ed. 1989. *Human Rights and Development: International Views*. New York: St. Martin's Press.
Goody, Jack. 1971. *Technology, Tradition and the State in Africa*. London: Hutchinson.
Hammarskjold Foundation. 1987. "The State and the Crisis in Africa: Towards a Second Liberation in Africa." Report on a seminar held in Uppsala, Sweden (September). *Development Dialogue* Nos. 1–2.
Hodgkin, Thomas. 1960. *Nationalism in Colonial Africa*. New York: New York University Press.
Holm, John, and Patrick Molutsi. 1992. "Democracy and Governance in Bo-

tswana." In *Governance and Politics in Africa*, ed. Michael Bratton and Goran Hyden. Boulder, Colo.: Lynne Rienner Publishers.

Howard, Rhoda. 1989. "Human Rights, Development and Foreign Policy." In *Human Rights and Development: International Views*. *See* Forsythe 1989.

Hyden, Goran. 1983. *No Shortcuts to Progress: African Development Management in Perspective*. Berkeley: University of California Press.

Jackson, Robert H., and Carl Rosberg. 1982. *Personal Rule in Black Africa*. Berkeley: University of California Press.

Kannyo, Edward. 1984. "The Banjul Charter on Human and Peoples' Rights: Genesis and Political Background." In *Human Rights and Development in Africa*. *See* Welch and Meltzer 1984.

Kopytoff, Igor. 1984. *The African Frontier: The Reproduction of Traditional African Societies*. Bloomington: Indiana University Press.

Lasch, Christopher, et al. 1991. "Who Owes What to Whom? Drafting a Constitutional Bill of Duties." *Harper's*, February, 43–54.

Legesse, Asmarom. 1980. "Human Rights in African Political Culture." In *The Moral Imperatives of Human Rights: A World Survey*, ed. Kenneth W. Thompson. Washington, D.C.: University Press of America for the Council on Religion and International Affairs.

Lemarchand, Rene. 1972. "Political Clientelism and Ethnicity in Tropical Africa: Competing Solidarities in Nation-Building." *American Political Science Review* 66, no. 1 (March): 68–90.

Lipset, Seymour Martin. 1960. *Political Man*. Garden City: Doubleday.

Lipset, Seymour Martin, Kyoung-Ryung Seong, and John C. Torres. 1990. "A Comparative Analysis of the Social Requisites of Democracy." Paper presented at the annual meeting of the American Political Science Association, San Francisco, 30 August–2 September.

Magnarella, Paul. 1990. "Promoting Peace, Human Rights and National Security: Focus on SubSaharan Africa." *Human Peace* 8, no. 2 (Summer): 3–8.

Marasinghe, Lakshman. 1984. "Traditional Conceptions of Human Rights in Africa." In *Human Rights and Development in Africa*. *See* Welch and Meltzer 1984.

Milne, A. J. M. 1986. *Human Rights and Human Diversity*. London: Macmillan Press.

Minogue, K. R. 1977. "Natural Rights, Ideology and the Game of Life." In *Human Rights*, ed. Eugene Kamenka and Alice Ehr-Soon Tay. London: Edward Arnold.

Needler, Martin C. 1968. "Political Development and Socio-Economic Development: The Case of Latin America." *American Political Science Review* 62, no. 3 (September): 889–97.

O'Donnell, Guillermo, Philippe Schmitter, and Lawrence Whitehead, 1986. *Transitions from Authoritarian Rule: Prospects for Democracy*. Baltimore: Johns Hopkins University Press.

Peter, Chris Maina. 1990. *Human Rights in Africa: A Comparative Study of the African Human and Peoples' Rights Charter and the New Tanzanian Bill of Rights*. Westport, Conn.: Greenwood Press.

Rehof, L. A., and C. Gulman, eds. 1989. *Human Rights in Domestic Law and Development Assistance Policies of the Nordic Countries*. Dordrecht: Martinus Nijhoff.

Rothchild, Donald, and Naomi Chazan, eds. 1988. *The Precarious Balance: State-Society Relations in Africa*. Boulder, Colo.: Westview Press.

Schwartz, Richard D. 1990. "Human Rights in an Evolving World Culture." In *Human Rights in Africa: Cross-cultural Perspectives*. *See* An-Na'im and Deng 1990.

Singer, Marcus. 1964. "Lamont on Rights and Duties." *Philosophy and Phenomenological Research* 26: 112–16.

Vincent, R. J. 1986. *Human Rights and International Relations*. Cambridge: Cambridge University Press.

Wai, Dunstan. 1979. "Human Rights in Sub-Saharan Africa." In *Human Rights: Cultural and Ideological Perspectives*, ed. Adamantia Pollis and Peter Schwab. New York: Praeger.

Walzer, Michael. 1977. *Just and Unjust Wars: A Moral Argument with Historical Illustrations*. New York: Basic Books.

———. 1980. "The Moral Standing of States: A Response to Four Critics." *Philosophy and Public Affairs* 9: 209–29.

Welch, Claude E., Jr., and Ronald I. Meltzer, eds. 1984. *Human Rights and Development in Africa*. Albany: State University of New York Press.

World Bank. 1989. *From Crisis to Sustainable Development in Sub-Saharan Africa*. Washington, D.C.: World Bank.

Wunsch, James, and Dele Olowu, eds. 1990. *The Failure of the Centralized State: Institutions and Self-Governance in Africa*. Boulder, Colo.: Westview Press.

INDEX

Abraham, Morris, 101
Achebe, Chinua, 3, 7
Adegbite, L. O., 40
Affective economy, affection, 244, 246, 252, 259, 266, 273–74
African Bar Association, 263
African Charter on Human and Peoples' Rights, 74, 141; account of, 75–77, 99, 114, 264; analysis of, 77–82; collective rights provisions of, 11, 13, 15, 40, 46, 92, 101, 216–17; economic, social, and cultural provisions of, 6, 43
African Commission on Human and Peoples' Rights, 74–75, 79–80, 97
African National Congress (ANC), 97, 99, 177
Africa Watch, 3, 7, 248, 276
Ake, Claude, 92, 97, 99–100
Alatas, Syed Hussein, 237
Alcoholism, 181–82
Amin, Idi, 3
Amnesty International, 3, 4, 7, 90, 248, 276
Andreski, Iris, 122
Arendt, Hannah, 169, 184
Asante, 56, 57, 59
Ashby, Eric, 240
Assembly of Heads of State and Government, 80
Association of University Teachers in Zimbabwe, 235
Asylum: as a right, 146
Atlantic Charter, 99, 101–2
Azikiwe, E. A., 101

Babu, A. M., 276, 277
Baganda, 124
Baldwin, F., 34n5
Banjul Charter. *See* African Charter on Human and Peoples' Rights
Basic needs, 20–21
Basic rights, 42, 64, 77–78

Basotho Congress party, 173
Basotho National party, 173
Bemba, 56, 65
Benin, 63
Beti, 123
Beye, Alioune Blondin, 74
Bitek, Okot p', 250
Botswana, 18, 269
Boukassa, 3
Buganda, 59, 63
Burundi, 17

Canadian International Development Agency, 112
Capitalism, 39
Chad, 122, 150, 151
Charter for Women and Children, 101
Charter of Economic Rights and Duties of States, 102–3
Civic public realm, 271–72
Civil and political rights, 5, 258–59; relation of, to economic, social and cultural rights, 81, 82, 89, 100
Civil society, 29–33
Collective rights, 78; in African Charter, 11, 13, 15, 40, 46, 92, 101, 216–17; precolonial, 39, 40, 47, 55–56; vs. individual, 15, 44, 45–46, 97, 221, 258
Collectivism, 25, 35n10
Community and communitarianism, 36n11, 56; as determiner of rights, 42, 46; as provider of rights, 39, 40, 42–43
Convention Governing the Specific Aspects of Refugee Problems in Africa, 147, 154–55
Convention on the Elimination of All Forms of Discrimination against Women, 113–14
Convention Relating to the Status of Refugees, 146–47
Corporate rights, 6
Council for the Development of Economic

and Social Research in Africa (CODESRIA), 235, 248, 253
Court, David, 252
Crummey, D., 50
Cultural relativism, 12–13, 54, 76, 125, 143

Decision making, 93–96, 95
Declaration of Social Principles of the Americas, 102
Declaration on the Establishment of a New Economic Order, 102–3
Declaration on the Establishment of a New International Economic Order, 115–16
Declaration on the Right to Development, 102–3, 115–16
Democratization, 28
Dependency theory, 117
Development, 25, 81, 104, 253, 262, 264; defined, 115–16; effect of, on rights, 21–23, 169; effect of, on women's rights, 114, 116, 120–21; and public discourse, 242; as a right, 101, 115–16, 263; rights as prerequisite to, 264; role of universities in, 243
Division of labor, 124–25
Donnelly, J., 39, 41, 42, 45, 46–47, 49, 51
Duties: and obligations, 39; and rights, 6, 40, 78–79, 266–68
Dworkin, R., 42

Economic, social, and cultural rights, 6, 81, 82, 89, 89, 100
Economic Charter of the Americas, 101–2
Education: consequence of inequities in, 230–31; dependence of rights on, 215–18, 222–23, 232; as a right, 16, 228. *See also under* Nigeria
Egalitarianism, 43–44
El Naiem, Abdullah Ahmed, 54
El-Sheikh, Ibrahim A. Badawi, 74
Enahoro, Anthony, 191–92, 204
Endurance of hardship, 271, 274
Eriksson, L. G., 148
Ethiopia, 18, 61, 65
Ethnic conflict and government, 17
Eze, O. C., 47

Fairness, 9, 10, 35n8
Feierman, Steven, 60, 236
Feminist thought, 117–18
Fernyhough, Timothy, 13–14

First International Conference on Assistance to Refugees in Africa (ICARA), 148, 154
Forced labor, 5
Foreign aid: impact of, on women's rights, 112, 129–33; tied to rights, 277
Forsythe, David P., 277
Freedom Charter of ANC, 99
Free speech, 62–64

Gabon, Alexis, 74
Gender rights, 16
Ghana, 124
Global Consultation on the Right to Development as a Human Right, 104
Goody, J., 48
Gould, W. T. S., 149
Gramsci, Antonio, 30, 236
Gurr, T. R., 169
Guyer, James I., 118

Hadiya, Mahmoud Abou, 74
Hanga, Kassim, 246
Hansen, Art, 8, 276
Hausa, 126
Hausaland, 18
Hayek, F., 26, 35n8
Hospitality toward refugees, 153–55
Howard, Rhoda, 39, 41, 42, 45, 46, 47–49, 51, 276
Human rights: analysis of, in Africa, 90–93; based on human dignity, 39, 41–42, 47, 49, 94; based on human nature, 41, 42, 45; defined, 4–5; dependence of, on education, 215–18, 222–23, 232; and development, 253, 264; effect of colonial experience on, 259–61; effect of reason vs. tradition on, 257–58; embodied in lists, 5, 8; emerge from contention, 51; emerge from popular culture, 52–53; established through social process, 9–10; as field of inquiry, 3, 34n1; liberal model, 98–99; limited by ethnicity, 219–20; limited to legal embodiment, 9; methodological problems in, 53–55; narrow vs. universal view of, 94–95; procedural protections for, 61–62; prescriptions for African, 104–7; of refugees, 141–43; related to types of governance, 265–75; related to written law, 259; sources of, 8–11; theory, 89–90, 95–96; third-generation,

96–97, 99–100, 263; traditional, 11–13, 114, 195–96; universality of, 42, 141–142, 217, 275–278; Western concepts of, 44, 92, 100, 195–96. *See also* Basic needs; Basic rights; Collective rights; Refugees; Right to life
Human Rights and Equal Opportunity Commission, Australia, 97
Human Rights Commission, 264
Human sacrifice, 57
Hussein, Maamun Mohamed, 90
Hutu-tutsi, 17
Hyden, Goran, 3, 7–8, 10

Ibingira, Grace Stuart, 74
Igbo, 57
Igboland, 62
Iliffe, J., 48, 65
Individualism, 13–16, 35n10, 36n11. *See also under* Collective rights
Intellectuals: account of, in Africa, 237–41; defined, 236–37; effect of state power on, 246–47; impact of economy on, 247–48; political positions of, 250–51; response of, to Western ideological influences, 251–53
International Bill of Human Rights, 76, 103, 113
International Covenant on Civil and Political Rights, 141, 152
International Covenant on Economic, Social, and Cultural Rights, 6, 76, 152
International Institute for Human Rights and Democratic Development, 130
Isaacman, A., 52
Islamic culture and practices, 54, 56, 62, 65, 122, 126, 127, 218–19

Janneh, Sourahata B. Semega, 75
Jonathan, Leabua, 173–76

Kano, 126
Kaunda, Kenneth, 40
Kenya, 18, 127, 128, 211, 272
Kikuyu, 57
Kisanga, Habesh Robert, 75
Kongo, 63, 65
Kopytoff, Igor, 57, 60, 272
Kuba, 56, 57, 62

Lagos Plan of Action, 117
Language: choice of national, 211; integrative role of, 203, 207–9; and intellectual discourse, 249–50; "one nation = one language," 209–10; and rights, 10, 16, 203–7
Legesse, A., 40, 42, 43, 44, 47
Lekhanya, Justin Khetsing, 176
Lesotho, 269–70; politics in, 58, 172–78; violence in, 178–80, 269–70
Lesotho Liberation Army, 174
Levine, D. N., 61
Lima Declaration on Academic Freedom and Autonomy of Institutions of Higher Education, 235
Lovejoy, P., 60, 61
Lozi, 65
Lunda, 65

Mali, 61
Mandela, Nelson, 277
Mannheim, Kar, 236
Marasinghe, L., 40, 42, 43, 45, 47, 195–96
Marriage rights. *See under* Women's rights
Mazrui, Ali, 253, 277
M'Baye, K., 43
Mboya, Tom, 246
Mbum, 125
Meillassoux, Claude, 60, 123
Miers, S., 57, 60
Migrants, 145
Mkandawire, Thandika, 247
Mojekwu, C. C., 40, 44, 47, 51, 57
Mokoma, R. M. D., 75
Moral universe, 18–19
Moskowitz, Moses, 96
Mubanga-Chipaya, C. L. C., 75

Nagan, Winston P., 26
Naldi, Gino J., 142, 146, 155
Naming, 34n3
Nationalists, 242, 261
National security, 28–29, 154–55, 262–63
National Youth Service, Nigeria, 222
Nations vs. states, 160–62
Ndiaye, Youssoupha, 75
Nguema, Issa, 75
Nigeria, 17, 18, 28, 64, 126, 128, 271; education and employment in, 229–30; exogenous languages of, 197–98; hierarchy of language in, 201–3; indigenous languages of, 198–200; Islamic education in, 218–19; language and national integration in, 207–9; language and

political divisions of, 193-95; language complexion of, 191-93; language policies of, 204-5; language proposals for, 212-13; and language rights, 203-7; non-Western education in, 218-19; rights education in, 222-23; traditional education in, 218-19; use of Pidgin English in, 200-201; Western-style education in, 220-24, 225-27
Nkrumah, Kwame, 43, 261
Nupe, 63
Nyerere, Julius, 40, 43, 148, 261

Obbo, Christine, 125
Okoth-Ogendo, H. W. O., 28
Oral history, 53-55
Organization of African Unity (OAU), 74, 76, 92, 262-63, 275

Parkin, David, 169
Peoples' rights, 78, 81-82, 92. *See also* Collective rights
Personal freedom, 57-58, 60
Personal security, 7-8
Personhood, 4, 13, 34n3
Peshkin, A., 219
Planning, 26-27
Pluralism, 17, 262-63
Polis, A., 42
Political power, 243-46
Political violence, 169-72
Popular culture, 55
Postcolonialism, 24
Poverty, 64-66
Pressman, D., 26
Property rights, 15, 127, 128, 273
Protocol Relating to the Status of Refugees, 146-47

Redistributive economy, 48-49
Refugees: characteristics of, 151-52; defined, 144-49; end of status as, 151-52; as expression of rights abuse, 162; hospitality toward, 153-55; integration of, 158-60; national security concerns of, 154-55; numbers of, 149-51; powerlessness of, 156-57; repatriation vs. integration of, 152; rights of, 141-43; scheme-settlement of, 154, 158-60; self-settlement of, 153-55, 157-58; state of knowledge of, 143-44
Rights and duties. *See* Duties: and rights

Rights talk, 171, 263, 270, 272
Right to life, 56-57
Rogers, Susan, 121
Rude, George, 52
Rwanda, 17, 59-60

Sanday, Peggy Reeves, 122
Scale and scope, 12, 35n9
Schatzberg, Michael, 3, 169, 170
Schwab, P., 42
Schwartz, Richard, 277
Scott, J., 52
Seighart, P., 34n6
Shambaa, 60
Shanafelt, Robert, 7
Sherbra, 58
Shivji, Issa G., 47, 244
Slavery, 60-61
Socialism, 25
Social relations, 271, 272-73
Songhay, 61
South Africa, 90-91, 172-78, 185-85, 269-70
State power: detrimental to individual rights, 15; fails to support Banjul Charter, 84-85; narrow conceptions of, 83-84; restraints on, 50, 58-59; rights dependence on, 10
State societies, 123-24
Statism, 23-29, 224, 265-66
Staudt, Kathleen, 121, 126
Sudan, 18, 90
Swazi, 56
Swaziland, 58-59, 63

Tanzania, 18, 64, 122, 124, 126, 128-29, 211, 235, 244, 245, 272
Telli, Diallo, 91
Thiongo, Ngugi wa, 246, 250
Third-generation rights, 96-97, 99-100, 263
Tio kingdom, 62
Tocqueville, Alexis de, 30
Totalitarian vs. authoritarian rule, 268
Toure, Sekou, 91, 261

Uganda, 272
Underdevelopment, 82-83
United Nations, 115
United Nations Charter, 76
United Nations High Commissioner for Refugees (UNHCR), 142, 147, 152

Universal Declaration of Human Rights, 40, 44, 76, 96, 141, 142, 195, 217
Universities, 243
Urbanization, 15

Vansina, J., 62
Vincent, R. J., 5, 6, 41, 44, 45, 47, 51
Violence: economic roots of, 182–84; psychology of, 178–80; social context of, 180–82; and weak governance, 184–86

Wai, 47, 49
Wallman, Sandra, 181
Walzer, Michael, 275–76
War, D. M., 40
Weisfelder, Richard, 173
Wildavsky, A., 26
Wilks, I., 57

Women: in the African economy, 119–21; in development, 112, 116–19, 130; division of labor, 124–25; ideology of subordination, 121–25; in politics, 126
Women's rights, 54; account of, 113–15; to children, 127; dependent on social change, 129–30; education needed for, 131; foreign aid and, 112, 129–33; marriage and, 14, 64; organizational support for, 128–29; prospects for, 125–29; to property, 127, 128
World Bank, 120, 252
Woronoff, 149

Yoruba, 63

Zaire, 170
Zambia, 158–60
Zeleza, Tiyambe, 247

No longer the property of the
Boston Public Library.
Sale of this material benefits the Library

Boston Public Library

COPLEY SQUARE
GENERAL LIBRARY

JC599
.A36
H84
1993

The Date Due Card in the pocket indicates the date on or before which this book should be returned to the Library.
Please do not remove cards from this pocket.